58 A.D.

A Study of

1 Corinthians

Jonathan Couper

GILEAD
B O O K S
PUBLISHING

Gilead Books Publishing
Corner Farm
West Knapton
Malton
North Yorkshire
YO17 8JB UK

www.GileadBooksPublishing.com

First published in Great Britain, November 2014

2 4 6 8 10 9 7 5 3 1

Copyright © Jonathan Couper 2014

British Library Cataloguing-in-Publication Data:

A catalogue record for this book is available from the British Library.

ISBN-13: 978-0-9926713-6-5

The publisher makes every effort to ensure that the papers used in our books are made from trees that have been legally sourced from well-managed and credibly certified forests by using a printer awarded FSC & PEFC chain of custody certification.

Corinth Erastus Inscription p303, photo courtesy of Mike Fuller, www.mikefuller.org.uk

Cover design: Jeremy Couper

Contents

Introduction	6
🏛 Ephesus 58A.D.	7
1 Corinthians Chapter 1-4	
Summary	12
Overview Chapter 1-2	16
Greek text commentary	
Chapter 1	19
Chapter 2	36
🏛 Corinth	44
🏛 Recent Life	49
Overview Chapter 3-4	52
Greek text commentary	
Chapter 3	54
Chapter 4	64
🏛 Walking in Ephesus	75
🏛 To Corinth with Love	79
1 Corinthians Chapter 5-6	
Overview	82
Greek text commentary	
Chapter 5	89
Chapter 6	94
🏛 Church Life	105
🏛 Timothy, Trophimus and Tychicus	107
1 Corinthians Chapter 7	
Overview	111
Greek text commentary	
Chapter 7	116
🏛 A Dream	140
🏛 Erastus	144
1 Corinthians Chapter 8-10	
Overview	148

Greek text commentary

    Chapter 8   155

    Chapter 9   164

    Chapter 10   171

Paul the Jew   176

Aquila & Priscilla   179

1 Corinthians Chapter 11

    Overview   182

Greek text commentary

    Chapter 11   189

The Lost Manuscript   205

Apollos and Aristarchus   209

1 Corinthians Chapter 12-14

    Overview   214

Greek text commentary

    Chapter 12   231

    Chapter 13   240

    Chapter 14   247

Ephesus in Revival   259

Paul in Reflection   263

1 Corinthians Chapter 15-16

    Overview   266

Greek text commentary

    Chapter 15   270

    Chapter 16   289

Departure   294

Appendix A: Corinth in the missionary journeys of Paul   298

Appendix B: Background 51A.D. – 58A.D.   305

Appendix C: Background 58A.D. – 59A.D.   309

Appendix D: Possible Timeline of Paul's Life   316

Appendix E: The imprisonment of Paul at Ephesus reflected

       in the New Testament epistles   324

This book is dedicated with all my love to

Anne, my wonderful wife and great companion.

Who brings joy and completeness, insight and peace

on the journey we walk together in life.

Introduction

This book is designed to put, in a straightforward way for the 21st century, what Paul wrote in the first letter to the Corinthians.

The book includes a novel to give a flavour of the time 1 Corinthians was written and I have added some appendices to show the reasons for some of the events in the novel. The appendices also include a timeline of the life of the apostle Paul and other useful background material.

Each chapter includes my own translation of the Greek text.

This commentary is not intended to be a discussion of the different academic points of view but instead, is an attempt to look at the text itself as if read for the first time. Behind the interpretation of the text is my firm conviction that:

- The straight forward meaning is the right one.
- The letter Paul wrote is God revealing truth for every generation and every culture.
- The right interpretation of the text brings life and revelation to those who read it.

I hope you enjoy reading and are blessed through it.

Jonathan Couper
Bridlington

Ephesus 58 A.D.

Paul looked out over the thriving city of Ephesus. Spring was always a good time of year ending the cold of winter before the heat of summer, but today was a typical March day with the temperature in the mid 60's with a little rain earlier in the day. He could see in the bright afternoon sun the ancient harbour with impressive stone colonnades and the ships busy in their trade. He could see outside the harbour to the westward sea, the three masts with square sails of one of the vast grain ships from Alexandria and could just make out the smaller ships ferrying goods to and fro into the harbour. This was a common sight and his eye quickly moved from the busy harbour. His gaze moved from west to east and he noticed in passing, the light reflecting on the water in the aqueduct in the distance, weaving its way through the city to one of the market places. He continued to look eastwards. He could see the many buildings and dwellings with the hills beyond. This was no small city—it was one of the largest in the ancient world. Afar off he could see the top of the large temple of Artemis shining in the still bright, late afternoon sun. This was one of the wonders of the ancient world which pilgrims visited from all over the known world. A dog barking averted Paul's gaze to the street below his window. He could hear the hustle and bustle in the streets which, whilst constant during day time hours, had the mark of business ending for the day in the agora (the market place). There was a constant flow of activity in the streets below. It was one of the main streets out of the city, and it was never silent. It was, he supposed, to be expected in the Roman seat of power for the province of Asia which stretched to the edge of the Roman Empire in the east. Military cohorts travelled with their equipment as well as traders with their wares. It was always busy. Ephesus looked distinctive and interesting in the late afternoon sun as it cast sharp shadows over the buildings. How God had prospered the mission of Paul in those streets and houses of Ephesus. God's timing was always perfect. The revival fire of the Holy Spirit that had come on his arrival to Ephesus and then had spread to the neighbouring towns and cities in the whole province of Asia.

Paul stood at the open window taking in the view but no longer listening to the noise or noticing who was passing below. He was deep in thought. He wondered what this year held in store for him and those friends he had made who together were seeking to bring the gospel to the entire world region by region. Ephesus had been and still was a dangerous place for him. He still remembered that it was in this city he had been sentenced to face wild beasts in the arena, escaping this ordeal on a technicality and not without a little help from his friends. This was not the end to the troubles Paul did not yet know that the difficulties with synagogue on the one hand and local craftsman on the other would put the whole city in uproar reacting against Paul and his teaching. The spiritual barometer reading had registered stormy many times whilst he was in Ephesus. Paul was used to this. Revival and persecution often go hand in hand.

Paul's eye looked towards the hills around the city. He had been told the mother of Jesus used to live in a house on one of the slopes. Paul had never met her, for she died a year before Paul had arrived in Ephesus. This city was not the same place, and neither was the church. Both had changed from when John the disciple first brought Mary the mother of Jesus to Ephesus. When she died, John had travelled westwards to Rome where Peter now lived.

Seven years before, God's Spirit had forbidden Paul to come to Ephesus and the province of Asia. He did not know then that John was founding the churches in the region. He recalled seeking to enter the province of Asia when he and his companions could get no peace about it. All of them knew God's Spirit was saying "no" at that time to the province of Asia, but now, so he reflected, years later he could look over the province of Asia's capital city. Back then he had then had a significant dream which had brought about his first trip to Corinth in Achaia. In the dream he saw a man who he knew by the style of clothing was from Macedonia. In the dream the Macedonian was asking him to come to preach the gospel, and so they had travelled into Europe for the first time arriving in Philippi, the capital city of Macedonia. It was there that God had birthed a major church work which supported him through his journey southwards to Athens and then onto Corinth. How important that dream was, he whispered quietly to himself. If he had not had that dream, there may have been no mission to Corinth at all.

He had just finished a meal with Aquila and Priscilla, friends he had first met in Corinth over 6 years before. This was a regular occurrence for them but tonight was different because they had been joined by some influential members of the Corinthian Church. These had taken the opportunity to travel by sea to Ephesus in the more clement weather after the end of the winter. At the meal they discussed the news of the church but also the political changes in Corinth. Gallio the Roman Proconsul when Paul was at Corinth had had to resign his post on health grounds not long after Paul left the city. There was some debate about whether politics in Rome was really the cause of his ill health. Emperor Claudius had been assassinated about 3 years after Paul had left Corinth and the 17 year old Nero had been made the next emperor rather than Claudius' son Britannicus at the instigation of Nero's murderous mother Agrippina who commanded respect as a direct descendant of Emperor Augustus. Nero's tutor Seneca was the power behind the throne, but it looked like he was losing influence. All over the world there was rapid change. Aquila thought that Nero was making Rome safer for Jews now that Claudius was gone but was still uncertain and listened to his guests with interest about the political changes. They had left Rome nearly ten years before because as a Jew in the latter part of Claudius' reign, he was under a death threat. Priscilla his wife never really settled in Corinth and they moved to Ephesus when Paul had moved from Corinth. Aquila's tent making business was even more profitable in Ephesus than Corinth. They had now put roots in Ephesus but they planned to return to their roots in Rome one day. Priscilla and Aquila were making active plans to go now it seemed safer for Jews to live there. They would not sell up their business in Ephesus but put others in charge so they could travel. Whatever they chose to do in the future, they would both do this with care and caution.

It was some years since Paul had been to Corinth, so he was glad to renew his friendship with those in the delegation. He knew all of them though last time he was in Corinth Sosthenes one of the delegation was not a believer. It was some years since Paul had set foot in Corinth. Paul had travelled many other places since, and churches were forming all over the Mediterranean world. Paul had come to Ephesus 2 years ago, but he had never forgotten the Corinthians and the province of Achaia where he longed to revisit. The Corinthians for their part knew people in Ephesus. Key among them was an Alexandrian called Apollos. He had spent some time in Corinth but Paul first met him over a year ago when he had returned from Corinth. Apollos lived elsewhere in Ephesus, and their paths rarely crossed. The Corinthian visitors no doubt during their stay would meet Apollos but it was Paul they had come to see.

In the group from Corinth was Fortunatus who knew about the old days when the apostle had been the notorious persecutor of the church in Jerusalem. He was accompanied by two other godly men Achaicus and Stephanas who with his household was one of the first converts to Christianity in Corinth. This was the core team but there were others. Erastus the city treasurer was with them accompanied by Sosthenes the leader of the synagogue. This delegation carried political and religious clout. They had brought a letter from the rapidly growing church in Corinth. In the letter was a list of problems that needed Paul's direction and they were awaiting Paul writing his reply. Little did they realise that this reply that they were to take back to Corinth would be preserved for centuries and incorporated in the Bible as 1 Corinthians.

Paul sat down and thought about the precious people he had met and what God had done during the years he had stayed in Corinth. The arrival of the Corinthian delegation had stirred up his spirit and he knew he needed to visit them again but he also needed to write a letter. Timothy was already preparing to leave for Macedonia and then onto to Corinth. It had already been agreed that Erastus would carry Paul's reply directly to Corinth. Paul had spoken to them yesterday. Their task was twofold. One to prepare for Paul's visit where at this time he planned to travel direct to meet Timothy in Corinth and then onto Macedonia and secondly, to make sure the promised collection to relieve the Christians in Jerusalem was collected, He wanted things settling before his arrival there, and he hoped their visit and this letter would do this. For now Paul felt he needed to return to Corinth but he had to stay in Ephesus at least until Pentecost, because there were different opportunities and problems emerging to deal with in Ephesus which affected the whole region.

Paul's plans to leave Ephesus for Greece were already advanced. Aristarchus a Jewish businessman from Macedonia had been with him over the winter and had shared in Paul's travels before. He was planning to return with Paul to the Greek mainland. Gaius a man who headed up a successful business in Philippi was already on his way from Macedonia to Ephesus to escort him on the first part of his travels west. None of them knew what would happen after Gaius' arrival in Ephesus, but that was for another day.

Paul looked around the room. His eyes rested on Sosthenes. God had done a remarkable work in this man's life. It seemed like yesterday when he recalled the turmoil in the synagogue at Corinth and the founding of the church in the house of a neighbour called Jason. He recalled the encouragement he received at the conversion of the ruler of the synagogue Crispus. For this was the first time he had really noticed Sosthenes. He succeeded Crispus as ruler of the synagogue and at first with many others in the synagogue opposed Paul and what the church stood for. It was remarkable that now he too had made the same steps that Crispus had done and become a member of the church. Jesus was now Lord of his life too, and he had a place of influence in the Corinthian church. Paul turned to him directly "Sosthenes, we should send a letter to our brothers in Corinth answering their concerns. Would you be willing to write down the letter which I dictate?" Certainly Paul, I am ready" and with that Sosthenes unrolled some blank parchment, took a pen in hand and dipped it in the ink." Let us begin. Paul started to speak,

From Paul, called to be an apostle of Jesus Christ through the will of God, and from Sosthenes our brother to the church of God which is in Corinth...

1 Corinthians Chapters 1-4
Summary

The Corinthian church was a lively church in one of the most important cities in the Roman Empire. The church was growing in a pagan, immoral city and was doing well, but Paul wants that life to be more than skin deep. It is the spiritual life of a church community which dictates its survival and impact on its community not its activities. Jesus said it was the love we had for each other in the church which would convince those outside the church that we were followers of Jesus (John 13:35). It was not the acts of kindness or charity work for the community or for the poor that did that, but our love for one another. Spiritual life is the key.

Paul is concerned about the divisions among them. This was in their support of one person and their lack of support for another. Paul sees this as thinking as the world thinks (Chapter 3) and not as heaven thinks. Ever since the fall, our mind has become darkened so that "our thoughts are not God's thoughts" (Isaiah 55).

This was important because it dictated what they could see, what power they could move in and the effectiveness of their bringing the kingdom. The kingdom of God is not brought about by the wisdom or efforts of men operating out of the world. The Kingdom comes through men and women who are sent from heaven.

Worldly thinking means the church cannot receive the things God wants them to receive as these are received by the spirit .Worldly thinking will cause despising of spiritual things so that what is of God is rejected and will also make it impossible to understand what God is saying. Worldly thinking also closes the portals of heaven so that no revelation happens. This means the Corinthian church will be operating blind.

Adam and Eve in the dawn of the human race chose to find wisdom through independent knowledge of good and evil rather than in relationship with God. Down the ages human kind has made the same mistake over and over again. This worldly wisdom is not real wisdom as real wisdom comes from revelation. Someone who is acclaimed as wise by the world can be a fool in his character, choices and beliefs. Knowing what is good and what is evil does not of itself make you wise in life. This real wisdom comes relationally from the Holy Spirit.

Key Truth - Worldly thinking in the church is shown by division

Paul starts in 1:10 stating that his intention in the next few chapters is to bring about unity. To this end he exposes the current divisions with the source of his information so the facts he wants to address are true. He then exposes the problems with such a position.

There is no basis for disunity

a. They have no doctrine to justify division. The anointing with Paul or Apollos or Peter is the same. It is from the Holy Spirit and He should not be divided. Do not put asunder what God has joined together. (1:13)

b. They have no example to justify division. Paul had never acted or spoken to give any justification for such a position (1:14,2:1-4)

c. They have no history to justify division. The Corinthians have been able to experience the same blessings despite there being few of them who could be regarded by the world as having merit intellectually, spiritually or through status. (1:26, 27) To form a church in Corinth required ignoring the worldly distinctions such as society status, jobs or intellect. They could not make distinctions in these so they also should not be doing so for Paul, Apollos or Peter.

The bad consequences of Disunity

d. When Christians are agreed in the church, they operate like the thoughts of a well-functioning brain and think as Jesus thinks (2:16). When there is disunity they operate less as the mind of Christ and more like someone demented.

e. A demented person can give high priority and energy to some unimportant thoughts and dismiss or not even hear more important thoughts. Churches in the same way when they think in a worldly way (which is marked by how they view others especially comparing and contrasting leaders) act and speak in such ways that decrease the prospect of the kingdom of God in their vicinity.

f. Dementia causes you to forget places and names. Worldly thinking means God's people can forget what God has done in the past and make decisions as if God had never done anything in the past. The classic bible story reflecting this theme is of the Israelites forgetting what God had done through the deliverance from Egypt by the Red Sea and their preservation in the wilderness. As a result they were afraid to obey God and go into the Promised Land because of the giants.

g. Dementia is shown when there is a major disorientation when you are outside normal familiar situations. It is worth stating in this context that Churches without the mind of Christ do not manage change well.

h. Disunity is because of Worldly thinking. This stops growth in Christ to fulfil our destiny and calling in the world.

i. Paul also points out that disunity brought about by this worldly thinking defiles the temple of God, (3:16, 17) bringing impurity into the church making it something other than it is meant to be.

We have a responsibility to build. Building on the platform with worldly thinking is putting the church at risk. Worldly thinking makes the church look to the flesh and so Jesus does not build His Church through the spirit, but man does it through the flesh. This produces dross which is eventually destroyed. Change of heart and renewal of mind for a church means stepping out of these old attitudes and in doing so, the relationship with God and the power of the Holy Spirit becomes central. What is built of the Spirit has an eternal dimension and stands.

Paul uses the example (3:12) of building in gold or silver (spirit led obedience according to revelation) as opposed to building on hay and stubble (building according to worldly principles).

Paul knows the building or serving will not stay as it always was. There will be some disturbance and difference because our deeds are also our altar of sacrifice and this altar of sacrifice attracts the fire. When the fire falls there is the opportunity to increase. Just as the fire falls on

Elijah's sacrificial altar at Carmel (see Kings 18:38), so that blessing can come on the countryside of Elijah's day, so heavenly fire will fall on church ministries which will then allow blessing to come to the area. The fire seals and affirms what is good so it can be foundational for the future, but at the same time increases its glory or effects. The action of God's fire is never without effect. It either destroys a work or enables blessing to reach out further. There is nothing anyone can do to stop the fire. The fire from heaven will come on every altar of sacrifice. We must not build with worldly thinking or else the work done will be burnt up in the fire.

Paul's solution to move in unity - All things are yours (3:21).
This is the change of thinking which counters worldly thinking

"All are yours" means you see everyone who comes your way as for you. This at first glance can seem selfish as you are putting yourself as central to your world and everyone serves you. But as Paul points out that central world is not marked by you on the throne of a self-made empire but of a life surrendered to Jesus. He does not stop at "all are yours" but "you are Christ's and Christ is God's". Everything may be for you, but you are all about Jesus as He is all about God. Understand this and worldly thinking dies. Worldly thinking can be there in supporting one denomination against another, one church against another, and also in denying church or denomination. The only way to avoid this is to see that everything is there to benefit you as you serve the Lord.

Overview Chapter 1-2

The Problem in General

1:1-9 Introduction

1:10 Paul starts by showing the main point he wants the Corinthians to get hold of,

> *Now I plead with you, brethren, by the name of our Lord Jesus Christ, that you all speak the same thing, and that there be no divisions among you, but that you be perfectly joined together in the same mind and in the same judgment.*

He then addresses this by,

1. Stating the problem (v11,12)
2. Pragmatic exposure of their position. He reminds them of their doctrine, what they saw of the way Paul behaved and their own experience.
   a. v13-17 "Is Christ Divided?" their practice does not match their doctrine.
   b. Their witness (of Paul): Paul's example did not point to this either (v17-23).
   c. Their experience (v26-29). Calling is not from merit, skill or by worldly status. Judging one better than another on such grounds denies the road they have travelled.
3. The underlying problem. Holding divisions means they operate out of worldly wisdom rather than by the Spirit. This affects the church's ability to receive revelation or move in power. (2:12, 3:2-4, 2:5)

1:10-2:16 The thread of worldly wisdom identified with its accompanying problems

The effect of division means the revelation and leading of the Holy Spirit is affected.

Relating appropriately to the world, extending and bringing the kingdom to this world and bringing about the purposes of God requires a church which is thinking right. Just as a human who is thinking wrongly can destroy relationships and prevent possibilities, so can the church without the mind of Christ. We are meant to have same mind so we assess together the unseen and seen realms and can accurately discern the will of God (v10). The mind of Christ functions properly when there is real unity. Division makes us bi-polar making us become a church that the world is unsure how to relate to. Division also closes down parts of the church body so we are unable to be fully who we are meant to be. We become like someone demented, unable to process thoughts and feelings properly, and so unable to respond appropriately to a world in need or to God.

The human mind has thousands of thoughts a day which it processes. In the church of God we move in revelation which are thoughts in the mind of Christ (2:16). We move in revelation as individual believers and these desires, convictions, revelations and instructions are all thoughts within the mind of Christ which only properly function within the church of God in the world as the thoughts of individuals come together (v16).

Worldly principles or celebrity status is not good for anyone. When we ally to one leader as opposed to another or to a cause based on some principle or human perception we are eating from the tree of knowledge of good and evil. Worldly wisdom may create clubs, teams, groups but they will be worldly formed through self-interest or empty principle (or dare I say doctrine). Such structures do not enable increased manifestation of God in and to the world (1:12-1, 2:2-5.)

The Church and the Christian life should be far from this. Real unity and life with God's indwelling is only found from the tree of life. Also real wisdom is found in the life of Jesus and relationship with Him not in the world (1:v12-31). It is not from study but from revelation (2:7) through the Holy Spirit (2:10). So (2:12) "we have received not the spirit of the world but the Spirit who is from God, that we might know the things that have been freely given to us by God" (NKJV)

Communication of revelation is not even in the realm of human wisdom either. (2:13) The words themselves are from what the Holy Spirit not man teaches. So God reveals what to say and how to say it. (Note what Jesus said "The Father who sent me commanded me what to say and how to say it." (John 12:49)

There is a fundamental flaw if we think human wisdom might be of some benefit. The natural man cannot receive the things of the Spirit. (2:13)

You cannot receive what you do not honour (2:14). Worldly thinking causes us to despise the very words and actions or relationships which can give us life.

You cannot receive what you do not first see. You can only see it with your spirit (2:14). What you see you can have. This is why Jesus explained that the Holy Spirit would show us what was His (John 16:14, 15). The motive is so we can have it and so bring glory to Jesus (John 16:14) which will spread through us to the world (Habakkuk 2:24). When we see it we can have it. Elijah knew this when he answered Elisha's question about the double anointing of the Spirit. (2 Kings 2:10)

1. Paul called to be an apostle of Jesus Christ through the will of God and Sosthenes the brother

1:1a Paul "called through the will of God" (1:1). In a world of imperfection and evil, it is obvious that God's will is not always done on the earth. God's will requires obedience. We first discover the will of God through call. God's will on earth is done when people personally obey God. Man wants God to sort out famines, wars and troubles. For this to happen we have to be willing to work with God.

In the Lord's Prayer Jesus reminds us that it is through the Kingdom that God's will is done. When we obey God we are in His Kingdom. As we become sons of the kingdom we will discover the will of God and the call of God. The call makes the will of God personal which goes deep into identity and hope.

The human spirit is stubborn and rebellious, and our will is naturally opposed to God's will. As we encounter Jesus our hearts soften and our will becomes aligned to His will. This is a source of spiritual power and so evokes enemy reaction which is allowed by the Lord as he uses this to test our hearts to see if we are able to receive more favour which he wants to give us. Thus endurance is part of the path of obedience for every faithful servant of God.

1:1b Paul starts his letter in normal letter writing style of the 1st century AD which states from the source of the letter followed by greeting to those to whom the letter is written. Sosthenes is mentioned alongside Paul defining who is writing the letter. In other letters these were recognisable members of his team like Timothy or Silas who had specific links with the church where the letter was going. Sosthenes is mentioned only one other time and it is in Corinth. He took over from Crispus as ruler of the synagogue (Acts 18). And presumably has come with the Corinthian delegation mentioned in 16:17. He may also be included at the beginning because of his influential position within the Corinthian Church, but he is not mentioned elsewhere (for example at the end of Romans where he is sending greetings from members of the Corinthian church to those in Rome). It could be that he is the one who is actually writing the letter which is being dictated by Paul and so is indeed a letter from both Paul and Sosthenes (see how Paul finishes with his own hand (16:21). This could also be the case in Paul's other letters. It is quite feasible that whenever anyone is mentioned alongside Paul at the beginning of one of Paul's letters, it is indicative of who is writing down what Paul is saying. For example Silas and indeed Timothy are both mentioned as part of beginning greetings in other epistles when they were probably the writers of what Paul was dictating.

2. To the church of God which is in Corinth

The church of God has its being in Corinth. The heavenly community must have its existence on the earth. There is no such thing as a spiritual reality if it has no manifestation on the earth, just as there is no real engaging with Jesus if there is no difference in our lives. The people of God will have an earthly reference point, and in this case it is Corinth. The called out ones gathering around the truth and person of Jesus through the Holy Spirit are those who have discovered the kingdom and thus can discover the will of God. They have their existence in a specific time and geographical place on the earth. God's will is down to earth nor "airy fairy"; is real not fantasy and has a corporate relational dimension within it.

The gospels mention disciples many times but the word church only once. In the rest of the New Testament after Acts the word church is used at least 50 times but there is no longer the word disciple used at all. This is. I think, because the word church is really used as the plural term of disciple. The church is made up of disciples - called out ones who are following Jesus and thus being his disciples.

2. To those who are sanctified in Christ called to be saints.

We are sanctified in Christ before we are saints. We abide in holiness and so can become holy.

John 15:4 "Abide in me and I in you". For years I read this verse the other way around. I would read this to mean if I ask Jesus into my life I can then abide in his presence. But Jesus does not say "If I abide in you, you will abide in me"; but rather "abide in me" first and then "I will abide in you." This same truth is expressed in the phrase "sanctified in Christ Jesus before we are called to be saints". We are to become what we already are.

Abiding in God is all to do with abiding in God's presence. Saul of Tarsus comes into God's presence on the Damascus Road and as a result there started a process whereby he eventually carried the gospel around the Mediterranean world planting churches through the power of the Holy Spirit within him. The presence of God comes into a house of a centurion called Cornelius and the whole family turn to Jesus and are baptised (Acts 10.11) and we cannot forget of course the Holy Spirit overshadows Mary before Jesus is conceived in her womb. In all of these cases if God's presence had not been there these events would not have happened.

Many people encountered God's presence and did not make the right responses so they got no benefit from this. Those sanctified in Christ may hear the call to be saints but can only become what they are by obeying the call. Responding to the voice of God is the way the environment of God's presence becomes internalised within our spirit and soul

The presence of God has a voice, but not everyone responds positively to that voice. In the beginning Adam and Eve hear the sound of the Lord God walking in the garden and they fled and hid. Sinful man has been doing the same ever since.

Moving out from abiding in Jesus means our life experience changes as it did for Adam and Eve but it is also true that coming back to abiding in Jesus will also change our life experience from curse to blessing; from ignorance to revelation; from emptiness to fulfilment and from fear to intimacy.

From the time we are born we can be in God's presence and not recognise it. This was certainly the case for Jacob before "the penny dropped" and he recognised God was speaking to him (Genesis 28) and it is true for all of us.

Many recount how they asked Jesus into their lives unaware that they had been in God's presence. This should not surprise us because just as we cannot see the kingdom of God without our new nature (John 3) so we cannot recognise God's presence either. We may see the effects but not recognise the cause. Someone, for example, may recount their conversion to Christ at a Billy Graham crusade, remembering the moment of appeal or even aspects of the sermon preached, and the response and the difference Jesus has made as a result of that response. What is missing from the memory and testimony is their awareness of the presence of God that was there. They omit to say what they felt at the arrival to the meeting and the surprise at being amongst so many people; or perhaps the awareness of an atmosphere which felt good and right, or even a feeling which felt different and yet familiar at the same time. Signs of God's presence went unheeded at the time. Most would not make the connection. Other signs might be the rapt attention being given by young people to old people singing songs or the effect of the sermon on the inner soul or the many who responded at the end of the meeting. These are all signs of God's presence, but few would recognise it as such.

When we respond to the presence of God; the presence of God can stay within. Within God's presence is his voice. The moment we respond to God's voice, that which is not experienced by us in the presence of God then becomes internal and a part of us. We may for example be in God's presence seeing healing or other supernatural phenomena. We may hear the voice in the presence speaking the invitation for us also to move in healing or be healed. At that moment as our faith responds to the word; what is happening around us suddenly is at work within us. What is more, when God is in us wherever we go He is with us. Staying in God's presence is a skill we learn. When we first experience God our lives are rooted in self, with its cares and regrets, its dreams and its battles, its responsibilities and its questions, and then if self asserts , our experience of God's presence can ebb away or become a one off experience. God desires us to learn to walk in his presence all the time.

As we experience God more, and when we recognise God, we become thirsty for more of Him. Natural thirst is quenched by drink, but spiritual thirst grows the more we "drink" in God's goodness. This thirst attracts heaven to our experience for heaven hears our cry and leads us to pivot our life less on relationship with self and more on relationship with God. This means we become quicker at recognising God in action and hearing Him and responding. These are the key skills we need to abide in his presence.

So - You may experience his presence but do not recognise this until you hear the call and then God changes your life and you become different (sanctified). The call is to everyone and when we have heard the call and obey we also become part of that call.

There is no holiness which has no call; nor is there any call which does not arise out of holiness. We are saints not sinners. We step into the sanctification/holiness wrought for us through the cross of Jesus. Into that place God calls. As we respond to that call we become in our experience holy. So holiness from an earthly perspective is gradual, but it is only fulfilling the reality made available for us in the heavenlies through the cross.

2. With all those who call upon the name of our Lord Jesus Christ in every place.

The word επικαλουμενοις is the same word which is used of Paul when he appeals to Caesar in Acts 25:11 the word is the middle form of επικαλεο which is used in normal usage to call upon a deity or to call upon someone for aid or as a witness. What Paul is saying here is that saints stand with others who pray, who cry out to God and share the same attitude of dependency upon God. We do not trust in our holiness but in our God. Such people do not have a holier than thou attitude but appear really normal and never unconcerned about issues in life or a person's need. Real holiness has a corporate dimension. Being in his sanctification means hearing his call, but we are not the only ones who hear his voice, so when we hear his call we find we are gathered with others. (See John 10:3, 4, 16)

2. Both theirs and ours

He is not just **our** Lord Jesus but **theirs** as well. This seems an afterthought as the "theirs and ours" is added at the end of the sentence. It would seem in the word order of the sentence to connect to "every place" but that does not seem to make much sense, so I judge this an afterthought adding to the earlier phrase "our Lord Jesus Christ". This "afterthought" is none the less important. It tells us that everyone can access the Lord Jesus. He belongs not just to the apostle Paul but to all who call upon Him. As soon as we respond to God we are on the same level as Paul.

> ## 3. Grace and Peace from God our Father and Lord Jesus Christ.
>
> ## 4. I thank my God always concerning you because of the grace of God which has been given you in Christ Jesus.

Sometimes Paul writes "Christ Jesus" and other times "Jesus Christ". I believe this is because of different emphases. Jesus Christ is focusing on the man Jesus who is the messiah, Christ Jesus is focusing on the anointing which Jesus had and has given to those who follow Him. This shows up well in 2 Tim. 1:1-2 *"Paul, an apostle of Jesus Christ by the will of God, according to the promise of life which is in Christ Jesus."* Paul puts Jesus before Christ when emphasising the person of Jesus and Christ before Jesus when emphasising the anointing more than the person of Jesus. This is an important distinction which has been lost by many who read the New Testament. For example Romans 8:1 "there is no condemnation for those who are in Christ Jesus" is often referred by many to being no condemnation because of what Jesus has done on the cross, whereas what Paul is actually referring to (as the rest of the chapter shows) is that there is no condemnation when you are in the anointing of Jesus, and the clue is in the order Christ Jesus; not Jesus Christ Similarly Galatians 3:28 "all one in Christ Jesus" or Ephesians 2:10 "created in Christ Jesus for good works" are verses which are referring to the work of the Holy Spirit (the anointing of Jesus) rather than the person or work of Jesus Christ.

5. Because you are enriched in everything in Him in all speech and all knowledge.

Christ means anointing. It is not used by Paul as a surname of Jesus but rather a reference to the fact Jesus was anointed with the Holy Spirit. (See Acts 10:38) The point Paul is making here is that it is the anointing that Jesus has which is enriching them in all speech and knowledge which is made available to them through the grace that Jesus has availed for them through his death and resurrection. Without the cross and Easter day there would be no anointing for us.

6. Even as the testimony of Christ was confirmed in you

What Paul had told the Corinthians about Jesus they had begun to know in their own experience. What they had heard from Paul they now knew for themselves. This is what is called Christian assurance. The phrase "even as" is καθως which means "in proportion to" So we learn from this verse that the enriching we receive from the anointing is proportional to the assurance we have.

7. so that you are not lacking in any grace at all.

The assurance we have enables us to move in the gifts which always go along with our calling. (See Romans 11:29) The more assurance the more we will move in spiritual gifts. We have a faith echo within which enables us to step out into the tasks God has called us to do. This assurance is marked by boldness. This is what the Sanhedrin saw in Peter and John (Acts 4:13). This is what the gathered apostles prayed for when the building was shaken (Acts 4:29). This boldness happens when our conscience does not condemn us (Hebrews 9:13). Assurance and a good conscience go hand in hand. Boldness and sensitivity are necessary twins which reflect the assurance in our hearts.

Jesus said that the Kingdom of God comes from within (Luke 17:21) "Neither shall they say, Lo here! Or, lo there! For, behold, the kingdom of God is within you". (John 7:38) "He that believeth on me, as the scripture hath said, out of his heart shall flow rivers of living water". The assurance is within and our obedience comes from within. It is no surprise that this is also the source of the kingdom coming to our communities, church, families and environments. God has to flow out from our inner life. It is not from the books we have read, the analysis of current trends or the doctrines that we teach. Luke 17:20: *Jesus answered the Pharisees and said, "The kingdom of God cometh not with observation".* It is all about our hearts.

> **Waiting for the revelation of our Lord Jesus Christ.**
>
> **8. who indeed will confirm you right up to the end being without accusation at the day of our Lord Jesus Christ.**

Moving in gifts points us forward to the final day when Jesus is fully revealed. The gifts are a taste of the kingdom which will only be fully known at the last day. Paul will return to this theme in 1 Corinthians 13 onwards, but for now we take to heart that sight of the second coming and indeed its nearness becomes more evident when spiritual gifts are manifest among us. All revivals have a last day aspect to them. Indeed, because of this, around the fringes of every revival there can be prophets of doom with their "the end is nigh" message, whilst the revivalists bring a message of hope to a dying world. Revivals are the powers of the Age to come breaking through into our present age, and within each revival there is an invitation to come up higher and to abide in that which God is bringing to the world. Our response to revival should not be as a prophet of doom or even a teacher of principles, but rather be as a follower of Jesus carrying the presence of God wherever we go, inviting others to dwell with God now and inhabit His Kingdom on the earth.

Notice εβεβαιωθη in verse 6 and εβεβαιωσει in verse 8. One is past tense and the other is future; one refers to the assurance we have and the other refers to the assurance we will have. In verse 8 the future the assurance looks to is the final day of judgement. It is not that we will only have assurance when the final day happens. It means rather that the assurance we have now lasts until the final day. We will feel the same assurance on judgement day as we do when we are moving in spiritual gifts now. This means that assurance is a permanent rather than a fleeting experience. We will feel the same now as then. The final day holds no fears on the inside of our life.

We saw in verse 6 that this assurance is linked to our gifts and our calling. It is the theme of calling to which we now return in verse 9.

> **9. God is faithful, though whom you were called to the fellowship of his son Jesus Christ our Lord.**

The assurance comes within the fellowship of His son. What feeds our assurance is not our past success: for after a success can come a fear of possible future failure or an alternative view which brings a different evaluation of the past undermining such assurance. This will always occur when our inner assurance and wellbeing is rooted in worldly confidences. Our assurance lies at a deeper level in the area of the human spirit. This domain is relational. True assurance is rooted in a relationship with Jesus and with His people.

You cannot be in real fellowship of Jesus without being part of the church so we conclude that continuing assurance needs real relationships in the church.

> **10. I entreat you, brethren, through the name of our Lord Jesus Christ in order that you may speak the same and there be no divisions among you but that you be knit together in the same mind and the same thought.**

Where fellowship is destroyed through contention, there will be a consequent lack of assurance. This confidence which amazes and confounds the world, which is ours in Christ, withers in the wake of relationship break down. So Paul in 1:10 asks they be "perfectly joined together" which shows in their attitude and speech (cf. Philippians 2:1,2)

If our assurance is an ingredient in moving in spiritual gifts, it is not surprising that when there is relationship break down there is also a decline in the use of spiritual gifts. Christian history is full of examples of spiritual gifts in use being stopped by controversy (Tertullian and the Arian controversy; the Celtic church and the dispute with Rome, the miracles of healing and visions in the church and the East/ West divide, and we remember the absence of spiritual gifts for 300 years after the disputes surrounding the reformation, and what about the lack of confidence amongst many because of contentions following the Welsh revival and other Pentecostal movements where they were branded as false cults in the early 20th century or those over Billy Graham in the mid-20th century or the suspicions and contentions regarding John Wimber or the Toronto blessing. Church history is full of examples of contentions destroying assurance which meant a diminishing of spiritual power.)

It is also no surprise that without signs of the kingdom there will be less or no growth, but rather decline because there is nothing to distinguish the people of God from any other religion or group of people on the earth. Spiritual gifts demonstrate the Kingdom of God, sourced in heaven and made known on the earth. Assurance is key for this and contentions damage the growth of that assurance.

> **11. for it has been made clear to me concerning you, my brethren, by those who belong to Chloe that there are arguments among you.**

Here Paul mentions his source. Chloe was a woman known to the Corinthians who had connections in Ephesus for part of her household (probably a slave) had passed news to him from her about the divisions in the church. Chloe was probably a business woman based in Corinth and because of her work had links with the Roman province of Asia. This means that the first issue which Paul tackles in the church is not one that is within the letter that Stephanas and his friends brought with them from Corinth. This he starts at chapter 7. Stephanas and his friends must have also discussed church life with Paul before he wrote this letter and I think some of this may be referenced in the "it has been reported" in chapter 5:1 when talking about sexual immorality in the church. But he first deals with the subject of divisions in the church about which has been told.

12. I say this that each of you says "I am of Paul, I of Apollos, I of Cephas I of Christ."

Paul now begins to go deeper into the subject of contentions and divisions. He makes two observations which we will draw out of the passage as we progress.

(a) Contentions will seem right to man, but they can twist your calling; positioning you in a different place than God's intention for your life. God never intended Paul to have a loyal fan base where he became the focus not Jesus. Paul was not sent to baptise. He was not crucified for them. He points out his calling. For he is an apostle, and indeed has a calling to them, but he is not their saviour or even called to pastor the church. He is called to preach the gospel.

(b) Contentions are to do with the wisdom of words and empty the cross of any effect. How? Because contentions lean towards human wisdom and so there is trust in the wisdom of men, and this is never the same as the power of God. (v18) What our faith is founded on makes a difference in our experience.

Paul will expand this theme as the letter proceeds.

13. Christ has been divided. Paul has not been crucified on your behalf or were you baptised into the name of Paul?

Some translate all these sentences as questions, and indeed the word order and sense does point to the last clause being a question. But the Greek text of the first two clauses indicates statements rather than questions. Paul has not been crucified, and Christ has been divided. Paul is making a statement. There is no need to think this is a rhetorical question. Paul is making the powerful observation that their attitude has actually divided Christ. We can split the anointing. God gives the anointing (Christ) in His Holy Spirit to one and to another and the result should be a drawing together superseding the divisions created by the world of different tribal or people groups or languages or nations even superseding the natural division of male and female and social class divisions so we can be "all one in Christ Jesus" Galatians 3:28 (see also Revelation 5:9; 7:9). Yet in the Corinthian church and indeed in other examples within church history instead of a coming together there has been a dividing. In such divisions the anointing flows in a divided way. There is an anointing in the eastern and western churches, an anointing in catholic and protestant, in Methodist and Anglican yet there is also division which has brought much damage and hurt to the work of the kingdom. The anointing, instead of flowing in the unity of the Spirit flows down divided streams. We shall see in this chapter that Paul observes that when this happens, the people of God go blind because the worldly unspiritual thinking which feeds division makes them unable to receive revelation from God.

The world has loyalties and distinctions which it seeks to make for its security and control. Religion as a world system can do the same. But the anointing of the Spirit is not of this world but from the Father and Son. Jesus said in John 18:36 that his kingdom was not of this world. If it was his disciples would fight (because in the world there are distinctions - some are in while others are out). This is not so with the kingdom. The only thing that keeps us out is our choices and our judgements. Because we have free will which can affect the way we relate to God, we can also divide that which God has given to bring the Kingdom of God to the earth. This hinders the effectiveness of that anointing and so the Kingdom of God is not seen in power everywhere in the world. Psalm 133 reminds us that it is in unity that God has decreed His blessing.

> ## 14. I thank God that I baptised none of you except Crispus and Gaius:
>
> ## 15. so that no-one could say that you were baptised in my name.

Crispus the converted synagogue leader (Acts 18:8)and Gaius in whom the church gathered (Romans 16:23 mentions Gaius as hosting the whole church in a city where Erastus was the treasurer which we know is Corinth (In recent years a marble pavement from the first century AD has been discovered in Corinth stating it was paid for by Erastus). Crispus and Gaius were probably two highly significant founder members of the new church. It was probable that these alongside others in leadership there baptised the other converts of the Corinthian church.

> **16. I baptised also the household of Stephanas. Besides that I do not know if I baptised anyone else.**
>
> **17. For Christ did not send me to baptise but to evangelise.**

Paul describes in Acts 26:16ff what Jesus said to him on the Damascus Road when he was converted. This has dictated his priorities and his journey. He saw the fulfilment of this as not leading individual churches or baptising or pasturing the flock. He was sent to preach and teach Jesus crucified to pay the price of our sin. His life call had rather given him a message, revelation and understanding of scripture which was foundational for the church made up of Jews and Gentiles (non-Jews). For Paul he knew he was called to the Gentiles to bring them into the people of God. This involved him in debate with others and in travel. His object was that all could become part of the people of God walking in the blessing of Abraham because he knew that they are set apart through faith not biological DNA or good deeds.

> **not in wisdom of speech so that the cross of Christ was not emptied.**

The Greek word κενωθη can mean empty or in vain and many translations combine these two ideas by translating it as "emptied of power". But the focus is not so much a contrast between wisdom and power but rather wisdom bringing about a lack of effectiveness in the experience of the hearer. Wisdom of man does not so much stop the Holy Spirit of power; it more affects man's soul which renders him unable to receive the full download from heaven that is possible through the cross. Worldly wisdom causes us to dismiss the benefits through the cross.

31

18. For the word which is of the cross is foolishness to those who are perishing but to those who are being saved it is the power of God.

19. For it is written "I will destroy the wisdom of the wise and will nullify the shrewdness of the shrewd"

20. Where is the wise man? Where is the scribe? Where is the debater of this age?

21. For since in the wisdom of God the world through its wisdom does not know God, God was pleased through the foolishness of the preaching to save those who believe.

22. Since both Jews ask for a sign and Gentiles seek wisdom,

23. we preach Christ crucified, offensive to the Jews and foolishness to the Gentiles,

24. but to those who are called whether they be Jews or Greeks, Christ is the power of God and the wisdom of God.

Notice that it is our call which spans the divide between Jew and Greek. It is the calling which can make denominational walls irrelevant. There is no distinction in the world that can stand against a calling coming from assurance and shown by gifts of the kingdom of God.

25. Because the foolishness of God is wiser than humans and the weakness of God is stronger than humans.

26. Look at your call, brethren because not many of you were wise according to fleshly standards, not many very able, not many well-bred.

Here Paul defines the three areas which the world respects and indeed where there is competition. The first is in the area of intellect, the second in the area of physical ability, and the third in the place of social standing. Paul makes it clear that the Corinthian church should not return to the values they inherited when they were in the world. Applying worldly values to the church would tear it from its proper place. It would be to allow the yeast of the world to change the church into just another religion, club or society. The church needs revelation, spiritual life and adherence to the living God to maintain the church as it is meant to be. The very things which the world calls foolish are the very things the church knows are essential.

> **27. But the foolish things of the world God has chosen to shame the wise people and the weak things of the world God has chosen in order to shame the strong things.**

Paul is applying what he sees in the Corinthian church to a more general principle in the way God works which is present in creation and history and is not just within the new Kingdom of God for "God has chosen" it this way from the foundation of the world. We are reminded of this principle every time the unlikely win over the strong, or the wise. Examples that come to mind are the animals that survive in the deserts of our world or the flowers that bloom in the Arctic, the strange creatures of the deep which make a better life than some wise human beings on the planet. In history there is the deliverance of weak England from the might of the Spanish Armada, or the weakness of Ghandi before the might of the British Empire. There are many other examples. God has left within creation and history reminders that human wit of prowess is flawed and the whole of creation including the human race is dependent on its creator.

The Greek case endings on the words tells us that Paul mentions "things which are weak or strong or foolish" but yet has people in focus when using the word wise. The reason for this is that wisdom is only seen in the choices and words of living creatures. Wisdom is a bi-product of life where there is choice. It cannot be manifest without it. Human beings can be wise in a way that other animals cannot, because of the gift of choice that they possess in the created order.

28. What is insignificant of the world and the things which are despised God has chosen and the things which are not in order that what is may be made ineffective.

This follows the same thinking yet it is making an additional point. This is not focused on a possible mind set change or recognition on the part of those in the world who see this, but rather is concerning actual differences to the plans and purposes the world may have. This verse is illustrated every time there is a revolution of nobodies who render ineffective the plans of those who are in a position to plan or rule. Every time ordinary members of the public thwart evil counsel or make impossible what was possible, this verse becomes true. The greatest illustration of these verses is Jesus who though untrained by worldly standards confounded the learned and educated at the age of 12 (Luke 2) and birthed a movement which changed the world though born in an obscure town of Bethlehem in an insignificant part of the Roman Empire. He who had no strength to fight yet won the greatest battle of all against sin, the world and the devil. The thwarting of the powerful, or rich, or well thought of, by the despised has occurred down the ages. We think of Wesley, Wilberforce, Churchill and others of old who although respected with the hindsight of history, were, in fact, thought little of at the start of their life call.

29. This means that no flesh could boast before God.

Flesh is our life without God. "Flesh" is singular emphasising there is not a single part of our flesh that can boast before God: whether it be our strength our wisdom, our status or even our position through what we have done, none of this can we boast before God. When God acts, no flesh can glory. Real life is found with the Holy Spirit not flesh; God not man is the source of all that is good and worthwhile and the world and the flesh mind set will militate against it and the flesh (self) part of us will find it hard to disagree with what the world says. The world glories in intellect, ability and social standing and honours such. The flesh likes the honours the world gives and it also glories in a job well done whether the world recognises such or not.

> **30. From Him (God) you are in Christ Jesus whom he became our wisdom from God (which is shown by) both righteousness and sanctification and redemption**
>
> **31. in order that as it is written "He who boasts, should boast in the Lord"**

Wisdom from God is defined as righteousness, sanctification and redemption. I think these are effects of the wise choices and words God has made which have enabled us to become righteous in life so we can exercise rightful authority despite the fact we used to be unrighteous. Wisdom, also shows itself in times when we choose different ways than the world which brings God's blessing to us and others. Our righteousness challenges the deceitful righteousness of the world and sanctification is all about us being set apart and different from the world and our old life and values.

God's wisdom means we can operate in sanctification – in our holiness we learn how to access the Lord's throne room and move in His purposes when our past experience outside Christ has just been being a sinner. We also demonstrate wisdom in our redemption - when we walk aright free under the mercy and favour of God out of past slavery. Christ Jesus is the source of all these blessings. He is indeed the way the truth and the life!

Chapter 2

> **1. And I coming to you, brethren, came not with prominence of speech or wisdom as I announced to you the mystery of God.**
>
> **2. For I did not intend** *(Paul puts himself deliberately in this frame)* **as knowing anything among you except Jesus Christ and that this was the man who was crucified.**

Paul knows two things. He knows Jesus Christ and then secondly he knows about the crucifixion. Both areas are crucial to his teaching and to the faith and development of the church.

> **3. And I was in weakness and in fear and in much trembling towards you.**
>
> **4. And my speech and my proclamation was not in persuasive words of wisdom, but in demonstration of the Spirit and of power**
>
> **5. in order that your faith should not be in human wisdom but in God's power.**

Faith comes by hearing (Romans 10:17). Paul knows God speaks his invitation amidst the works of the kingdom - amidst things that the world sees as suspicious, futile, foolish or false.

God speaks through revelation, miracles, and testimonies. Faith can be engendered by any of these three. A work of healing can bring others to faith, and talking about that event can do the same as can revelation which speaks to your soul.

Paul also recognised that faith could be birthed through presenting God's word through human wisdom, but then that faith would be limited in expression by the intellect. The environment of power encounter for faith makes the sky the limit and leads to quicker and more manifestations of the kingdom as right from the start the faith that is birthed is fully engaged with the unseen kingdom and is not mixed with the intellect and education that the world acclaims.

6. We do speak wisdom among those who have reached completion.

Paul uses the technical term for an initiate into a mystery, He is referring to those who have become Christians who are in the people of God; who have completed their journey to reach faith in Jesus and a relationship with Him.

As Christians who are "born again" we have a new nature which makes us complete and fulfilled. It is this new nature which enables us to recognise and receive the wisdom from God.

It is not the wisdom of this age, nor (wisdom) of the rulers of this age who will be made ineffective.

7. But we speak the wisdom of God in a mystery which was hidden which God ordained before the ages for our glory,

We get glory because we receive the effects of understanding the wisdom

8. a (wisdom) which none of the rulers of this world recognised.

The events around the cross, the execution of Jesus, are a permanent reminder of the foolishness. What the world calls wisdom or politically expedient or helpful is actually not wisdom at all.

If they had recognised, they would not have crucified the Lord of glory

Glory attracts the rulers of this age. That is what they are after (see Isaiah 60:3, Revelation 12:4. Haggai 2:7) If they had recognised Jesus as the source and Lord of glory they would not have crucified Him.

9. But as it is has been written "What eye has not seen and the ear has not heard and what has not been gone upon the heart of man

επι καρδια. Επι with the accusative is to do with place and means "upon". Our inner thoughts arise towards our consciousness and are carried by our heart where our self-esteem with its perceptions, desires and priorities lie. Isaiah 64: 4, which Paul quotes here, states that throughout history "from the beginning of the world" the only God that can be seen or heard with the ear or perceived (presumably with the heart) is the Lord.

Paul here is making the point that this verse shows that only God gives real wisdom. The world cannot get wisdom without relating to God. Before the fall, wisdom was connected to relationship with God. It only became distanced from relationship when man sought independent knowledge of good and evil without the tree of life. This means that worldly wisdom is not real wisdom at all. Real wisdom needs relationship with God.

that is what God has prepared to those who love Him.

All that is not seen, heard or understood by the world, those in relationship with God can receive. It is ready; indeed it has been made ready by the Father for us.

10. that is what God has revealed to us through the Spirit. For the Spirit investigates everything, even the deep things of God.

We may feel scrutinized by the Spirit in every area of our life including our motives and thoughts, our priorities and our loves, but Paul wants us to know the Spirit does the same with God. This reminds us that when we are walking with the Holy Spirit it is possible for us to know the motives, thoughts, priorities and loves of the Lord. We can enter His private world in the same way as God enters our private world. This is truly amazing!

11. For what human agency can know the things of a human being unless the spirit of the human being is in him. In the same way, no-one knows the things of God except the Spirit of God.

12. We have not received the spirit of the world but the Spirit (sent) from God in order that we might know that the things given freely to us from God,

Or possibly "that we might know the things from God are freely given to us". I suspect it is more likely to mean that we might recognise all the gifts that are from God - as Paul's emphasis is on the contrast between world attitudes and God centred attitudes. He is not saying we will discover right doctrine regarding the free gift of grace, but rather that we can discover the things freely given to us by God, things we would not recognise , understand or move in without wisdom. V 13 then follows in the same theme of spiritual words bringing spiritual revelation to spiritual people.

13. What we speak about, not in the wise words taught by man, but (words) taught by the Spirit bringing together (this is what συγκρινο means) **spiritual things to spiritual people.**

14. Man who pertains to this life

ψυΧικος translated pertains to this life could be translated "soulish" as the word at root refers to the soul. Paul is referring to a person who does not see beyond the soul with its natural feelings and its ties to the physical world. It makes our public and private worlds, together with the facts and wonder of the physical world, its only spiritual domain. Soulish people can be awed at creation or perceptive of spiritual atmospheres, even engaging in some spiritual activity but they never relate to God. "Soulish" describes the human condition without God. Our spirit is dead to God – naturally we do not see or hear Him. When we are "born again" our spirits come alive to God and we begin to recognise His voice and see what He is doing. "Soulish" is not as strong a negative term as σαρκινοις which is the word used in Chapter 3 to describe the Corinthians. This word σαρκινοις is translated carnal in old versions of the Bible The part σαρκινοις of man is the part Paul later describes as in which "no good dwells" and which will be stripped away from the soul in death. Carnal is not what Paul is talking about here. He is talking about "Soulish". The soul (ψυΧος) has an eternal existence (in the way that σαρκινοις does not). Paul is reminding us that Christians can still operate at this low soul level and be miles away from our God-given destiny of walking with God moving in His Spirit and understanding the Lord on the earth. We are to be filled with the Holy Spirit relating to God by our human spirit (Romans 8:16) and as such that becomes central to our lives not our souls. Our relationship with God becomes more important than what we choose, feel or think (which is to do with the life of the soul).

If the mind, will and emotions are not impacted by our relationship with Jesus we are "soulish" rather than spiritual in the real sense of the word. One of the results of this is that we cannot receive the things of the Holy Spirit. We must be careful not to go on our feelings or our thoughts or our past decisions or perceptions because that soulish approach will mean we will despise what the Spirit says and does.

does not receive the things of the Spirit of God. For they are foolishness to him, and he is not able to understand them because it is spiritually examined.

The activity of the Holy Spirit is one of an investigator. God's Spirit searches our hearts and minds. He is a detective on a case with the authority to act to on our behalf in blessing where there is righteousness or truth. He searches not just to see, but so He can act. He analyses the motives of prayer, he looks at the capacity we have to bear the blessing or opportunity we are asking for. He recognises the enemy's advance or retreat, the genuine love of God, the state of our heart with its thoughts and intentions. The Bible: describes the Holy Spirit as the eyes of the Lord which go over the earth (Revelation 5:6 – see 1:4b). It is this investigative capacity which is his primary characteristic. (2 *Chron. 16:9 for the eyes of the Lord run to and fro throughout the whole earth, to show himself strong on behalf of them whose heart is perfect toward him*. See also Zechariah 4:6, 10) He notes our reaction, our welcome or lack of it and assesses by our reaction whether we are not ready or worthy of further call, revelation or opportunity. Our reaction dictates our destiny. Whether when we see what He brings and we welcome this or regard it as foolishness does make a difference to our lives and the course our life takes.(Matthew 22:5-9)

---

15. But he who is spiritual judges all things yet he is not worked out (judged) by anyone.

16. For one knows the mind of the Lord who is knit together with him. We have the mind of Christ.

The word" knit together" is also used in Colossians 2:19 and Ephesians 4:16 referencing relationships in the church that form the temple where the Holy Spirit can dwell. Colossians 2:19 - "the Head, from which all the body by its joints and ligaments (which enables the body) to be supported and knit together, increases with the increase of God." The body increases by the joints and ligaments which refers to the relationships some which give structure and some for activity. When they are operative there is nourishment, support and a knitting together. The body then increases the increase of God. The knitting together and the support structure that relationships bring allows the body to build on what God does. To the church God resources these relationships. It is here that God dwells by his Spirit. He may provide 5, 2 or 1 talents (to quote Jesus' parable) but we can increase that because of the quality of our relationships. Ephesians was written at the same time as Colossians and parallels many verses and Ephesians 4; 16 being a parallel verse to Colossians 2; 19. Here Paul explains that it is to these relationships that God supplies His power.

δια πασης αφης της επιχορηγιας κατ'ενεργειαν εν μετρω ενος εκαστου μερους"which is translated in an amplified manner " each ligament has support in relation to the power (it has) in the area of its responsibility. Each in its own area of responsibility."

The amount of supplies into the relationships which brings growth is according to the work being done by them.

By way of summary: Church growth comes through an increased presence of God in church life. This happens relationally. The more we obey God together, the more power to grow happens. The various linkages and relationships God resources with anointing increase His presence and bring church growth.

In those passages Paul refers to Christ being the head. We are knit to Jesus in the same way as we are knit to one another.

The result of this being knit together with the head is that we have the mind of Christ. His thoughts become accessed by us through the knitting together. The closer we are knit the more this happens. This is why he says we have the mind of Christ. The unity of the church is made up of members who know the mind of Christ. The human mind has lots of different things going on at the same time, with thoughts and memories and reactions and emotions all weaving together. A right mind can distinguish right priorities and importance to each so we act wisely. Together we can have the mind of Christ, so our actions and our responses are like Jesus. We will have different gifts, characters, thoughts, reactions or expressions but we can together make manifest the mind of Christ. The more we are in the anointing of the Spirit in the Unity in the Spirit the more this is seen in the church and evidenced in the world.

The knit together verbs used by Paul in his epistles echoes psalm 122 where the people of God (Jerusalem) are described as being compacted together. Perhaps it is fitting to finish this section with these verses.

Psalm 122:1-7 - I was glad when they said unto me, Let us go into the house of the Lord. [2] Our feet shall stand within thy gates, O Jerusalem. [3] Jerusalem is built as a city that is compact together: [4] Whither the tribes go up, the tribes of the Lord, unto the testimony of Israel, to give thanks unto the name of the Lord. [5] For there are set thrones of judgment, the thrones of the house of David. [6] Pray for the peace of Jerusalem: they shall prosper that love thee. [7] Peace be within thy walls, and prosperity within thy palaces.

Corinth

Paul looked over at Sosthenes. "We will continue in the morning." The light of the day was fading fast and the lamps were giving more smoke than light tonight so chapter three of one Corinthians as it would be known would be written in the morning. Paul picked up the manuscript left by Sosthenes as he departed to bed. Paul could just read the writing though his eyes were never good in such light. He reached over to the two jugs provided by their hosts and he poured first some wine and then water from the other jug into his tumbler size glass. This was a time to relax, but also to pray.

In the quiet of the room, he recalled the Church in Corinth. There were many people from all ages and all backgrounds. There were doctors, teachers, fishermen, farmers, slaves and free. There were specialists in linen, makers of quality furniture as well as a range of those who sold imported and local goods. The wealthy were those engaged in trade, for Corinth had come into prominence because of its ideal harbour positioned west towards Rome. There had always been a close link between Corinth and Rome as Corinth had originally been full of retired Roman soldiers who had been rewarded with land there. Although Athens was the capital of Achaea, Corinth was much larger. Achaea had been for over 40 years an imperial province alongside Macedonia which it bordered to the north, but for the last 16 years there had been an even closer integration between Rome and Corinth. Emperor Claudius had marked its closer link with Rome by restoring the proconsuls of Achaea and Macedonia to the Senate. There were those in the church at Corinth whose family had always lived in Corinth. They had heard stories passed down to their grandparents about the destruction of old Corinth by the Romans, but those same grandparents could recall as children the rebuilding of what was now a beautiful modern Roman city. The city of Corinth was big, bustling and a cosmopolitan hub city and it was still expanding with new building happening all the time as the riches continued to increase. The heart of the city, the forum, was filled with temples and shrines to the emperor and various members of his family, built alongside temples to the older Greek gods such as Apollo. Apollo's son, Asklepios, the god of healing, had a shrine there also. The city was young, dynamic, and not hidebound by tradition. It was a mix of dislocated individuals without strong ethnic identities seeking to shed their former low status by achieving social honour and material success. There were elements of the city which was influenced by the debate and philosophy of Athens, but trade and business dominated everything. Though both Athens and Corinth had large harbours, Corinth was a very different place from Athens, and five times the size. It had been built just over 100 years before with some innovative architecture and latest design. Corinth was a major city of trade and the church was made up of a gathering of travellers who were born in other parts of the world as well as those born in Greece. Most of the older families in the new city of Corinth could trace their ancestry back to an esteemed servant of the Roman Empire or a less known member of one of the Roman legions. Freed Slaves and conscripts from Italy, Greece, Syria, Egypt and Judea had been given land as the city developed as a roman colony under Julius Caesar. The new city was cosmopolitan from the start and within just a few years, the enormously profitable commerce at this crossroads of the nations had brought thousands more eager settlers from all over the Mediterranean. Many of these accumulated enormous personal wealth and formed a new local ruling class of self-made women and men under the authority of a proconsul who was a servant of the Roman Senate appointed by the emperor.

Paul had arrived on his own from Athens when he first came to Corinth, and he met Aquila more or less straight away. They were both Jews and they quickly formed a friendship. Aquila recognised Paul was not a wealthy man and so employed him in his tent making business. Paul quickly found that Corinth had a synagogue. Crispus was the ruler of the synagogue when Paul first came there. When Silas and Timothy eventually joined him from Macedonia, he started to debate every Sabbath in the synagogue with the Jews there about the truth of Jesus as Messiah and the wonder of the gospel. It was a great day when Crispus turned to Christ, but not everyone in the synagogue was happy, and caused a lot of trouble for Paul, and the other Christians. Paul and Crispus moved out of the synagogue to a large enough house next door owned by a Gentile and were joined by many households. The church grew and grew and it was not too long before the church had groups of Christians all over the city and beyond under different leaders and teams. There were groups of Christians throughout Achaea, and Paul hoped to visit some of these groups when he visited Achaea in the next few months.

Paul had made some deep friendships during his time in Corinth and longed to renew his acquaintance with them. Paul recalled Phoebe who lived in Cenchrea where the smaller eastern port of Corinth was located, who first became part of the church whilst Paul was in Corinth who has continued to be a church leader and there was also Stephanas, Achaicus and Fortunatus who between them had links with most of the church in the city and beyond in the wider Achaia region. Some of those he had known at Corinth had now moved onto Rome since Paul had left , and fresh leaders had taken over. The church had grown. There were now established church groups in every part of Corinth. The Church benefited from meeting together from time to time at the house of Gaius a prosperous business man who had a house large enough to have all the church meet for special occasions especially when important letters were to be read or announcements made. "They will be gathering to listen to this letter in a few weeks' time" mused Paul. He looked back with wonder at how God had brought the church into being. Paul had followed his preferred method of starting in the synagogue in Corinth. Unlike Philippi, Corinth had enough Jews to form a synagogue in the city, and Crispus and then Sosthenes had been their leader. Paul thought how things had changed for him over the years. Sosthenes in the early days had opposed Crispus and the advance of the Christian faith in the synagogue at Corinth. He had been elected leader of the synagogue when Crispus resigned. This had happened when the synagogue opposed the church Paul had started.

Now Sosthenes was also a Christian and Sosthenes and some of those who had opposed Paul were now part of the church. The church was much larger now. Though there were still many Jews in the Corinthian church, there were many more non-Jews than Jews in its gatherings. The church was now so numerous that they met regularly in different houses in the city (as they now did in Ephesus also) and the leaders and others gathered from time to time in Gaius' large house in Corinth. The rapid growth and life of the church there was wonderful.

There was Stephanas. How could he have forgotten about baptising one of the first converts in Achaia and his household. It was a good that Stephanas who was there at the start of this letter had interrupted and said he and his family were also baptised by Paul. We must have the record straight. Paul put the parchment safe on the desk where Sosthenes had left it and sipped his wine. God had blessed the Corinthians in the wake of their first visit there. God had then sent others to encourage the new faith of the church. Amongst these were Apollos who was a good preacher, eloquent from an Alexandrian background, which was one of the centres of learning in the ancient world. There was also Peter who visited various places in the ancient world accompanied by his wife. He spoke of the teachings and actions of Jesus, and helped every church he went to get more in touch with Jesus. He was someone who had actually known Jesus during his earthly ministry and was a Jew many could understand and relate to, and he brought encouragement and authority wherever he went. Paul had arrived in Corinth before any of them just eight years before and had started the church.

He turned to look out the window which looked westwards to the red sky as the sun had already passed the rim of the earth. How he longed for heaven to reach more on the earth through the gospel. There was so much more! Ephesus was on the brink of another revival. There had been in the last year or so many miracles of healing. There had been an increase overflow of power so that people had even been healed who Paul never met. He had given handkerchiefs he had blessed to caring friends and family who had placed them on the sick and they had got well. This had not happened like this before, as far as he knew, but it was the Lord. There had also been open repentance from the occult and now new converts were opening new doors to the whole of proconsular Asia. Thousands in Asia just as in Achaia now knew that Jesus had died for all and risen from death and many had received the Holy Spirit.

Paul looked down at the desk where the parchments had been neatly arranged by Sosthenes. In the wake of the growth of the church in Achaia there were many concerns. Paul knew he had much to say in the letter, but that would wait for the morrow. For now bed and rest was needed to refresh him. Paul put his glass carefully down on the side, put the lamps out and left the room, already thinking about the next day.

Recent Life

Paul and Sosthenes were up early as usual at first light. They had both slept well and felt refreshed. When Sosthenes entered the room, Paul was looking out taking in the view of the city whilst stillness still pervaded the air. Ephesus, with a population of over 250,000 people was seldom still during daylight hours. Paul had a cloak around his shoulders for there was a definite chill in the air. Sosthenes joined Paul at the window and looked out. He could see the white marble towards the harbour and agora gleaming even in the early morning light holding a promise of the heat that would soon come. Paul turned to greet him but soon returned to his thoughts as Sosthenes prepared to get ready to write. Paul was recalling to his mind the last few months. He mused how different the view was from the house where they were staying than from the fortified watchtower on the hill overlooking the harbour where he had been imprisoned facing a possible death sentence. It had been touch and go whether he would survive this but Aquila had risked his reputation and even possibly his life to get Paul's case reviewed and Paul was now a free man. He knew there were many enemies still in the city and though he was free to move wherever he chose, caution still guarded his heart. In the last few weeks he had said goodbye to Epaphroditus who had spent the winter with Paul. He had travelled from Macedonia to visit and help Paul in prison. The cold winter climate and damp conditions had affected Epaphroditus badly and he had caught a fever and nearly died. He had returned to Macedonia with Paul's letter to the Philippians, which prepared the way for Timothy. Timothy was due to leave Ephesus in a few days' time to go to Philippi on his way to Corinth. The plan was that Erastus and Timothy would sail together for the first part of the trip, but then Erastus would not disembark at Macedonia but would instead continue on to Corinth. Paul knew he had to finish the letter so they could take it with them. Erastus would travel direct to Corinth with the rest of the Corinthian delegation, and Timothy would travel overland to Corinth via Macedonia probably arriving three or four weeks later. This would be ample time to prepare for Timothy's arrival.

Jentaculum, as the Romans call breakfast, was eaten quickly .They both had an air of urgency, but Paul more so. The task of writing the letter captured his full attention, and he was keen to continue the writing or rather dictating of the letter. Sosthenes was still enjoying a drink of milk enriched with honey but was at least moving to the table at the side of the room where light fell from the open window overlooking the street. It was still early, and it would not be long before this busy city started to return to its daily noise of cart wheels moving, people talking, children shouting and dogs barking which accompanied the constant movement along the streets providing throughout the day fluctuating and varied sounds. It was never quiet. For now, however, the only noticeable noise was the early birdsong greeting the dawn. Paul picked up the parchment and read what had been written so far. He knew he needed to continue the teaching he started the night before concerning the general attitudes within the Corinthian church and its divisions around personalities. He had made a start with the letter last night but now he needed to go deeper into the roots of the problem and provide at the same time a road map so the Corinthian church could walk aright in the future. This would need God's Spirit of revelation, and he felt already the stirring of the anointing within, which he recognised as a feeling of well being with excitement in a background of peace. Paul knew what he needed to say and he prayed in his heart that He might say it clearly and as God instructed. Paul moved over to the part of the room where the writing table was. He placed the letter in Sosthenes' hand who placed it carefully in front of him. Sosthenes had been arranging the other parchments making space for the task ahead. He looked up at Paul showing he was ready to start. Paul did not want to delay. There was much to cover before lunch. Sosthenes dipped his pen in the ink and started to write as Paul spoke,

"And I brethren could not speak to you as spiritual people but as carnal, as to babes in Christ..."

Overview Chapter 3-4

The Way Forward

The root of the problem - worldly thinking in the church.

This brings fruit which is not good, but there is a way to counter this. Paul now turns to the way ahead.

Paul moves from the individual to the church as a whole - "Brothers"

3:1-4:16 The effect: Worldly thinking affects what they can receive and how they build. Linked to this is the destructive attitude towards Paul and other servants of God.

Paul as apostle could be a blessing to Corinthians only if they had a right attitude towards him which would come about as they ditched their worldly viewpoints. The blessing and grace of Paul the apostle would have maximum benefit for those who related to him correctly with the right attitude. Worldly viewpoints would affect that attitude and therefore the grace Paul could give.

Paul was not attractive to worldly wisdom. He came with trembling and fear. (2:1). His content would not be the diet suitable for spiritual people but carnal, and worldly wisdom would conclude Paul was inferior to others, and therefore not obey what they heard.

His defence against that possible accusation is that he accurately assessed them as carnal because carnal shows in divisions (3:1-4). He asks for a proper attitude towards him and to the others (3:6; 4:1) the reason is so they can receive the grace that comes to Paul for them (4:14-16)

Some truths to hold onto when worldly thinking assails

1. When God sends, he imparts an anointing which will accomplish in those to whom he is sent if the relationship is right. Grace transfers relationally. These relationships have right attitudes and relate appropriately. Inappropriate attitudes cause relational withdrawal. In order for grace to pass from Paul's calling to the church, there must be good relationships.

2. The Holy Spirit teaching will be according to the state of our heart. The less carnal the more revelation we will receive. The more our togetherness in our relationship with Jesus, the more revelation will be imparted. For God sends Paul to speak to their carnal hearts, if they had been spiritual (and together they would be), the more Paul would have shared as God would have sent him to a different environment.
3. Recognising all things are yours turns the worldly thinking upside down. Instead of putting yourself as belonging to Apollos or Paul, you are with Christ above every power so everything can serve you including both Apollos and Paul. God will use everything in life for blessing but we need to see it that way. Moving away from worldly thinking will help that process.

Greek text commentary 1 Corinthians Chapter 3

1. And I, brethren could not speak to you as spiritual but as carnal,

σαρκινοις "fleshly" belonging to the realm of the flesh (σαρξ) and so is translated carnal. We are made body soul and spirit (I Thessalonians 5:24) and Paul knows that any one of these can be areas where Christians rely on for life, but it is the area of the spirit rather than the soul ψυχινοι or the body σαρκινοις where real life can be found in relationship with God.

Carnal v Soulish

Paul earlier (2:14) calls the Corinthians ψυχινοι because they rely for their life within the soul instead of pressing through to relate to God with their human spirit, and as we saw in the last chapter such a stance prevents them receiving the things of the Holy Spirit. The soul is designed not to operate outside a partnership with the spirit. We are made for life which is from a relationship with God interacting with our human spirit. When this happens Paul calls this "being spiritual". The soul, however, can instead of partnering with the human spirit, look away from the Lord towards the body for its life. Results of such is that life is seen in what gives pleasure to the body – what makes it look good or feel good – and which does not bring life at all. We remember the words of Jesus "Man shall not live by bread alone" (Luke 4:4) and "Life is not found in many possessions" (Luke 12:15). This position Paul refers here. He calls it "being carnal". Paul can tell the Corinthians are looking in this wrong direction – to the body rather than to the spirit- because of their competitive divisive attitudes.

The soul realm is the natural place for all humanity (1 Corinthians 15:44). It is the place of inner identity and meaning, and responds to both the seen and unseen creation. But if we try to live our life in the soul without God we are to be pitied. The soul is not the same as the spirit, and cannot produce the life the spirit desires (see James 3:15; Jude 1:19). Relationship with God is from the Holy Spirit who relates with our spirit (Romans 8:16) rather than our soul. Being psychic does not bring real life.

Carnal v Spiritual

In this verse Paul is talking about Christians who seek their life from the body. Human beings are unique amongst God's creation because they are flesh and spirit; made eternal like the angels yet earthly creatures as well. This means we live in two different realms. One is within the realm of our creatureliness (flesh) with its instinct, self-preservation and its drive to succeed, and the other within the realm of our relationship with God. At the beginning of human history, people chose to rebel against God and so humankind was left with only one option –to live within his creatureliness. His spirit though still hankered after God, but there was an ignorance deep in the heart of man which meant he did not seek after the true God and the drive for life within his soul he sought not from God but from the body i.e. from appearance, or strength and achievements, or skill and knowledge. Living without God in the world (Ephesians 2:20) and drawing our reference frame from our humanity and the world in which we live is what Paul means by being carnal. The carnal (flesh) is the part where desires are against the spirit, where the dreams are not as God intends (Romans 8:5; 1 Peter2:11). The carnal (flesh) is the part that feels temptation which draws us into sin.

Paul knew that Jesus had won a solution to the problem of man's ignorance of God. Because of his death and resurrection, Jesus had made it possible for us to connect to God again. It was now possible for man to find the life his spirit and soul longed for.

The Corinthians when they turned to Christ had been spiritually awakened to this new life. His expectation was that they therefore would no longer live as they used to do - in the old life where God was absent but rather in a new life where the Holy Spirit would be listened to, followed, and obeyed. Jesus demonstrated during his life on earth what it is like to be spiritual rather than carnal:- to be a spiritually awakened man. Not since the fall of man had there been a perfect example, but now humankind had Jesus. He became a real man so he was tempted just as we are yet did not sin (Hebrews 4:15). He could do this because he chose to relate to the Father, to abide in the Kingdom which meant living in the realm of the Holy Spirit where sin is seen for what it is and where God's purpose causes us to look forward towards

God rather than to the trigger points of the flesh. Sin uses our natural desires to lead us into sin. Jesus had these natural desires but he refused them, preferring instead the desires of the Spirit. The commonest trigger points are (1) personal appetite often amplified by loss or inner accusation; (2) intimidation from those we want to please or fear or (3)the promise of results or rewards from the world we live in.

as children in Christ.

As a result of their "being carnal" they have not grown to maturity - they had not become whom God designed them fully to be. They are therefore as "children in Christ" unable to carry the responsibility God would love to bestow on them, or be trusted to act appropriately or wisely in the complex battles of life and death. Their lack of maturity means God cannot even trust them to understand properly what they hear, so what they are taught is less than God would intend them to hear.

2. I gave you milk to drink not meat. For you were not able, but even now you are still not able, for you are still carnal.

3. For whenever there is competition or division among you are you not carnal and walk (as mere) men?

4. For whenever anyone makes the statement

($\lambda\varepsilon\gamma\omega$ used here focuses on the content whereas $\lambda\alpha\lambda\varepsilon\omega$ focuses on the speaking)

"I am of Paul." Whilst another "I am for Apollos" are you not on a human (Greek word for "men" not "carnal") **(rather than spiritual) basis.**

5. What is Apollos? What is Paul? Servants through whom you believed, and to each as the Lord has given.

6. I planted, Apollos provided water but God grew you.

7. So neither he who plants nor he who waters is anything but only God who gives the increase.

> **8. He who plants and he who waters are one. Each one will receive his own reward according to his own labour.**
>
> **9. For we are fellow-workers with God. You are God's field, God's building**

There is a link between the theme of reward and being fellow workers of God. The reward they receive from God is not from any belonging they may have as servants of the Corinthian Church calling or mission. It is rather because they are working with God. Paul and Apollos will be getting their reward from God not from them as they are fellow workers with Him. They should not regard themselves as of Paul or of Apollos or of anyone else. God alone is their master and gives the reward. Their focus also should be not as belonging to Paul or Apollos or Peter or anyone else as fellow workers, but rather belonging to God as His fellow workers. It is there where true rewards are to be found.

The Church at Corinth is God's field where they as fellow servants with god are sowing seed of the kingdom; they are God's building where they are working with god to build the church. Part of their reward is that the seed bears fruit and the church is built.

> **10. According to the grace of God which was given to me so I have laid a foundation as a wise architect, and another has built on it. Each person should look how he builds.**
>
> **11. For no-one is able to lay any other foundation beside that which has been lain which is Jesus Christ.**
>
> **12. If anyone builds on the foundation with gold or silver or precious stones or wood, hay, straw,**
>
> **13. the work of each will be made clear. For the day will show it because it will be revealed in fire.**

Every time we are granted more favour because of past faithfulness there has been a day of the Lord; every time there is revival and judgements on the earth there is a day of the Lord. Whenever there is an ending of a phase of church life and a development into another, we are living in a day of the Lord.

In the first chapter of Genesis each new day starts in the evening and proceeds to the day, so the final outworking and judgement "God saw that it was good" is clearly seen in the day (as opposed to the earlier work in the night). Each work of service will start small and grow to a point where it can be clearly seen in the day when God then exposes the work for what it is (or is not). The "day of the Lord" refers to the time when God assess a past work and opens or closes paths of favour or future opportunity.

All service especially done in God's name and out of obedience to Him attracts fire. When the fire falls and the sacrifice is true, there is increased favour and blessings from that sacrifice. A significant "day of the Lord" for Jesus was his baptism day which ended the "first day" of his birth and upbringing and brought in the "second day" of his earthly ministry. On that day if his baptism he received the judgement "you are my beloved son in whom I am well pleased" and as a result received more grace through the indwelling of the Spirit to start a ministry of power. His previous sacrifice as an obedient family member living a normal life with God central in humility was affirmed on that day and brought to the light. It ushered in also a new day through the Word and Spirit from heaven which heralded and empowered the earthly ministry of Jesus. Our service for God will attract God and His presence brings testing judgements which are to do with the fire of God. Whenever this fire falls, it is on a "day of the Lord" when God visits the work. This happens to the tower of Babel (Genesis 11:5); it happened to Belshazzar in Daniel's lifetime (Daniel 5:27), and to Job (Job 42:10). It happened in the experience of Abraham (Genesis 22:16-18), Moses (Exodus 3) and all the characters of the Bible. It is this "day of the Lord" that Jesus teaches about this in his parables, the wise and foolish maidens, the unjust steward and the unmerciful servant to name just a few. I will just chose one:- the parable of the talents where those given talents who act faithfully are set over cities at a day of the Lord (Matthew 25:23) and servants are judged faithful or not at the sudden unexpected return of their master (Matthew 24:46). These parables teach about such days of the Lord, when we enter into the joy of the Lord (Matthew 25:23), when there is an increase of the Kingdom for all of us (Isaiah 9:7) There are many days of the Lord not just the one final day. The teaching of Jesus in these parables does include the final day of the Lord for the work of creation. This final day of the Lord is Judgement day. Peter mentions this "day of the Lord" (2 Peter 3:10) referring to the time when the creation ends, but Paul here is referring to the time when what we have done shows up for what it is during our lifetime and this could be before the final day, as Jesus himself taught.

And what sort of work is of each person (i.e. the quality of each person's work) the fire will test it.

14. If anyone's work remains, which he has built upon, then he will receive a reward.

15. If the work of anyone is burnt up, he will suffer the loss, but he himself will be saved without further ado as through fire.

16. You do not know that you are the temple of God and the Spirit of God lives among you.

17. If anyone destroys the temple of God, God will destroy this man. For the temple of God is holy which is what you are.

Dividing into groups destroys the temple of God's Spirit. The Corinthians are building wrongly on the foundation treating Paul and Apollos instead as different part of the building and thus building a divided fellowship. When testing comes Paul sees such a divided place will not be able to withstand the heavenly fire and all their words and deeds will go up in smoke. He also reminds them how he started the letter to them. They are holy in Christ and they have heard the call which saints hear because they are holy. Holiness and rivalry do not go together. They are embarking on this division because they do not know who they are. I think Paul states this in verse 16. This is not a question. This position is reinforced by verse 17 where Paul is making a statement about who they are which I do not think they had realised so they did not know they were a temple of God and that this was being destroyed by their divisions. Now hopefully they would amend their ways. Paul then returns to his theme of wisdom as the next verses form a rounding off of the subject before he embarks on the next strand in this issue (Chapter 4).

18. No-one should deceive himself. If anyone seems to be wise among you in this age, let him be a fool so that he may be wise.

Personal choice to count our human wisdom (which is anything sourced by or affirmed by the world) as foolishness is the only way we should be. God is the source of all wisdom, and this is found in revelation and relationship with Him. The problem with human wisdom is it filters out much of what God is saying, trusting instead in some other view

Paul observes here that it is easy to deceive ourselves into thinking we do not need to do this. There is something deep in our nature which says we are wise when we are really fools. For example: - The Bible describes as a fool those who in their heart say there is no God (Psalm 14: 1; 53:1). There are many examples of people wise in the world's eyes who fall into this category.

When we decide to regard our human wisdom as folly, we are standing against our fallen nature and returning to the original place of humankind (Genesis 2-3). Our wisdom is not found in some independent place made possible by the tree of knowledge of good and evil where we think we are wise because we know what is good and what is bad. Wisdom is not shown by correctly answering facts or by doing the right thing as men think but rather by listening to God and from his revelation understanding the way the world is, the reasons behind something and the future path to take to fulfil God's purpose. The right choices to make flow out of this understanding which grows as our relationship with God grows.

True wisdom is what creation needs, and in the spiritual realms of creation this is what matters more than power. Jeremiah 10:12 says that whilst the earth was formed by power, the world (culture) was formed by Wisdom (wit) and the heavens stretched out by wisdom (design, strategy). This verse tells us that

1. Wisdom not power is what the supernatural world is awed by. Whereas the flesh of man on the earth is awed by power.
2. The nations in the world like power because it desires the respect of man, but culture is formed by wit.
3. Wisdom forms cultures which have a supernatural dimension to it.

Wisdom was never designed to be divorced from relationship (Proverbs 9:10; Isaiah 11:2) as it was through wisdom that God created the earth (Jeremiah 10:12) and gave life to its inhabitants. (Ecclesiastes 7:12; Proverbs 3:13; 4:10)

Wisdom has an alertness about it, a wit, an ability to say or do what fits the moment (word of wisdom) (e.g. Joseph before Pharaoh or Winston Churchill before wartime Parliament and the nation). Wisdom also has an ability to design, envision and strategize (word of knowledge).

19. The wisdom of this world is foolishness in God's presence

παρα τω θεο. παρα with dative means "near" a person so I have translated this in "God's presence". When we are near God the wisdom of the world shows up for what it really is: it is seen as foolishness. It is shown by its results which though clearly seen are perceived clearly by those who walk with God. The wisdom of the world draws its followers into an enclosed place where they are blind to what God is doing and unable to move with Him.

For it is written "He is catching the wise in their cleverness"

The word used for cleverness also means deceit. Paul is saying here about the peril of being deceived and thinking you are clever. The area where the wise in this world think they are clever is the very trap that will catch them. We cannot risk being "know all's", experts or the indispensable fountain of wisdom to problem solve, organise or impart teaching. Each one of these attitudes provides us with traps which destroy us. Such traps can bring distancing from people, overwork, poor health, rivalry, pain, unbelief and discouragement as well as worldly perspectives which make others who follow these so called wise, become fools before God even whilst they think that they are wise.

> **20. And again "The Lord knows the opinions** *(διαλογισμοσ is a thought, a reasoning, an argument).* **of the wise that they are empty.**
>
> **21. so that no one might boast amongst men.**

Boasting is not possible on two grounds before God. One is that their thoughts are not new to God "The Lord knows what they are thinking" and, two, their content is empty.

> **For all is yours**
>
> **22. whether Paul or Apollos or Cephas or the world or life or death or the present or the future. All things are yours. You are of Christ and Christ is of God.**

This passage is one of the most significant of the whole section and yet it can be read as a mere platitude rounding off the chapter! This is in fact the key to the answer of how to live avoiding the pitfalls which had brought about the divisions in the Corinthian church. It is the antidote to the attitude of "I am of Paul or I am of Cephas (Peter)". "All is yours" turns the loyalty of celebrity or the support of leadership upside down. The real position the Corinthians have is the very opposite of their worldly wisdom. Instead of they being part of rival teams belonging to Paul or Apollos or Peter, Paul and the others belong to the Corinthian Church members. These leaders are all servants sent to bless them.

This does not just apply to leaders but to everything: to "present and future" because this same truth is also true of time. The years do not rule us; they are there to serve us. God has given us time and the different seasons in life are from God for us to enjoy. The future too is something we can make a difference on. It is not inevitable fate as to how our future unfolds. We can change the future by our choices in the present. It belongs to us. The same truth is there for the world, and even life and death.

This can seem selfish, as if everything operates around you and for you, but what stops that is "you are of Christ and Christ is of God". We are about pleasing Christ and obeying His will just as Jesus was about pleasing the Father and obeying His will. We in Christ can find everything serves us. We can experience the changes of the world; we can have experience of both life and death. All of these can be a blessing to us. They are sent to serve us because of our position in Christ who has all authority. We have choices. We can step out of Christ and be dominated by the changes in the world or life or death, but if we remain in Christ our inheritance is to be able to find that everything serves us in one way or another. God intends to bless us. We are bigger than these just as Christ is bigger than us, and as Christ came to fulfil the Fathers will the same can be said of Christ in this context regarding God, for he made himself nothing (Phil 2), a little lower than the angels (Psalm 8, Hebrews 1). It is God who exalted Him. Everything should be subjected to the will of Christ who Himself was subject to the Father.

Chapter 4

Paul has not yet finished with this subject. He has just explained the right heart attitude to counter the attitude of "I am of Paul, Apollos, or Peter" but now he wants to turn his attention to how they should view him and Apollos. He will show in what ways Paul and Apollos belong to the Corinthians (as opposed to anyone belonging to them –"I am of Paul, Apollos etc."). He could not start teaching this until he had explained the teaching of the last chapter, but now he is ready to embark on this so that they receive the full benefit from those whom God sends to them whether it be Paul, Apollos or anyone else.

---

1. Thus should man consider us, as assistants serving Christ. *The word υπηρετης points to the relationship to Christ rather than the work they do.* **and stewards of the mysteries of God**

So the two main points of relationship to others is firstly as servants of Christ which focuses on their relationship with God and God's purpose, and secondly what they carry as stewards to the Corinthians in anointing and revelation.

"Mysteries" reminds us that unless there is disclosure in word (revelation) or action (anointing) there is nothing to steward. Tragically in churches "being good stewards" is often linked to how we spend or rather don't spend our money supporting faith engendered ministries (which because they are of faith are seen as risky) or moving in compassion. Once we place stewardship into anointing and revelation, new possibilities and perspectives open up before us.

What we steward can be given personally in dreams, impressions, visions and conviction, but it can also be in the way we keep what has been handed down from past generations, and also what has been revealed through others.

The Greek word "steward" is the normal word for steward but the word literally translated would mean "house – orderer" (i.e. one who organises the household). This reminds us that stewarding of mysteries has a church dimension to it. We steward the vision, the teaching and the revelation that we or others have given to the church (not just stewarding what God has shared with us personally). We are called to help steward the vision, giving understanding to develop this in the experience of the local church, as well as preserving the prophetic words connected to it. We are also called to steward the truths received by the church in the past, Stewards will need to be proactive sometimes to defend these and keep them, whilst at other times taking them and applying them to the choices they make and the priorities they hold.

2. Furthermore, it is required in stewards that each be found faithful.

3. It is of little concern to me that I am judged by you or by a "day" brought about by man

The word "day" has the word $\alpha\nu\theta\rho o\pi\iota\nu os$ which means the day is to do with people and not God (day of the Lord). Some have thought this refers to a civic court. The reasoning is the context is of examination and the word " day" can be used in the day of the Lord where judgements are made (see teaching above in chapter 3 text) but I do not think there is any reference to civic court.

He is stating two sources of judgements which he is not worried about because he is faithful. One is from the Corinthians "It is of little concern to me that I am judged by you" and the other is where men in general (not just the Corinthian church) judge the work because of events that happen originating in a human rather than divine cause. Not every time of pressure or difficulty is a "day of the Lord".

For I do not even judge myself.

Jesus did not judge and nor does Paul. This refusal to judge even reaches to a refusal to judge himself. In Luke 6:36-37 Jesus explains the path of non-judgement as a path of mercy involves no condemning (no writing anything or anyone off. Dead bones can live!) Forgiving, giving and no judging.

When we judge we appeal to the heavenly law court where Satan is the chief prosecutor. We have no need to go there for when Jesus died on the cross sentence was passed on our sin as it was taken by Jesus. The price is paid. We have no need to enter the law court again. Once we have received Jesus into our life. We now live in grace not law. We can choose to return to the law court but then our experience will be to face accusations from Satan, and miss the anointing and life which only comes by grace.

We choose to be in the law court when we refuse to forgive or only give to deserving causes. (Only after we have judged something to be deserving). Paul refuses to judge because he does not want to step out of the river of grace where the anointing flows, into the law court where there is no such anointing flow and also where Satan operates in his role as prosecuting council. Paul and other wise Christians steer clear of this and remain in the river of mercy bringing life to a needy world.

Judging can stop us receiving a messenger from God or recognising and valuing what they bring. It happened in Jesus' ministry where people judged Jesus by the town where he was from, the failure to not heal on the Sabbath and his challenging of the religious and devout to a greater devotion and experience of the kingdom, and so despite Jesus' call for them to look at what he was bringing (the works he was doing John 5:36; 10:37; 14:11), many could not recognise or accept him. (John 1:11)

Judging also can pivot us into that divisive belonging to Paul or Apollos based on flesh rather than spirit. So judging is toxic for the Christian and must be avoided. We should instead of judging eagerly receive what others bring. If they bring nothing then they are exposed as not stewards and servants but that is not our problem but God's. Nothing stops us benefitting from all that God brings.

4. For I do not know (about anything wrong) in me, but I am not justified in this. The Lord is the one who judges me.

5. So do not judge anything before the time until the Lord shall come who will make clear the hidden things of darkness and enlighten the motives of hearts.

When judgement day comes the criteria for right judgements will be made known which are not known now so our judgements can be faulty for we do not know the hidden things and we do not know the motives. These are both crucial parts of the evidence in forming a judgement. Only judgement day will expose these things.

> **Then shall you have approving recognition to each from the Lord.** *The only judgement that really matters is what God thinks.*
>
> **6 These things, brethren, I have made this a figure of speech in reference to myself and Apollos for the sake of you in order that you may learn in not to go beyond what is written in order that one is not proud on behalf of one against another**

Paul wants them "not to go beyond what is written" (i.e. that they are ministers of Christ and stewards of the mysteries of God). Paul wants to erase the distortions about who he and Apollos are so the relationship can be true between them and the Corinthians

He wants the Corinthians to relate to them as (1) servants of Christ. He does not want the Corinthians to relate to them either as superstars or as people who can be dismissed as irrelevant because they are not as good as others. (2) Stewards of the mysteries of God, Paul is making the point that how they administer this is not for anyone except God to judge. Paul is wanting to remove the performance critique out of the relationship between them so the relationship is unencumbered by judgements. The law court with its judgements creates fear and distinctions which thwart and hinder relationship growth. Relationships which work to nourish each other in love and respect need friendship. This is found in mercy rather than through legal proceedings.

> **7. For who judges me correctly? What you have that you did not receive? If indeed you received, why do you boast as if there was no receiving?**

Paul then outlines the inadequacies of a law court approach

1. They are not in a position to make judgements because they cannot know all the facts which are before the throne of God
2. They are not in a position to make judgements because they are not in the strong position they think they are. They have no inherent authority. They have received (from Paul and other servants) whatever spiritual grace they have. Is it right that they should turn around and judge the hand that had blessed them?
3. They are not operating in real authority. They are misreading what it is to have authority and what it looks like and feels like on the earth. Paul is now going to enlighten them on this

8. You are already full; you are already rich, *he now broadens his point to include Apollos by "us"* **You have ruled without us. Even so would that you had ruled so that we could rule with you.**

9. For I think God has shown the apostles (to be) least as condemned to death because we have been made a theatrical play to the world, and angels and mankind.

Acts 19 tells us that immediately before his departure from Ephesus, there was uproar in the city. It is probably within the year after this is written that this riot occurs, but Paul had already faced many threats and imprisonments in Ephesus as elsewhere. For wherever Paul went various trials accompanied his steps.

Behind the imagery in this verse are the gladiatorial contests and other "sport" events involving those condemned to lose their lives in the theatre which were so popular in Roman times especially in the reigns of Claudius and Nero. This is the surprising picture behind Paul's view of apostleship into which he includes Apollos. The world, angels and men look on like the crowd whilst the apostle stands in the theatre under a death sentence. This picture was never truer than when Jesus was on the cross, but this is also true for Paul and indeed all of Jesus' followers. Paul writes from his own experience of what it is like. He also knew the imagery first hand if he had actually fought with wild beasts in the Ephesian theatre (1 Corinthians 15:32).

The three segments who watch on are the world (which refers to the culture, traditions, and structures of power), angels (the supernatural unseen dimension comprising both angels and demons) and humankind (those men women and children who live at the same time as Paul and interact with areas he influences and also those future generations who interact with the influence and teaching as it is passed down from Paul). There are a lot more looking on than the few we see with our eyes when engaged in the service of Jesus.

10. We are fools for Christ but you are wise in Christ. We are weak you are strong. You are distinguished, we are without honour.

The attitude of the Corinthians Paul seeks to relate to is made clear to them. First is he is regarded as unwise saying what does not need to be said or doing what does not need to be done. Moreover he is regarded as weak and as a result of all this he is mocked and not respected

The world does not understand the spiritual and so they are considered fools. Whilst the world might do that because they are unspiritual, Paul did not expect fellow believers to do this. Paul sees the reason for such worldly thinking as originating in pride within and listening to the acclaim of the world. Worldly thinking comes from the human heart within or from the attitudes around us. This is part of the leaven of Herodians and Pharisees that Jesus warned the disciples against (Mark 8:15). Such thinking Paul seeks to change. He starts by contrasting their aspirations of what is godly with the reality of the experience of Paul and Apollos.

The Corinthian Christians in their worldly thinking might have been close to modern Christians who think that if they follow Jesus they can avoid trouble. Poverty, destruction, contention and slander only occur, so they might think, if the follower of Jesus does something wrong. Such people who are often on church committees and concerned about the church expect churches to have the money for all God wants **before** they start a project; or expect everyone to agree, or expect it to not upset anyone if the Lord is in it, and furthermore expect some end result to prove it was the right thing. None of these

69

however may be guaranteed as we obey Jesus, and to trust ourselves to this betrays worldly thinking.

> **11. Up to this present hour we both hunger and thirst, and we are naked and are assaulted** *(the Greek word means hit with the fist.)* **and without a place to be,**
>
> **12. and we toil working with our own hands. When we are reviled, we bless: when persecuted, we have endured, slandered we encourage. We have become as dirt of the world, the rubbish of all even to now.**

The word translated "dirt" is formed from the verb περικαθαιρω meaning cleanse all round and so it means that which is removed as a result of thorough cleansing. As such the meaning is almost identical to the word περιψημα translated rubbish which is from a verb to wipe all around, so it means that which is removed by the process of cleansing. These are however distinctly different words with the same themed idea. The first however is plural and the second singular, I think Paul is stating two aspects of being regarded as dirt. The first is referencing that as individuals (hence the plural form) they are treated as dirt (i.e. they are seen as irrelevant, dishonoured and even as dangerous and are therefore avoided) whilst the second word being singular is referring to way they are regarded as the cause of the trouble in the world). Paul and the other Christians already knew this, but they would continue to experience this in the future. He is blamed for the economic downturn of the silversmiths and related tradesfolk in Ephesus (Acts 19) and it is probable that Paul was martyred by Nero in Rome where Christians were blamed for the fire which devastated the city. Blaming Christians for the troubles in the world has not stopped in the 1st century. In our recent history Christians were openly blamed initially for the troubles in Ireland until they were the first to confound the world by facing loss with the message of forgiveness rather than revenge.

> **14. I am not writing these things to make you ashamed, but am instructing you as my children whom I love.**

15. If you had thousands of guardians

Paul uses a word translated guardians which has a meaning of child leader or teacher and was a technical word used for a slave who would take a child to school and look after him. A carer or nanny might have a similar role but I have chosen the word guardian)

in Christ but you do not have many fathers. For in Christ Jesus through the gospel I begat you.

Jesus described the gospel as seed. Paul sees this seed sown by him into their hearts through the anointing of Jesus makes him their spiritual father. The word translated with the old English word begat is probably the nearest English meaning of the Greek word. The word is used in other contexts to mean generate but in the context of fathering begat is probably better.

I ask you to be like me.

As a son is to a father. The likeness is to be in their thoughts and ways. In heaven it is these which are important, - not our words or our appearance. It is our thoughts which are not as God's thoughts; our ways as his ways (Isaiah 55). It is our thoughts which speak into the supernatural realm so God will search our hearts and our inmost thoughts, and we are to keep every thought captive so we can obey Christ. It is the fact that all thoughts - even the imagination of hearts - were evil that brought the decision to act in the judgement of the flood (Genesis 6:5). Proverbs 23:7 reads "For as he thinks in his heart, so is he"

Our heart condition and who we are, is shown by our ways. Paul is seeking to change thinking which will show in their ways (see Psalm 51:13; 119:5). Our ways as well as our thoughts affect our destiny Proverbs 16:7 says "When a man's ways please the Lord, he makes even his enemies to be at peace with him". Jeremiah writes (17:10) "I the Lord search the heart, I try the reins, even *to give every man according to his ways*, and according to the fruit of his doings". (Also Isaiah 57:18; Jeremiah 6:16)

16. For this reason I have sent Timothy to you

Timothy is possibly the postman who hand would deliver this letter to the church and would probably be in attendance as the letter is read out to the gathered Corinthian church. Acts 19 records how Paul sent Timothy with Erastus the city treasurer of Corinth from Ephesus to Macedonia and then onto to Achaia. Timothy is the one Paul has entrusted with the teaching ministry accompanying this letter.

who is my beloved and reliable child in the Lord who will bring up to your remembrance

The verb αναμνμησει has the basic word remember with the preposition ανα which means upwards. Memory is a response to things coming up which require action. This happened to the Lord in Acts 10 with Cornelius, but it happens to us. Bringing to remembrance in this context is not to engage in some self-indulgent reflective journey, but rather a call to analyse Paul's teaching and ways see any shortfalls or differences from this and change accordingly.

my ways that I have in Christ just as I teach everywhere in every church.

In Acts 15 we read that Paul had guidelines for his teaching in the mission God called him. Within those guidelines he was to teach on idolatry and sexual immorality as well as some aspects of food laws. These are some of the subjects covered in this epistle, so it is probable Paul is building on some of the teaching he gave to the church as it was forming around the gospel of Jesus Christ. It is this that he refers to here when he talks about the ways which he teaches in every church. He is certainly not expecting Timothy to say anything different from what is said elsewhere

18. Certain people have been puffed up as if I were not coming to you.

19. I will come quickly to you if the Lord will desire it and I will know not the word of the puffed up ones but the power.

20. For the Kingdom of God is not in word but in power. What do you want? Should I come to you with a stick or in love with a spirit of gentleness.

τε is used to connect phrases: In this case spirit and gentleness. The word gentleness has courtesy and consideration as well as meekness to describe its meaning. It is a word pointing to how Paul will behave with the Corinthians.

SUMMARY: Paul's teaching to get the relationship between him and the Corinthians straight. Paul knows grace is incarnational, flowing from his heart to them and bringing about God's purpose in Corinth. The relationship had become so twisted that little grace could flow to them so his motive is to encourage the Corinthians so that the relationship becomes healthy.

Paul is teaching the right attitude to have towards him and the others.

1. **Remove the distortions** about who they are. Relate to them as servants of Christ. Neither superstars in their own right or of people who can be dismissed as irrelevant for they are servants of Christ. Paul wants to remove the distortions about who he is so the relationship can be true

2. **Remove the judgements** over how or what they do. They are Stewards of the mysteries of God. How they administer this is not for anyone except God to judge. Paul wants to remove the performance critique out of the relationship between them again so the relationship is unencumbered. To this end he spends verses 4-7 speaking to the performance mind-set. Real achievement only comes in what God thinks who looks not at the outward but the inward attitude of the heart (v5). Competition is pride and is no longer there when you recognise what you are that makes you different is what you have received. Competitiveness and proving oneself loses its power when what we have is seen not as inherently belonging to who we are, but rather in what we have received so we can steward this to the blessing of others

3. **Be challenged to think differently.** He shows up the difference in experience between Paul and the Corinthians, and asks them to think

again about what an apostle looks like. What we think about someone affects that relationship. The thoughts may not be verbalised in word but are communicated through attitude or body language or lack of response to relationship development. Thoughts matter and they need to be agreed together.

4. **Stay together on the common ground and avoid independence**. Real relationships require reality and they require a walking together in that reality. Paul is identifying the common ground they should walk together. They thought they had arrived and did not need Paul and the others (v8) but Paul states that if they did indeed reign. If they were really operating in the kingdom of God, they would be alongside Paul as He operated in the kingdom too. Instead they are saying they do not need him. The closer we are to God and His Kingdom the closer we walk with those who walk in the kingdom. Independence (not needing Paul etc.) is a trait of the fall not of the kingdom.

5. **Recognise those who are special in your life and honour them** Paul is their spiritual father. He has a place of blessing that others cannot occupy. They can follow him so they can be blessed and enter their inheritance.

Walking in Ephesus

Paul was aware of the hum of a fly as it buzzed around the room. It had escaped the rising heat of the day by staying in the shadow of the room. It may have been there for some time but it had gone unnoticed. His attention had been fully captivated in writing the parts of the letter which would be known as Chapters 3 and 4 of his epistle. He was still uncertain whether what he had written would fully restore the relationship between him and the Corinthians, but he hoped it would be a good start to a full recovery. He thought with sadness at the puffed up Corinthians who were not operating appropriately or wisely. There was more to say but he would keep that back for a second letter. He needed first to see what the response of this letter would be. Paul decided he should go for a walk, and with a short explanation went down the stone staircase into the street. The air was hot but the breeze was noticeable and refreshing. He was not far from one of the main entrances into the city - where the Magnesium gate would later be built. He, however, turned westwards following the street leading towards the centre of this cosmopolitan city, and walked quickly down the spacious streets lined with buildings on either side. The road was widening or rather the houses were lessening as he approached the courtyard which made the space for one of the two marketplaces in the city. This State agora was a Public Square now about 190 X 520 ft. since being enlarged by Augustus, and was the centre of civic life with government offices and imperial shrines surrounding it. There was always a small military presence here and Paul chose a route across the agora which avoided them. To the west of the agora lay the temple of Isis which needed some repairs but it did not mar the magnificence of its other buildings with 3 rows of columns on each of the other sides of the square. All around the front of the buildings money lenders and the wealthy mixed with entrepreneurs, administrators, and politicians. The silversmiths making coins and idols were plying their trade. This was the official hub of a vibrant city and from here many were engaged in the many major building projects in the city. Law and order in Ephesus was one of its hallmarks especially since becoming part of the Roman Empire, and the influence and authority of the Empire was felt everywhere. The recent temple of Augustus obscured the old temple of Isis from view and Paul glanced northwards at the municipal palace with its Doric columns and the council chamber which was a theatre type structure called the Odium, where the city council met for debate and decision. The agora was full of people as usual, with the vendors under the shade of the Royal Portico which ran the full length of the front of these key civic buildings. Paul passed by some of the stalls. There were the usual mix of Ephesus items for sale, mementos for the thousands of visitors who came through the city on business or as a pilgrim visiting the world famous temple of Artemis. Not everyone was allowed to trade here. They had to be part of one of the temples or the government to do business at this place. Paul passed the offices where the taxes and imports were recorded and where the payments of military and civil servants was managed. Soldiers were on guard here protecting the money contained within. Paul walked firmly on through the crowds. There were people from countries Paul had only heard of but not seen. They came from the west and from the east including from countries far beyond the reach of the Roman Empire. He passed the famous aqueduct which brought water into the city and at its finish formed a refreshing pool at the south part of the civic agora. He kept walking at a good pace onto Curetes Street, one of the three major streets in the city. On both sides of the street were shops monuments and fountains. The shops were well built with living accommodation above and open shop beneath. Travellers could step off the street into shops of all shapes and sizes some with mosaic floors and all with plenty to sell. These were wealthy shop owners on this prime site in the city. The street was built entirely of marble and led to the impressive marble Mazaeus & Mithridates Gate which marked the entrance into the commercial agora. The gate had been built about 15 years before Paul arrived in Ephesus. Once in the agora you could buy anything you wanted. Paul passed by the sellers of cloth of different colours, the meat and the stalls selling produce from other parts of the world including pottery and ivory. He had to pause as some men brought fresh fish up to sell in the baskets at the edge of the agora. This was a prosperous business and there had been just built a toll house for the fishing paid for by donations. There were the usual sellers of nuts, spices and fruit as well as the famous perfumes of Ephesus of which "megalleion" was the best known. There were also "physicians" who sought to help and advise clients with lots of healing potions or charms, as well as bakers, carpenters, bed builders, wine growers and artists all making a good living. There were guilds in Ephesus where tradesmen would help others of the same trade with funeral expenses or sometimes in hardship. Some of these guilds especially the silversmiths had had special meeting recently concerned about their business since the public burning in the autumn of the magic scrolls and charms because of the preaching of Paul. The burning of the scrolls was last autumn and Paul had been imprisoned since then. He was no longer a regular here as he had been when he had spoken daily in the hall of Tyrannus. It was unlikely now that he would be recognised, but he still needed to be cautious and so without a pause he continued past the stallholders selling other fresh produce and vegetables, local produce from the surrounding farms and villages. This agora or "market place" in English was full of people, and it was hard to make quick progress so Paul pressed through the columns onto the eleven metre wide marble road with its colonnades providing welcome shade which brought him past the theatre on his right, and he turned left to walk to the ancient port of Ephesus past tax collectors and those taking charge of the animals from the ships and delivering them into the pound near the small prison about 500 yards westwards from where Paul was standing. There were also a small detachment of soldiers there to ensure order amidst the hustle and bustle of unloading cargoes including slaves as well as spices, and luxury items. Most merchant ships had their own guards who loaded and unloaded the cargo, and they were efficient and experienced. Very little went missing at the harbour.

Paul moved northwards well away from the prison which overlooked the harbour. Paul during his stay in Ephesus had found several quiet places where he could be undisturbed. This one was by an abandoned farm house or barn – there was not much left of it – just a couple of walls. It overlooked the marshes and he could still see the Cayster River flowing towards the coast. Here he paused, found a large boulder and sat down. This was a familiar place for Paul. It was shaded from the sun by an old wall which had crumbled through neglect but still provided at this time of day welcome shade. This was a distance away from the business of the harbour and where Paul could safely pray. It was some time before he got back to his feet. He knew it would take him about an hour to reach the house in the neighbourhood where he was staying, the land sloped upwards from the harbour, and so the walking would take longer than on the way down. Fortunately where Paul had to go was not as far as some of houses he had visited during his stay. So leaving the ancient port of Ephesus Paul quickly past the harbour baths and walked the mile or so east toward the city along Arcadian Street facing the theatre. Being near the sea had refreshed him. As a boy he had grown up in Tarsus, the capital of Cilicia and a cultural and intellectual centre for the region. He had spent time as a boy walking around his home town. Parts of Ephesus reminded him of home. He thought back to the ancient streets of Tarsus and the river Cydnus as it flowed by Tarsus on its way to the sea. But for the last 18 months Ephesus had been his home, and he knew he would soon leave this behind. As he approached the house again, Timothy greeted him and they walked the last few yards together into the house.

To Corinth with love

Timothy turned into the gateway and rushed up the stairs. Paul watched the young man effortlessly ascend the stairs, but he was going to take his time. Life had taken its toll on his outer frame. He had suffered many assaults since becoming a Christian and these had left their mark. Walking was fine. He could do that all day, but running quickly and up stairs was not something Paul would relish, so he took his time. At the top of the stairs he heard voices He entered the familiar room but to his surprise the voices belonged to those in the rooms beyond and the inner courtyard below. He looked down and saw people engaged in their business which reminded him that he would have to return to his task. He sought a place to sit away from the sun and was grateful for the drink brought to him by one of the younger members of the household. Sosthenes was not in the room on his return. His young informant told him he had wanted a brief rest and had left the room for a short walk, though Paul had not seen him .However Paul was grateful for the space this afforded. He had much to think about to prepare for writing the letter. Timothy was busying himself with the others getting lunch ready, and he now had time to gather his thoughts for the next section of the letter. He knew in this letter he had to deal with some pastoral issues with this church. Top of the list was sexual immorality. The old Greek playwrights mentioned Corinth and immorality in the same word. To be immoral was to be like a Corinthian. The old city of Corinth had been destroyed over two hundred years before. The Romans had rebuilt it 100 years later but it's culture remained from the old days. Immorality did not characterize everyone in the city, but it was a definite issue in the culture of the Corinth Paul had known. This culture had invaded the church where there was continuing bad practice and the last letter Paul wrote to them on this subject had been misunderstood. Paul had been concerned that issues of sexual immorality should not be swept under the carpet by the church, and had said that church members who were immoral should find a difference in how other church members relate to them. Some, however, had taken his words to mean to not associate with sexually immoral people anywhere!. This meant distancing church members from most of the adult population of Corinth! This brought a possible increased distancing between church and community which Paul never intended and in fact would hinder evangelism as the gospel spread from one Corinthian relating with another. If barriers were to exist between the church and the unbeliever based on the immorality of those unbelievers, few would be saved. There would then result in friendships being confined to members within the church. This was never Paul's or Jesus' intention. The other consequence of this misunderstanding was to introduce a judgemental spirit on the part of the church towards the Corinthian community. This was something which God had not intended for the church either! The church like Jesus came to save not to condemn and to act like Jesus meant to not judge others. Paul knew he needed to make clear that those who were unbelievers and therefore not yet part of the church were God's problem not the church's. They should relate to such without judgements. The church did, however, have a responsibility for those within the community of the church and they should operate properly with each other without even a hint of immorality amongst them. The church needed to be genuine, and holiness was part of that genuineness which made church life real and their message trustworthy. Immorality within the church was a serious matter and the person by refusing to repent had put himself out of the beliefs and values of the church community, so the church had to make this clear. Holding onto their values and beliefs and preserving the holiness of the church meant excluding the immoral brother from their gatherings and not relating to him as a brother. The exercise of this painful discipline was to preserve the church but also to give an environment where there can be repentance on the part of the immoral persons and then future reconciliation. To build a proper understanding for the church on sexual purity, Paul would also have to teach the reasons why sex outside marriage was wrong, and at the same time not demonise sex itself. He knew sex in the right place of marriage was good and he knew also that Satan will actively attack when sex is not part of a marriage relationship. He wanted to teach about divorce and also singleness. There was so much to say. The Corinthians had given him a list of related subjects linked to various pastoral situations in the church, and he would seek to address each one by one. He looked out of the window and saw Sosthenes turn in to the house. He would be up in a moment and then he would turn the page and start writing again.

1 Corinthians Chapter 5-6
Overview

Life Issues: - Immorality

Relationships Matter

God made people to relate to him and one another and there is power in relationships. The Holy Spirit is designed to flow between us and God, and God and us. This means it is also His purpose that He flows in our relationships. This is supremely true of marriage where we become one flesh in the Lord. The first half of the 10 commandments refers to our relationship with God, the second half of the 10 commandments refer to sins which either abide or destroy in human relationships. It is in relationships where spiritual power can reside. Immorality quenches the Holy Spirit and seeks to oppose God's purpose, whilst freeing Satan to work more easily his purposes to outwork on the earth.

Immorality is bad news for the church (5:2) because it can change the church (5:6, 7) from relationships where God dwells to relationships where God cannot dwell because sin is welcomed and hearts are hard. The Church cannot operate the same way with an immoral brother or sister as they can with their other Christian friends because this relationship defilement affects everything (5:9-11). Paul makes the point in this chapter that Immorality in the church is something which the church has to deal with whereas immorality in the world is what God deals with (5:11-13). In England during my lifetime, Satan has tried successfully to get the church to moralise about the culture outside the church. When the church does this, it steps out of its mandate and power and becomes weak, strengthening immorality through its prohibition (Romans 7:8-10)

What is Immorality?

Immorality is a general word covering every aspect of sexual sin from fornication to adultery, from sodomy to bestiality, from pornography to prostitution; from incest to rape – in fact anything which is not within a loving committed relationship called marriage. Immorality hurts, can destabilize at a deep level, and can affect important relationships in family and community.

People are deceived into thinking immorality is alright because sex is natural, or because it is legal. Both these arguments were there in Corinth and Paul addresses both in these chapters. Paul also says in these chapters that immorality affects the body in a way God never intended and sex accesses the human spirit which is then united so two become one. This is wonderful when there is a right and committed relationship (marriage) but sex unites even when there is no love or commitment. Paul cites the example of a man with a prostitute to illustrate what he is talking about. Paul also says in this passage that in Christ there is deliverance from past immorality "You are washed, sanctified and justified in Jesus" 6:11

There are no winners with immorality.

Immorality is literally playing with fire. The immoral commonly fall into two camps:-

1. **The Predators:** the ones who are trapped in it as a lifestyle and like an addict who has given up everything else to pursue the addiction, so there are those who use sex to feed their addiction trapped by past or present immorality. Some will try to recreate the patterns of the past (e.g. the man who continues to "sleep with" young girls even when he himself is very old); others will be victims of past choices unable to change their lifestyle, and needing to find another victim.

2. **The Victims:** There are some who have been unwilling victims – date raped or soiled through the demands and expectations of their family or peers or culture. There are others who never thought immorality would be part of their lifestyle. They have "found themselves" falling into it.

Sin can stain anyone, and temptation seeks to use our natural sexual desires to bring about sinful actions.

Chapter 5

The Church has a responsibility to stop sexual sin spreading in the church

5:1-8 Dealing with sexual sin in the church involves making judgements

Sexual immorality spreads more easily when there is a non application of truth and an uncertainty of making judgements. Immorality has a strong drive which welcomes hell at any cost, but a culture of truth application gives pathways that believers can walk to avoid immorality. As we shall see, without some appropriate action being taken the church itself is at risk.

5:9-10 Relating to sexual sinners who are outside the church is different from relating to those inside the church.

A Church exceeds its mandate when it seeks to pontificate about the sexual morals of unbelievers. The Church is within its mandate when it is bringing the Kingdom of God and as part of that believers are being instructed to avoid immorality and to seek Jesus.

When a church operates outside its mandate, it loses spiritual power and has to rely instead on carnal power based in money, privilege, manipulation or oppression. This earthly power by persuasion and pressure lead the religious away from the reality of Jesus and the empowerment of the Spirit. It also is understood by the world and its rulers and the church can easily become a pawn in some minor political issue rather than being God's people for God.

The church is in a nation to be a blessing and to help the citizens of that nation find Jesus and walk in new life. This process blesses a nation and the nation can as a result of the church enter its God given destiny in the earth. A Church can through its history of being a blessing have close ties with the state. When this happens there can be increased blessing. The Celtic revival, the Norman parish system, the missionary movements from this nation all happened through helpful partnerships between men of God and political leaders of the day this is one of the fruits of discipling nations which Jesus spoke about in the Great commission (Matthew 28).

However the church's primary role is not to tell the nation how to behave, but to encourage that nation to come to Jesus. Our own values and beliefs will communicate from our hearts when we really love those around us.

Behaviour is not the dictate of the church, but people cannot behave without knowing the truth, so the proclamation goes out, but not so that people can behave (for this is law) but rather so they may believe and be saved (this is all about good news and promise). The message the church gives if it is law will alienate many and encourage oppressors - for there will be some who will support the legal "how to behave" teaching and will thereby condemn those who do not behave the same way. But no-one can behave perfectly. Law and life does not go together, and lessons about behaviour should be reserved for those who claim to belong and believe so they can steward the rich life they have in Christ. In these chapters Paul encourages the church to make judgements about life issues so that all can enter into the fullness of the kingdom of God (6:10).

The Church should never sway from its invitation to ordinary people to "Belong, Believe, and Behave". Those outside the church should be encouraged to belong, knowing that if they relate to other believers it will not be long before they too have faith. In the 1950s in the Church of England, people would get ready for church wearing their Sunday best. There was an emphasis on what you wore and your behaviour in order to belong; and belief was taken for granted and rarely challenged. In the 1960s especially after Billy Graham crusades, there was an emphasis in the evangelical churches on belief in order to belong. Either dogma or behaviour as a way to belong characterised the church in those eras and taught the ordinary people in our nation subliminally that they cannot belong. Today millions claim they are not religious because of their lifestyle or because of their scientific or social beliefs and resultant scepticism about issues of faith. But belief does not come from intellectual dogma or discussion. It is something we have when we are encountering Jesus. This is possible for anyone. Faith comes by hearing (Romans 10:17). Faith is birthed not in a classroom but in a relationship. Faith means trust. This is not an educational word but a relational one.

The message of welcome allows someone to find Jesus for themselves. This leads to a following Jesus. Obeying Him will involve purity in every area including sex, and the church becomes a safe place when those who belong and believe also behave. Church morals are for Church people.

Chapter 6

Introduction

Paul started in Chapter 5 by saying the Corinthians had to exclude the immoral from the church, but not have the same judgements for those outside the church. Having explained why they should operate differently with those who are non believers, he then explains why the Corinthian church should make judgements. This leads him to expose how the lack of judgement in the church has not only led to the immoral brother possibly contaminating the rest of the church, but also that the culture of lack of judgement in the church has encouraged brothers to make decisions according to secular values than Christian ones. Paul says this is dangerous and shameful. It would be better to bear being defrauded etc. rather than be in this position. So instead of the world seeing how the Corinthians love one another, the world sees dispute and argument and is given access to give verdicts between brothers. Paul says Christians will be involved in judging angels in the future judgement and in the present time the world's ways, values, policies and decisions, and so they also have responsibility to do the same with "life issues" especially how we behave with one another. The church needs to act and not procrastinate

The Church has often acted in ways Jesus never did. "Ye judge after the flesh; I judge no man" (John 8:15) and "Do not judge". (Matthew 7:1) Jesus judged no-one yet the church has formed judgements of those outside the church which have alienated whole swaths of society from having hope in the gospel for themselves. We need to lay the law book down, and start to engender belonging where trust can gradually grow as belief and behaviour are demonstrated. Judgements put people into a box and gives them an external identity which destroys team, hope, relational development and God's indwelling.

6:6-8 Church members rather than outsiders should resolve sinful conduct with church goers.

6:8-11 Sin does not bring about the kingdom of God

In this section Paul shows sins that are related closely to the sin of immorality all of which do not lead anyone into the kingdom of God

6:12ff The false premises of sexual immorality exposed

1. **1st false Premise – It is legal.** Sexual Immorality is not against the civil law v12

   Answer: I might not be brought before a law court, but I can be brought into bondage through sin.

2. **2nd false premise – It is natural.** What are genitals for if not for sex in the same way as stomach is for food" v1

   Answer: "the body is not for immorality but for the Lord". We might have expected Paul to say "the body is not for immorality but for chastity, but instead he says for the Lord. Immorality has much greater potential consequences than losing virginity in a non married relationship.

a. The body being for the Lord means it has a spiritual dimension. We know we are spiritual beings able to relate to the supernatural unseen world by our human spirit. What happens in the area of the spirit affects the body and our life destiny. A person prospers in life as his soul prospers; we neglect our spirit at our peril. It happens this way because we are made spiritual beings who are clothed in a body. After the fall, the spirit died and the body was the only reference point in the ignorance of man's

b. Being a Christian involves the body and soul not just the soul. Our bodies become the temple of the Holy Spirit. The anointing will be within our bodies and that will also include those things we own especially what we are attached to.

c. What is in our spirit will flow into our bodies. (Romans 8:11). Sex affects our spirits. heart, but that did not change the reality of the fact that what happens in the area of the spirit affects the body

3. **3rd false premises - It does no harm.** this is the implication from the its natural argument
    Answer: sex is designed to bring male and female together, and this unity happens spiritually even when we have sex without love (as in the case of a prostitute) (v 15, 16). It is also by its nature not external like other sin is to the body.

The list in 6:9 are sins clearly to do with immorality, and therefore verse 10 must also be linked. Paul is not following the 10 commandments because drunkards in the list are not part of these. The reason Paul mentions these is this is the outcrop from lives where there is a link to the spirit principality accessed by immorality. So in an immoral society we would expect thieving, drunkenness, seizing of property and slander to increase as well as idolatry (worship of something which is not God). Immorality harms communities as well as individuals.

1. It has been said that there is actually immorality among you, *(immorality is something which should not be in the church of God)* **and the immorality is of such a kind of which is not acceptable even amongst those who are unchurched** *(Paul used the word for gentiles here, but his meaning is the culture outside the church which would not accept such behaviour.)* **that one is living with the wife of his father.** *(Paul makes clear what the problem is. This is a son having sex with his step mother.)*

2. And you have become conceited and not instead mourned

Conceit creates a bubble effect in which the conceited live where they cannot address real issues and bring holiness. Conceit and Compassion never go together. Compassion (which flows out of mourning) is a precursor of action and it does not flow when conceit is present. Conceit is a form of lying to yourself, and compassion needs truth and reality. It is compassion rather than pride which enables effective action. The facing of the problem (mourning) is the first stage of effective action. There has to be a problem to solve (see Nehemiah 1)

Pride makes us out of touch, protecting self-interest rather than reaching out to and meeting the need, or believing lies which help Satan rather than facing the truth. Compassion is essential for action and this comes from recognising truth with a desire to meet the need that is presented. This is a principle which operates in every strata of human life. This is true in offices of our land as much as with the jobless young or in parents organising their children and home

in order that he who has done this deed should be taken from the midst of you.

3. For I, although not present in the body being present in the spirit, already have decided as being present that this absolutely should be done.

the word "brought you all together" is from a verb συναγω meaning to gather from which the word synagogue comes. C.K. Barrett[1] says it became a technical expression for the church gathering in later years, but it could have been in use to describe the gathering of the synagogue before Paul's day which was then transferred to the church gathering, the church being a gradual replacement for the synagogue as the Church emerged out of the Jewish religion to take its stand as a major religion in its own right. We see the same in the word church (ἐκκλησία). This was also a term used elsewhere but this time from a secular setting. In secular Greek it is a term used for an assembly of people (see Acts 19:32 where ecclesia describes the civic gathering of Ephesian citizens). Ecclesia does also however have a religious connotation because the Jews who translated the Old Testament into Greek in the first century translated the Hebrew verb 70 times by "ecclesia" and the rest by "sunagoge" to describe a congregation and an assembly.

and my spirit with the power of our Lord Jesus,

5. (you are) to hand over this man to Satan for the destruction of the flesh in order that the spirit might be saved in the day of our Lord Jesus.

6. Your boasting is not good. You do not know that a little yeast leavens the whole dough.

7. Remove *(this word is used of purifying yourself so you can meet with God. It is not clear whether it was used in normal kitchen use to mean getting rid of the old dough. I suspect it was, but it also is an ideal word for Paul to use in the current context)* **the old dough in order that you as new dough without yeast. For the Christ your Pascal lamb has been sacrificed.**

In Jewish practice the yeast would be got rid of before the Passover feast. Because Christ the Passover lamb has already been sacrificed they are already late in getting rid of their old yeast.

The specific subject Paul is addressing:-The old yeast is in the dough of the immoral church member and therefore he has to be excluded. (There is no mention of his stepmother with which he is having an affair. This is probably because the woman was not part of the church and an unbeliever). In the second epistle where there is a man addressed who had been excluded from the fellowship. It seems to me this is the same person in which case as a result of this action he is led to contrition and probable restoration in the church (2 Corinthians 2:6-7).

> **8. So let us celebrate the festival not with the old yeast nor in the yeast of evil and wickedness, but in the unleavened (breads)** *(the word unleavened is in the plural. Each one in the church is unleavened in his own right. It is not the church life in general but individuals who are in focus here. The yeast starts within motives and belief of those individual members of the church.)* **of pure motives and truth.** *We must avoid and move away from scheming or believing lies.*
>
> **9. I have written to you in the (previous) letter not to associate with** (literal meaning of the verb is to mix up together with) **the immoral.**
>
> **10. This is not every single immoral person in this world** *i.e. Paul is saying "I did not mean this to refer to every immoral person"* **whether it be the greedy for gain who takes (things) or the idolaters**

I think this verse should not be translated as if Paul is merely referencing three unconnected areas - immorality, greedy for gain and idolatry. Paul is not introducing some random illustrations of sinful actions to be judged (amongst the many other possibilities). Rather he is continuing his theme of immorality. Paul is defining the two ways which lead to immorality – one way "greedy for gain", and the other closely linked to this is idolatry. Paul makes the same connection in Ephesians 5:5. Greedy for gain is all to do with taking what is not theirs. This happens in fornication, rape or adultery. Idolatry happens when the images created through lust evoke awe. Included in this way is voyeurism and pornography, but it also includes the worship of powers of creation or money or drink or drugs which lead to immorality.

> **(for to do this) you would have to come out of the world.**
>
> **11. But now I have written to you not to associate if anyone is called a brother if they are immoral or greedy for gain or idolatrous, or a slanderer, or a drunk, or someone who takes things.**

This is a similar list of sinful traits to the list in chapter 6:10.which is identical except it expands the specific references to sexual sin – i.e. the word immoral is expanded to specific adultery, fornication and homosexual acts. Here all this is just covered with one word for immorality (the same word translated fornication in 6:10). These are all sins linked to sexual immorality and as such require some clear judgements within the church life for those who claim to be Christians being involved in them; but to whom we do not bring judgement on those who do not belong to the church.

> **Do not even eat with such people.**
>
> **12. What is it for me to judge those outside (the church), but should you not judge those inside,**
>
> **13. for God judges those outside. Expel the wicked man from yourselves.**

There is a distinction between how we operate within the church family and how we operate outside that community. Within the community we adhere to God's values and principles and laws which means exposing and dealing properly with those which claim still to be Christians on equal footing with other believers whilst these same Christians are behaving in ungodly ways. But the same does not apply to those outside the Christian community. When Great Britain had most members within a Christian community context it might have been viable for the church to speak to the nation about its morals, but when the Christian community is weak and small, it should never do this.

The weakness of the church in my lifetime is it has ignored sexual sin in the church whilst exceeding its mandate by telling the secular society how it ought to behave. Such has contributed towards increasing alienation between church and society and moved sections of the church to become a spiritual ghetto alienated from the community around it. What is worse, it can be risky to join such ghettos if sin within it is not being adequately addressed, and a sense of reality has been lost. Many spiritual people have made the right decision to avoid joining such church clubs, and there are many in the UK thirsty for true church communities which are actually what they say on the tin. Where there is obscurity or uncertainty of what that church believes (i.e. what it says on the tin), there is no hope of finding out whether a church is safe or not. There are good churches. They do exist, but it is hard to tell as an outsider which is good and which is best avoided. In the confusion many avoid joining a church even though they might want to. Children's work (Sunday school) and Community projects which really help are more important indicators of reality to an enquirer than what choruses are sung or what spirituality is demonstrated.

Chapter 6

1. Who of you dares *(the world is a place where Satan rules (John 16:11), and the world hates Christ and the Christians (John 15:19-20) so it takes some guts to let the world judge them)* **having a matter (to settle) towards another, let judgement be made before the unjust and not before the saints?** *This is the key point which Paul is addressing throughout this passage. He wants to encourage the Corinthian church to sort out its differences with God's Spirit rather than by worldly secular values.*

2. Or do you not know that the saints will judge the world and if the world is judged among *Greek εν reminds us that Paul sees the gathered church as the place for judgements* **you, are you not good enough** *(i.e. competent enough)* **to settle lawsuits (on what is on such a) very small level?** *(i.e. Surely the church which is called to judge the world can sort out the issues upon which the lawsuits are being formed, because these are after all is on a very small scale compared to judging the world)*

If Christians have the right to judge the old world order with its values and priorities then they are able to judge, and not have lawsuits in the secular courts. Christians, who rightly make judgements according to their new nature, should not be allowing judgments on worldly criteria. Within the church, issues of sexual immorality should be judged according to God's Word not the secular society in which the church is placed. Furthermore to let the secular culture judge this means it remains not dealt with in God's way and can thus still be a damaging influence. In addition it can put the church at risk when you allow the world to access the church in this way. All these are reasons behind Paul's teaching here.

The Ephesians were proud of the legal system (Acts 19:38, 39) and lawsuits were a normal and common way of life. It looks like from Paul's comments here that Corinth was also similar in this regard. Paul uses 2 words in this passage κριτερια (v2, 4 criteria) and Κριματα (krimata) in verse 7. Both words mean lawsuits, but though the usual meaning of κριτερια (v2, v4 criteria) is law courts /tribunals, this does not fit well in this passage and I think it is closer to the English expression of criteria -i.e. The content, cause or basis of the law suit - whereas Κριματα krimata in verse 7 Paul focuses on the verdicts and judgements made in the lawsuit. So in verse 7 it is about the verdicts themselves and who makes them, whereas in verse 2 it is to do with the issues which bring about the dispute.

3. Do you not know that we will judge angels, not to mention the ordinary things of life?

Paul is making the point that the criteria they need to use must be of the Spirit in any judgements they make. He will in the next verse show they judge in the important things of angels (i.e. the unseen parts of creation) as well as the seen creation in the world systems. He, therefore expects them not have lawsuits. The point of this is made explicitly in verses 5-6 –*"is not a wise man among you? But brother goes to law with brother and that before the unbelievers."* He builds his case up towards this sentence by sentence. First, Christians judging the world order and second judging angels. He then mentions the "ordinary things of life". He knows Christians have to make judgement calls about their career, their family, what they should eat, and the exercise they should take, the priorities they hold in life and so on. He says he is not even bringing this into the argument, preferring instead to stay on judging territory exclusive to born again believers

The Greek μητι infers that the probable answer to the question is no, which is that they do not know that they will judge angels. Paul says he knows this is true because they are not making God-led judgements which take into account the unseen as well as seen worlds. The way they have not dealt with immorality in their church life is an example of this. Paul says the Corinthians put their case before judges who do not follow Christian values but adopt standards that are from the old life. They may not be in all cases professional judges in secular law courts. They could also be friends or people of standing in the community who are not believers.

> **4. Whenever you have** *(verb "to have" can mean "have the opportunity")* **to have disputes in the ordinary things of life you appoint people whose way of life is not respected in the church**

I think this is not a question as most translations put it but a statement. (The original text has no punctuation and we have to work out the punctuation from the meaning of the verse.)

Paul throughout this passage is addressing a principle of church people dealing with issues rather than outsiders in a secular court of law. Paul is referring to the way the Corinthians resolve their differences or establish their rights or redress wrongs done to them. He wants them to do this within the church amongst those who acknowledge Jesus and obey the Holy Spirit rather than involve those outside the church with their different value systems. Paul is not advocating new structures – ecclesiastical courts to match secular courts. (Although this would happen after the Roman Empire became Christianized in the 3rd and 4th century). In Paul's day the gathering where verdicts are made in the church would look more like a prayer meeting rather than a law court. It would be similar to the gathering where the Holy Spirit is present mentioned in Chapter 5 when the immoral personis handed over to Satan. A similar prayer type meeting where judgement was given is possibly described in Acts 5 in the church where Ananias and Sapphira belonged

Thus far is clear but who is referred to by "despised" in verse 4 and why. Different translations make different points.

Possible views

a. King James *1 Cor. 6:4 If then ye have judgments of things pertaining to this life, set them to judge who are least esteemed in the church.* This is saying it is better to have people in the church even if they are the lowest of the low than to go to those outside the church. In this case the shame statement in verse 5 is because they have not appointed anyone in the church as judges. The problem with this view here is that Paul does not say that they have not appointed anyone, but rather that they appoint people who are despised to judge and this is the cause of their shame.

b. So the American standard *Version* follows this" So if you have cases dealing with this life, why do you appoint as judges people who have no standing in the church? This view is that Paul would be saying that the Corinthian church is not putting a strong enough emphasis on its judgments by appointing people who have no influence in the church and therefore any judgements they give carries no weight. This translation seems unlikely as it is introducing a fresh element (i.e. the quality of judges within the church) to the debate whereas Paul in the rest of the verses is making the argument that Christians should not go to secular people/ unbelievers to be judged

I therefore agree with the NIV which translates verse 4 *Therefore, if you have disputes about such matters, do you ask for a ruling from those whose way of life is scorned in the church?* This is saying why should the Corinthians ask verdicts from those who do not follow Christian values but adopt standards according to the old life they used to live which as Christians they no longer honour in the same way since discovering a better way in Christ. This fits better the next phrase "I say this to your shame", and in my view fits the context better.

This whole subject of judging is about "life's issues" and includes sexual immorality and ways of behaviour in life. We shall be reminded of this fact when he lists various criteria which need judgements from the church so that such people practising such evils can begin to repent and move in the kingdom (v9).

His conclusion

5. I say this to your shame.

Shame is not just about doing something wrong, but also about not doing what is right. This includes not entering into all that God has made available to us. For many, shame will only be known when the truth of all that God intended for us and made available to us is fully known at the last day. For now, entering fully into the kingdom is a must which we are foolish not to pursue.

Is there no-one among you who is wise who can be enabled *(passive of verb to be able, so it might be that Paul expected the church to see who was wise and release them into this role of judging between brothers)* **to judge in the affairs of his brother** *(ανα μεσον can mean in the region of see Mark 7:31).*

6. but one brother is judged against a brother and this before unbelievers.

7. This is already an utter defeat for you because you have judgements *(verdicts made by the secular people)* **amongst each other.** *Seeking justice through law courts is a worse problem than putting up with the wrong done to you. Love must rule everything. Love is there in the church judging the immoral person to bring a hope of repentance and restoration. It is not there in lawsuits. So Paul continues.* **Why not rather be wronged? Why not rather be defrauded.**

8. But you do wrong and you defraud and that (to your) brothers or do you not know that the ones who are unrighteous *(this term is explained in v9, 10)* **do not inherit the kingdom of God?**

9. Do not be deceived. Neither the immoral, not idolaters nor adulterers nor homosexuals *(the word is "to be effeminate" and used of those who allow themselves to be used homosexually)* **nor those engaged in sodomy** *(this is the other part of a homosexual relationship.)*

10. not thieves nor the covetous, nor the drunkards nor slanderers nor rapists

---

This list is to do with immorality. Whilst some of the list are indeed in the 10 commandments, there are some that are not e.g. drunkenness (though it is condemned by Paul in Ephesians 5:17). They are all actions linked closely to immorality Paul is defining the nature of the principality behind sexual immorality with its characteristics.

The word translated "rapist "refers to people who seize things. In the King James Bible the word used is "extortioners", but the word refers to more than money. It is people who take what is not theirs to take. As such it refers to those who take power or possessions they should not have and includes the fornicator, adulterer as well as rapist and paedophile. The sinful actions mentioned in verses 9 are linked to the same principality which sexual immorality is linked. In an immoral society there will not just be a rise in pregnancies outside marriage and sexual diseases, but there will also be a rise of theft, drinking, slander and rape and possibly fraud. Taking what is not yours in immorality can spill over into other areas in power games or economic fraud at other stages of life. The immoral young do not always become the righteous old.

Paul is seeking to help the church form right judgements around the area of sexual immorality (5:1) and is therefore deliberately outlining various sins which are linked to sexual immorality. There is certainly some detail in some of the words used. The passive and active member in a homosexual relationship both receive judgements as does fornicators (those who have sex outside marriage) and adulterers (those who have sex with other partners whilst in marriage). In the list there are some words you would not necessarily associate with sexual sin, idolatry, covetousness, thieves, drunkards and revilers. But as mentioned earlier I think this is referring to the sins around sexual sin.

Idolatry is present when there is worship involving sex or worship of sex.

Thieving is there in sex trafficking, sex slaves, but also stealing someone's virginity or love through immorality.

Covetousness is a desire of another's partner or to have something you should not. Drunkenness is the cause of sexual sin for many, but if I am right, there is a deeper connection than that;

Revilers refer to the people who speak against their partner or the opposite sex. Gossip as well as despising is included here.

Extortioners is sometimes translated in English bibles , but the original is a Greek word which refers to those who snatch things and in a sexual context would refer to all abductions for sex, as explained above, including the crimes of paedophiles and rapists.

> **will inherit the kingdom of God.**
>
> **11. And such were some of you. But you have been washed, but you have been made holy, but you have been made righteous in the name of the Lord Jesus Christ and in the Spirit of our God.**

This whole passage has sexual immorality in focus but the solution for sexual immorality is true of all sin. We need to be washed so the Holy Spirit can come to our life and change us (which involves being set apart with a purpose). Getting into the river of God washes us clean. It is highly relevant however to victims of sexual sin who when they recognise what has happened is wrong feel dirty as a result.

The washing is in the realm of the Holy Spirit and the new nature which comes from being born of the Spirit (see Titus 3:5). This is not surprising. Paul is dealing with redemption from what happens to us. Sexual sin defiles and enslaves. Redemption takes us out of that slavery and we are transferred into the realm of the Holy Spirit where we are washed clean. The Holy Spirit washes, sanctifies and leads us into righteousness (Romans 6:16 just as sin leads to death so obedience leads to righteousness which leads to holiness.)

Now he brings into focus the false thinking which justifies the sin of immorality

> **12. All things is permitted for me but not everything is useful or helpful. All things are permitted but I will not be mastered by anything** (the word is a Greek verb which in active form means having the right or power over someone.)

The "All things permitted to me" seems a phrase known to both Paul and the Corinthians. This is not part of the letter they had written to him for he refers to the letter they had written for the first time in chapter 7. These are probably phrases which are used by the Corinthians and because Paul actually quotes them, it might indicate that they originate from him but in a different context. This may be a truth which they had learnt from teaching they had heard before about grace and our position in Christ.

The first phrase "All things are permitted for me" could come from teaching about their heavenly position in Christ, but it had become warped to justify immorality. The answer is given

a. It may be permitted in law, or by others and all things may be subject to you as you are Christ's, but you still need to analyse whether it is profitable or helpful,

b. It may be permitted but the reality of sin is it masters you so you do not get involved in what may be permitted in law because sin brings bondage.

The second phrase (in next verse) which could come from teaching about their earthly position in Christ "Foods for the stomach and stomach for foods" referencing how you cannot find Jesus by natural means. We only find Jesus through prayer and seeking him with our hearts, and obeying Him in our lives.

Both phrases are true, but they have been taken through wrong emphasis or exaggeration as a basis for immorality that is wrong. "Sex is like food. We have stomachs so we eat, and we have genitals so we have sex. Morality does not come into it, just function." This is the implication which Paul now disputes.

---

13. Foods for the stomach and the stomach for foods: *So Paul realigns their thinking. He does not repeat the earlier argument of whether it is profitable or not, but rather argues about the nature of the body and its destiny and purpose.* **But God will make ineffective both this (stomach) and these (foods).**

The body argument has no relevance in the new life brought about in the kingdom of God. For the Christians it is the life of the kingdom of God which should be the focus and basis for our actions. The Greek word καταργεω has meanings like make ineffective, wipe out, put an end to childish ways (1

Corinthians 13:11), be released from an association with someone (Romans 7:2). Paul may be looking forward to a time when the kingdom of God comes fully when food and stomach will no longer have relevance to us. I think he is looking forward to the resurrection body which like Jesus' risen body can eat, but does not have to in order to live. He assesses the values of the present in the light of the future. In this same context "he will raise us through his power" in the next verse.

Then the next principle to realign their thinking is about the purpose of the body,

The body is not for immorality but for the Lord and the Lord for the body. *"The Lord for the body" The body is not just the animal tissue. It is the full part of us. The Lord can become part of our life on earth. He can step into our inner life and walk with us in our physical life.*

14. God raised the Lord and he will raise us through his power. *This verse certainly will be fulfilled at the final day when our earthly bodies are resurrected to be like Jesus, but it is also talking about the present. Our bodies can experience power and the purpose of that is so we are raised to a new level in God.*

15 You do not know that your bodies are the limbs of Christ.

Colossians 3:5 uses the word limbs and says that we are to put to death the limbs which are on the earth. Limbs are an extension of our body. We manifest where we abide. To use Paul's analogy - If we live on the earth limbs form which then impede our walk with heaven. Conversely when we abide in God, limbs form in Christ and we act like Jesus.

When we make a decision to follow Christ and ask Jesus to come into our lives, it brings about a radical change. New lifestyles, hopes, understandings and grace operate, so it makes no sense to go back to immorality.

Taking the limbs of Christ, shall I make them the limbs of a prostitute? May it not be so!

It is possible for those who are part of the Church to belong to evil as well. As Christians we surrender our bodies as living sacrifices to God (Romans 12:1). Being a Christian is a body and soul experience. Our bodies contain the anointing of Jesus. (Remember the anointed Elisha, whose bones raised someone to life 2 Kings 13:21). Every part of us is designed to line up to the anointing of Jesus and everything we are will then extend His purpose and Kingdom. But those who have sex with prostitutes spiritually aligned their whole bodies (spirit soul and body) to that prostitute. Sex is designed to make us "one in spirit" (see also Malachi 2:15). It affects our spirit as well as our body.

Just as the Christian when he interacts with God's Spirit enters the realm of the Kingdom of God, so the one who has sex with an immoral person will access whatever roots the immorality has – attracting spirits from the family line, or past partners or from the place or from the situation. In fact whatever spiritually the immoral partner abides in. Immorality lies in the house of the dead (Proverbs 9:18; 2; 18) a demonic principality which meets out infirmity and seeks to destroy life. What Immorality links the human spirit to is not good or of Jesus.

The word prostitute does not just refer to those who provide sex for money. It is any immoral person (either male or female).

Paul is about to make the point that sex brings about an oneness in the realm of the spirit which means that a prostitute spirit operates within our body and life to transform us instead of the spirit of Christ.

16. For do you not know that being attached to a prostitute is oneness in the body? For it says two shall become one flesh.

Paul says even in a relationship where there is no love at all – a man with a prostitute- a relationship of convenience for money – even at this level where there is no commitment beyond the act of sex; there is a joining of spirit to spirit. The flesh is human body, soul and human spirit. You can be in the bizarre situation of ones with a prostitute with all the spiritual problems that brings and still attached to the Lord. An adulterous immoral person can be worshipping God, and seem as devoted to the Lord. But in fact their relationship with god and their own body has been radically affected.

> **17. But being attached to the Lord is in the spirit.**
>
> **18. Flee immorality. Every sin that man does is outside the body.**

This is true of all sin including immorality. Sin does not originate inside the body. But immorality is sin against the body in that this is not what the body is meant for. It is meant to be a place where Holy Spirit dwells. Other sins cause us to fall short of God's plan but do not directly affect our body, but immorality does!

> **But he who is immoral sins towards his own body or**
>
> **19. do you not know that your body is a temple for the Holy Spirit (to dwell) among you? (What) you have is from God not from yourselves**
>
> **20. for you were bought with a price. Honour God in your** (plural) **body** (singular). *We have a responsibility to honour God as individuals in our bodies.*

Church Life

A sound of people talking excitedly in the courtyard below alerted Paul that it was time to stop. Time for the church to gather was fast approaching and they needed to be there.. Paul and Sosthenes stood up and walked knowingly through to the adjoining room onto the short wooden balustrade and down the stairs into the private courtyard away from the street. Paul was staying overlooking a rear courtyard lying behind the shops which lined the main route from south and west into the city. It had been a business centre for many years, but Aquila and Priscilla had bought the premises when they first came to Ephesus. The large gates of the courtyard were shut and locked, and the new arrivals were coming through the mosaic and fresco lined living rooms of the wealthy home where Paul was staying. The downstairs rooms were cool in the heat of the day, and Priscilla had simple tasteful pictures on the walls with elaborate vases and ornaments placed tastefully on tables in the main reception area and rooms. Today none went into the rooms but instead proceeded directly to the courtyard beyond. Already some of Paul's friends in the church were putting up a large table in the courtyard shaded from the afternoon sun. Others were setting out the food they had brought and adding to other side tables other delights for people to share. It was always a great occasion when the church met together and there was lots of fun and laughter even before everybody had arrived. Paul descended the wooden stairs into the courtyard below. Children greeted Paul as his feet touched the paved floor and the women setting up the tables with the men looked up and smiled. It reminded Paul of some of the family occasions he had enjoyed as a boy in his Jewish home except this included Gentiles and in the gathering were people from many different parts of the Empire as well as very differing positions in society. Some very wealthy and some poor; some traders and some politicians, some influential in society - women as well as men and also some slaves. All this was not unusual in Ephesus. What was different was that these slaves were joining the gathering on equal footing with the others. The church indeed cut through the class divisions and created new communities. Paul looked around at the crowd already assembled but knew there would be some latecomers. There always were.

Friday night was often a time when parts of the Ephesian church would gather together but this was a special day as tonight they were welcoming the visitors from the church in Corinth. Paul knew he would feel in two different worlds as he would step back into his time at Corinth and his continuing time at Ephesus. The provinces of Achaia and Asia were meeting tonight over a meal. Ephesus everyday in its culture and setting was both indigenous to the eastern Mediterranean and also Roman with its inherent Greek influences so the occasion would not feel at all alien, but for Paul he would still feel the deep pull in two directions for he loved both churches in their differing culture and characteristics. Both Ephesus and Corinth were newish cities built by Romans, but below the surface the culture of Ephesus was very different from Corinth. It was proud of its Middle East culture influenced by ancient Mesopotamian beliefs and customs, and with an inbuilt resistance of change to their own identity whilst maintaining compliance to the foreigners who ruled their land, for they were also proud of their position and ability to trade and valued the wealth that trade brought. The expansion of trade with laws to match suited them and they were more than content to be part of the Roman empire rejoicing in the stability it brought to the world they knew. It would be some weeks before Paul would leave Ephesus behind to travel towards Achaia, and for now he could enjoy the people from both worlds in one place. For now he would put his letter to the Corinthians to the back of his mind. There was the Sabbath followed by the church meeting early on Sunday. It would be Monday before he and Sosthenes would resume, so for now Paul relaxed into the company of so many varied people to enjoy the meal and the family atmosphere in which he found himself.

Timothy, Trophimus and Tychicus

Paul paused. In the light that shone brightly through the window he picked up a crumpled parchment left at the edge of the table. He unrolled it and read the first section of it. This was the letter Stephanas had brought with him. It was time to address their concerns but it would wait until later in the day. Lunch had been good, and quickly eaten because downstairs was collecting the returning team from Colossae as well as most of the Corinthian team. They were joining Paul and his friends for prayer during the heat of the mid-day. Paul and Sosthenes quickly went down to greet the group. The only one not there was Erastus who was at the harbour seeking to find a ship leaving next week for Greece, so he and Timothy could start on the return journey with their friends to Corinth. At one side of the room was Timothy who was already in discussion with Trophimus a young man who was a member of the church group to which Paul belonged, and Immediately to his right as he entered the room was Tychicus had led the team which had just returned from a mission trip to Colossae and Laodicea which were two major cities just over 100 miles to the east of Ephesus, and Paul wanted to know all that had happened. Tychicus turned and greeted Paul warmly as he entered the room. He had left when Paul was still in prison and it was a great delight and relief to him to find Paul at liberty once again on his return. He knew the time in prison for Paul had not been easy especially in the winter, but Paul was now free again and for that he was thankful. Paul was grateful for this opportunity to find out all he could and in as brief a way as possible, Tychicus gave Paul an overview of the success and events of the last few weeks. There were many friends in the room and there was no opportunity to talk more with Tychicus. They walked together to the far side of the room and joined Timothy and Trophimus.

Trophimus was born in the city and Tychicus was from one of the surrounding villages so they knew each other well. Soon Paul drew Timothy away from the group to talk with him privately. Trophimus and Tychicus did not notice them go as they were deep in conversation about Asia and the churches there. Sosthenes joined them, but listened more than spoke. He enjoyed their company. Tychicus mentioned in passing to Sosthenes the changes he noticed in Ephesus just in the few weeks he had been away especially in the harbour and temple areas of the city. Ephesus was changing fast. There were new buildings everywhere. - and not all of them welcome developments by locals like Trophimus. Tychicus was pleased that there was renovation of the old theatre built on the slopes of Mount Pion. He was proud of the largest theatre in Anatolia with 25,000 seats on three banks of raised seating. The renovated theatre had been the venue for plays and political debates, and facilitated special displays enhancing a festival of events which had brought the whole city together. Less welcome were the gladiatorial contests and animal fights which this venue hosted. Trophimus agreed and spoke with dismay at the renovations of the stadium. Nero was changing the shape of it to give it a radical new look for chariot racing and duels, and wondered where it would all end. The stadium was built in a similar area as the theatre and was of a similar antiquity also using the slopes of Mount Pion for its raised seating. The culture in that part of the city had changed rapidly. It seemed that everyone agreed that it did not seem like the old Ephesus anymore. Greek and Roman influences were everywhere, and Trophimus said that there were new baths and a possible gymnasium to be built in that same part of town. Sosthenes enjoyed listening to the enthusiasm of Tychicus and the observations of Trophimus. He had for a moment got a glimpse of Ephesian life as these spoke together. As a non-Ephesian, he got an insight into the way they thought and the differences in the culture from Corinth. Ephesus was now the 3rd largest city in the world after Rome and Alexandria, and it dominated the region. The ancient road from Ephesus to Susa built by the Persians still provided a welcome route to and fro for traders inland. Trophimus made the observation that all roads from the east led to Ephesus and so from this city the gospel has spread far and wide affecting the whole Roman province of Asia. Sosthenes reflected to himself there was no doubt the gospel was spreading rapidly in Asia. But his thoughts were interrupted. Paul stood up and welcomed everyone introducing the Corinthian team to the mission team. In the room were a mixture of Tychicus' team, the Corinthian delegation and the team going with Paul to Macedonia and Corinth. He asked Timothy to lead the meeting. They worshipped together and then Tychicus spoke of his recent trip to Colossae, Laodicea and the other churches in Asia, and the responses to the letters Paul had written. Aristarchus asked after Onesimus who was a fairly new convert they had met whilst in prison, and found he had been welcomed by the people of Colossae and Philemon in particular. Paul asked after Mark who had set off with them, and as anticipated he had stopped off at Hierapolis to meet the church there for longer than the rest of the team. Tychicus was unaware of his movements returning with the team without him. They listened as Tychicus spoke some further reflections of his mission trip giving topics for prayer. Then they worshipped and prayed.

Timothy led the meeting well. The presence of God was strong and there had been revelation given through prophetic word, as well as tongues and interpretation. It was special having the Corinthians there with them. After the prayer ended, Sosthenes noted to himself how they all respected Timothy highly even though he was still young. Paul had told the Corinthian delegation in private that he was thinking Timothy would be the future leader of the Ephesus church, building on the foundation which Paul had laid down, but that was all for the future. Paul received from Tychicus the general letter Paul had written to be read in all the churches he had visited. He handed this letter to Timothy for safe keeping. As a general letter it might be of use on another trip. Ephesus was a safe place to store records and parchments. There were already many stored in safe places and there was talk of building a library like Alexandria had. Rome was building one and Timothy knew Ephesus would follow. Timothy took the parchment and stored it securely under his arm little imagining this letter would be known as a letter to the Ephesians by later generations.

Paul and Sosthenes said goodbye to their friends and by the time Sosthenes had ascended the stairs, he saw Paul had already taken up his favourite place by the window, waiting to dictate the next part of the letter. Sosthenes resumed his familiar position. He picked up his quill, stretched out the new parchment, and, began to write as Paul spoke.

1 Corinthians Chapter 7
Overview

Up to this chapter Paul has been responding to what has been said to him (1 Corinthians 1:11, 5:1) but now for the rest of the epistle he is relating to the letter that they wrote to him. (1 Corinthians 7:1, 11, 2; 12:1, 16:1). The two previous chapters have prepared the ground for the first issue Paul refers to in the letter which is on the theme of marriage, divorce and singleness.

Life Issues: Marriage, divorce, singleness and widowhood

The teaching Paul gives in Chapters 5-7 is:-

a. Sexual sin of whatever nature does not stop God working in your life, but you have to repent of your sin to be included in the company of God. (Chapter 5,6:9-11)

b. Sex affects the spirit as well as the body. There is an unseen spiritual dimension to sex. The place for sex is within marriage and it is only there it is safe sex. Damage is done when there is sex outside a marriage relationship. (6:13,16-18)

c. Sex is for marriage. Satan schemes work easier where there is no sex in a marriage. (7:5) Lives and careers have been destroyed through Satan's schemes

d. Whatever state you are in life, single, widowed, divorced. Married, stay in that place. (7; 8, 10, 17)

The death of a partner or the desire of a partner to be divorced changes all this. There are also other reasons. You want to get married. Do so! (7:9) or You are quite happy staying single and not getting married for a while but your fiancée is at an age where they should be married, you must marry then (7:36)

a. Marriage will disturb your desire to please God, because you will experience a tension between following God with the pressures the world, the latter being able to exercise its obligations through your (rightful) desire to please your husband or wife. 7:33, 34.

b. Divorce is never God's plan. It can happen though and if you are being forced into a divorce, God is in the divorce settlement and you should remain single if you can. Adultery is out. Divorcing your partner so you can marry another is not an option (7:11) Paul recognised some marriages would break down but there should be a cooling off period to see if reconciliation can happen.

c. Marrying again after a divorce is not a sin (7:27,28a)

d. Remaining a virgin is fine also. You are not missing out on real life at all. Immoral lifestyles will try to lie to you making the false claim that to enjoy life you have to be sexually active.

e. If you lose your partner in death, marry in the Lord (v39). Do not discard your faith when a widow or widower. God is still there. You are free to marry again but Paul says happiness is not impossible for the widow/widower if they stay single. In fact Paul says that it is more likely that happiness will accompany you.

Paul and Marriage

From the very beginning a committed relationship between a man and a woman for life was the definition of marriage and the only place where sex could not destroy and disturb the central areas of self-esteem, relationship sensitivity, perception and prayer. Genesis 2:24 still contains the definitive verse "For this cause a man should leave his father and mother and cleave to his wife and they become one flesh" so they can go forth and multiply (see Gen: 1:27, 28).

A marriage is still a marriage whether there are children or not, but whilst sex always unifies, marriage is only formed through choice and commitment. Sex in such a committed relationship builds within the marriage a secure friendship and a unifying which affirms common values and produces a family culture which blesses those who are part of it.

Marriage is not better than being single. They are just different callings and as such are equal in status. Paul's main point in this chapter is that each should be content in their calling whether they be a virgin, single with sexual experience, living together, married or divorced. God has a purpose for each.

He gives reasons why each should remain as they are.

1. The married because it is a command from God
2. The living together because the believing partner can still bring a blessing into that unholy relationship which can bless any children in that family
3. The single because they can more easily avoid the pressures the world brings. Families cannot avoid this as easily.
4. Those who have been married and are divorced can be free to be single with its benefits
5. Remaining in your calling can change however. Marriage partners die, living together relationships can end, divorcees can get married, content singles can get married when they see time passing, and people who are wanting to get married should not delay.

Divorce and Remarriage

It is alright to get remarried after divorce (v27-28a)

Within Chapter 7 there is a verse which has been mistranslated in most English versions of the Bible and is therefore unknown to most of Christendom. The verse is verse 27-28a. It reads in the New King James Version which is one of the few translations which seeks to translate accurately the original text "Are you loosed (divorced) from a wife? Do not seek a wife. But even if you do marry you have not sinned". The church for centuries made marriage after divorce a sin except in exceptional circumstances. This is what lay behind the difficulties Henry VIII had in wishing to divorce Catherine of Aragon in favour of Anne Boleyn and the eventual fall of Cardinal Wolsey in the 16th century and King Edward VIII and Mrs Simpson in the twentieth century. Until recent decades no divorcees could be married in the Church of England. In defence of the church, the bible does state that divorce is not God's intention (Malachi 2:16); and has not been God's original intention in creation (Mark 10:6, 7), but was a necessary measure because of people's hardness of heart (Mark 10:5). However there is no such law against remarriage of divorcees in the Bible. The Church to its detriment went beyond Scripture in this case.

The Old Testament

Malachi 2:16 *"I hate divorce," says the LORD God of Israel, "and I hate a man's covering himself with violence as well as with his garment," says the LORD Almighty. So guard yourself in your spirit, and do not break faith.NIV).* There are two things mentioned here which does not have God's favour (I hate) - One is divorce, but the other is what can happen in the period long before a divorce – where there can be accusation , assault on one's partner in argument or not valuing him/her. This is where his/her spirit is turned away from husband or wife. This troubles God as much as divorce. Your spirit is turned away from your partner the moment you are not bothered about your wife or husband. It can also be when your spirit is caught by drink, sex of drugs. In other words God through Malachi looks not just at the divorce but at other areas within the marriage relationship which can also restrict God's favour and can bring pain.

The teaching of Jesus.

Divorce is never easy, but Jesus does not focus on the emotional journey or legal process involved. *Jesus said to them, "Because of your hardness of heart he wrote you this commandment. But from the beginning of creation, God made them male and female. "For this cause a man shall leave his father and mother, and the two shall become one flesh; consequently they are no longer two, but one flesh". What therefore God has joined together, let no man separate." And in the house the disciples began questioning Him about this again. And He said to them, "Whoever divorces his wife and marries another woman commits adultery against her; and if she herself divorces her husband and marries another man, she is committing adultery."*

He focuses on the spirit unity brought about by sex. Jesus highlights the unifying of marriage "the two shall become one".

Paul in 1 Corinthians 6:16, 17 refers to sex as being the way this occurs. This unity man or woman can be broken "Whatever God has joined, let not man put asunder". Twice (Matthew 5:32; Matthew 19:9) Jesus says *And I say unto you, Whosoever shall put away his wife, except it be for fornication, and shall marry another, commits adultery: and whoso marries her which is put away commits adultery.* Jesus is not making some legal exception clause for acceptable grounds of divorce. He is rather stating the fact that unity in marriage is broken by sexual immorality either by fornication or adultery as the Greek word refers to both. It is possible for marriages to survive such events, but Jesus is not dealing with this. He is dealing with the subject of divorce in the light of the unity marriage forms.

The Church has made the mistake of taking the words of Jesus and stating that remarriage of divorcees are wrong. Paul says that whilst divorcees should remain as they are if they can (7:27), if they marry they do not sin. This is the advice Paul gives the divorced. The advice he gives to the married is do not divorce (7:10, 11) but if there is a marriage break down not rush off to get a divorce or to remarry. This verse is "to the married" and is not to be used (as it often is) as commands to the divorced. A couple who are married may after a time of separation move from the place of marriage to a place of being loosed. In which case they move from the advice in 7:10,11 to verse 27. God has a right path for us whatever our place, single, married or divorced.

Church history made some overstated affirmations which introduced a false doctrine that "Marriage is indissoluble". The fact is "Marriage is dissoluble". Jesus said people could put asunder what God had joined, precisely because they could dissolve what god had joined together. Alongside this has come the idea that a wedding in a non-Christian context may be dissolvable, but a "Christian" wedding is indissoluble. This is also untrue. It is sex not beliefs which unite the marriage bond. Because sex is such a powerful agent for unity, sex with others does affect future or present marriage. God can sort this out and some marriages can survive but not all. There is forgiveness from God to all who turn to him on any sin including these mentioned here.

Greek text Commentary 1 Corinthians Chapter 7

1. Now concerning what you wrote

This is the letter which Paul is responding to that presumably Stephanas and the others brought with him from Corinth. Before this he has been dealing with some of the things he has heard in discussion with them and others. Now he is turning to the concerns they had,

These concerns were,

1. **"Is it better not to marry**?" The reason for this question was how a Christian should view sex. Is it better to be celibate, what about if you are married or divorced or in a living together relationship

2. A further question was probably from a specific pastoral situation in Corinth **"If you become a Christian as a virgin, should you stay that way"**. Behind this question (v15) lay a pastoral issue of two God fearing people who were wondering if they should continue with their wedding plans (v36-37)

Paul knows God's will is for everyone in whatever place they are in life So God has a perfect way for the married and for those who are living together, divorced, widowed or single

The Christians in Corinth are to be commended because they wanted the Kingdom of God to reach every area of their lives including their sex life.

It is fine for a man not to touch a woman

The original Greek is a middle form of a verb which in its active sense means to kindle a fire. In the middle form the verb means to touch, hold someone. This verb "touch" is in a sexual context and Paul uses a verb referring to sexual excitement awakened through touch. This verse contains Paul's advice for sexual morals in courtship – "No petting" – touching the genitals. It is not the way to behave outside marriage and opens the door for immorality.

2. Because of immoralities, let each man have his wife, and each wife her own husband.

The reality of immorality in society makes marriage even more important for it provides the right and safe path amidst an immoral culture. Paul gives two reasons for the importance of sex (1) the safe way for sex (2) the responsibilities of the marriage relationship

3. The husband should pay the debt

Love always creates a debt which is an obligation (see *Romans 13:8 Owe (same word as here) no man anything, but to love one another*) and in the case of love in a marriage covenant that debt has a sexual dimension. You are obliged within the marriage covenant whether husband or wife to respond sexually to your partner

to the wife, and likewise the wife to the husband.

4. The wife does not have authority over her own body but the husband; likewise also the husband does not have authority over his own body but the wife (has).

5. Do not defraud (rob) each other

If a marriage has no sexual intercourse you rob each other. Sex adds more than children. Sex brings happiness, fulfilment, security, delight, and stability to a person in a marriage relationship. Sex without lifelong commitment is dangerous because the good fruits of sex return to bite and destroy what it gives when the other walks away or when it is no longer possible to pretend that the relationship is permanent. There are many immoral who cannot risk receiving the benefits of sex and instead use sex in wrong ways whilst at the same time trying to gain stability or security or happiness in other ways other than marriage.

except by agreement for a time in order to have time for prayer and then come again to each other *(active sex life renewed)* **so that Satan might not tempt you through lack of self-control.**

"Lack of self-control" is the term Paul uses for selfishness in a relationship context. Lack of self-control is where self is not submitted to the greater good of the relationship but so asserts itself. This makes us open to temptation in a way that would not be the case if self were firmly under control. Selfishness and love do not mix. Selfishness in fact produces a toxic atmosphere which stifles trust and prevents respect. In such a climate love cannot grow. Lack of self-control can lead to things said or actions taken which would normally not occur. The abstinence from sex brings about an environment where this is more likely.

Selfishness is the opposite of a husband giving to his wife and a wife to her husband. It allows Satan to tempt. Satan's temptation may be lust or relationship of death through adultery or prostitution (Proverbs 2:18; 5:5; 7:27) but can equally be temptation to selfish acts to pursue a hobby or responsibility which empty the marriage bond. The subtle first step is lack of self-control. This deadly blow can lead to other sins. Like the Indonesian Komodo dragon gives at first a weak but deadly bite to its prey and then waits whilst the poison gradually weakens its victim so it can be devoured, so selfishness gives a deadly blow to the marriage which allows Satan to eventually devour it.

When selfishness rules in a marriage, the relationship dies from within. One of the fruits of the Holy Spirit is called "self-control" (Galatians 5:22-23). Self-Control is all about the kingdom of God affecting our inner world providing us, through the Holy Spirit, boundaries which bring security and identity in Kingdom purpose and revelation from God as well as nourishment and comfort to our inner self so we can be strong. Self-control is God's rule in the arena of self. With this in place our marriages are strong.

The same principle of self-control operates in our relationships especially the marriage relationship. Self-control enables love to be expressed by hindering selfishness. It also provides boundaries (proverbs 25:28). Without boundaries, insecurity enters the home. Self-control brings a strong identity which can stand against lies, manipulation and oppression. Without self-control, the marriage may outwardly seems fine, but inwardly it is dying because selfishness is destroying the friendship which is its life.

Self-control means selfishness is kept at bay and rightful behaviour and motivation enriches the marriage

Satan develops schemes to undermine marriage through selfishness when sex is not part of the relationship: **1-7. Sex in marriage** During the whole theme of immorality Satan is not mentioned, but when abstinence from sex in marriage is referred to, so is Satan. Satan's main interest is not within evil but within godly structures and people who are in a proper place with God and His word. When Jesus went to his trial and death, Satan did not occupy the hearts of the Pharisees or Pontius Pilate, but rather the disciple Judas Iscariot (John 13:27). It is thus no surprise to have Satan mentioned in the context of marriage whereas he gets no mention in the teaching on immorality. Paul is saying if sex is missing from the marriage relationship, Satan will seek to tempt a husband or wife to indulge in inappropriate selfish behaviour which falls short of the purpose a married couple can have together. This "selfishness" takes many forms from moods or anger, to drug addiction, adultery or pornography. In fact any act which damages rather than enriches the marriage.

---

6. I say this *(turn away from each other if you need to)* **by concession not from command.**

What concession does "this" refer to?

To say Paul is referring back to the agreement in v5 would mean Paul is saying couples should keep on abstaining from sex as an aid to prayer and only come back together by concession. But this is the very opposite of what Paul had been saying in these verses where his main point is that there should be a physical relationship between married couples.

What is Paul saying here then? The clue is in verse 5 where Paul says do not rob (turn away) from each other unless. This word introduces the concession which is where there is a time of abstinence in a relationship. The concession refers to the time apart. Paul is saying that if they decide to abstain from sex in order to pray then this should be time limited and by agreement so sexual relationship is quickly restored.

7. I want every man to be as I am, but each has his own gift from God, one has one thing and another has something else.

What does Paul mean here? We think Paul was unmarried and therefore he could be summarising the passage which started with the statement "no-one should touch a woman". This is his experience and he desires others to have the same richness he has, but he also knows that celibacy is a gift from God – as is marriage- and so he knows not everyone will share the gift he has.

A single may need to get married; a married or living together relationship may not continue [because one partner refuses to accept the conversion of their partner to Christ bringing conflict either over lifestyle or doctrine, values or agreements, (but even in these cases it is still possible says Paul for the relationship to continue if the unbelieving partner wants it).]

Both these scenarios render the reader free to change their position of life; the single to marry and the married to separate. If the married separate they are not to form new relationships immediately, but to live as singles. There is no place for adultery in the church

Re. Celibacy: - There is a fulfilment in celibacy which few in the west would believe possible because most in the west have accepted the lie that to be fully human you must be sexually active at some point in your life and if you are not you are not a true man or woman and may even be repressing a true sexual identity as a Homosexual or Lesbian. This western view which has been influenced by Freud and others has caused a mind-set change which means that many accept the view that monks in the middle ages were secretly immoral or oppressed by religion. They never envisage a monastery or convent as a happy place with fulfilled "normal" people full of life. In the 1992 film Sister Act directed by Emile Ardolino and starring Goldberg, and Maggie Smith, "normal" balanced life is brought to the sincere nuns through the Las Vegas singer played by Whoopi Goldberg. Normal balanced happy fulfilment is not in this convent until she arrives. Those in the convent are either old, or legally bound, or desirous of life but insecure or possibly naive and undeveloped. Such is an untrue caricature of celibacy made possible by our modern preconceived western ideas. There are many examples in our churches and down the years of people who have been celibate and who have been genuine, joyful and righteous in life. From St Teresa to countless celibate servants of God in the ministry or in public life bear witness to this, and we cannot pass by the fact that Jesus was celibate and was the most fulfilled human being anyone has ever seen. Jesus was fully righteous in his celibacy His closest friends and also his enemies giving witness to his holy life in a Jewish culture where immorality was unholy. Celibacy is a mystery to most in the west and they have no paradigm for it. The Bible however treats this as calling to be honoured as much as marriage (not more so) and is part of a valid human experience equal in value to being married. (Matthew19:11)

---

8. I say to the unmarried men and to the widows, it is fine for them if they remain as I am *(Paul again states he is unmarried. See 7:7)*

If he were a widower as some suggest because Jewish rabbis were encouraged to be married, Paul states "as I am" which refers back to the word for unmarried man (not widower which would be a different word).

Why does Paul not include widowers or unmarried women in this verse? It is possible that he has chosen these two groups as representative of unmarried of both sexes and those who have lost their marriage partner by death whether male or female.

---

9. but if they cannot reign in this they should marry. For it is better to be married than to be burning.

Paul continues to say that for everyone who is unmarried or has lost someone in death, it is better for them to marry than to burn. In using the word. "burn". Paul describes accurately the human condition which is lit for sex and he advises for such, marriage as this is the only place sex should be i.e. within a long term committed marriage relationship between a man and a woman. To try to placate the burning by any other means destroys others and one's own soul /spirit receives damage creating unhelpful drives, false thought processes and leading to further destruction. All immorality is best avoided.

Where marriage is despised, sexual desire can spill over into many different inappropriate areas and sexual energy spent in sinful destructive ways.

10. But I announce to those who have been married, I am not (the source of this) but the Lord,

Paul is not referring to divine revelation he has picked up in his heart but the scriptures. He uses different Greek words when he is referring to revelation of the heart. (See verse 40). The New Testament scriptures – and the words of Jesus in particular were already beginning to be written down during Paul's lifetime. Paul knew Mark who is thought to have written the earliest gospel and his gospel could have been already written by 58A.D. (see 2 Tim 4:11-13, 2 Peter 3; 16). If this is so, the verse might give a clue that Paul had read at least part of that gospel by the time he was writing 1 Corinthians as Paul is referring to what Jesus said in the gospels (Matthew 19:6. Mark 10:9-11, Luke 16:18)

a woman should not be separated (divorced);

11. If she is separated let them remain unmarried or be reconciled to her ex-husband and the man should not send away his wife.

The verb meaning send away was used in legal courts to get a divorce. The verb for the woman means at root being separated whereas the verb used for getting a divorce for the man is "sent away". This reflects the legal processes in place at the time where divorce was initiated by the man and happened to the woman. The cause as today could be on either side of the relationship, but Paul is referring to the legal process of divorce at the time. This is advice to the married, and is not for those who are divorced. He will address these later in the chapter. His advice to the married is in a nutshell "stay married and if there is a fall out, stay in a place where reconciliation can happen".

The verbs "send away" and "separated" are the words used in Paul's day to initiate divorce proceedings. The word for actually being divorced is different; it is "loosed". This is the verb used later when Paul addresses the divorced directly and refers to those whose divorce proceedings have been completed for some time and they have no obligations felt or unfelt to their previous partner. Presumably one could imagine a marriage breakdown occurring so that divorce did happen. In this case they would need to take note, not of these verses, but of the verses to the divorced later in this chapter. This verse "to the married" is not to be used (as it often is) as commands to the divorced. A couple who are married may after a time of separation move from the place of marriage to a place of being loosed. In which case they move from the advice in 7:10, 11 to verse 27. God has a right path for us whatever our life situation- single, married or divorced.

When truth is overstated with further rules it undermines the truth itself as the extra rules are not the truth. People are then deceived by the extra rules to dismiss the truth. The church has taught the lie that Marriage is indissoluble. But Jesus said the opposite: "man could put asunder what God had joined" (Mark 10:9). People can put asunder marriage. It is dissoluble.

In the Christian community I have heard related false claims. One of these is that if it is a Christian wedding it is indissoluble, but if it is in a registrar's office or marriage to an unbeliever it is dissoluble. But marriage is the same whether in a registrar's office or church; whether a couple have faith or not. It is sex and commitment to each other not their beliefs which brings about the marriage bond. Paul is talking to the married Corinthians whether they were married in church/synagogue or not (most of them would have been married external to the church or synagogue)

Once it is accepted that people can make a difference and destroy a marriage; it is possible also to see that he/she has also the ability to restore what may have been broken in the past. A couple can have a rich marriage when they have previously been fornicators or adulterers. God can break soul ties created through immorality. Confession and repentance are two important steps in this process of experiencing the forgiveness of God (and of self) and the newness of life. God's intention is that we live in the freedom and joy married life can bring rather than in the regret or in the condemnation of Satan based on past sins or unforgiveness.

12. The rest

Who is Paul referring to? I think he is talking to people who are in a relationship but who are not married.

Some have suggested

1. Paul is talking about those who do not have a marriage where faith in Jesus is part of their relationship but that would imply that there is some distinction between marriages where there is faith and marriages where there is not. But Jesus did not and Paul does not make this distinction. Jesus affirms that marriage is a creation ordinance which exists regardless of faith, and we have already seen Paul adheres to the teaching of Jesus in this passage.

2. The distinction he draws by using the word λοιπos is not because of the doctrine of marriage, but rather the reference to the rest of the concerns in the letter to which he is replying (7:1). But the problem with this is that it seems " the rest" is embedded within the teaching he is giving rather than introducing a fresh subject. Paul is rather, bringing a fresh group into the same orbit as his teaching of remaining in the same calling. He has no new subject here, but rather a further category of people to whom the principles he is outlining applies

3. The distinction Paul is talking about with "the rest" is the distinction between married couples who agree together about God and those who have a partner who is an "unbeliever". This is advice for those who are living together but can also be relevant to those who are married to someone who opposes the Christian faith to the degree it affects the marriage. (see below)

I think however that this teaching is primarily for those who live together as husband and wife who are not actually married. My reasons for saying this is:-

a. Paul is drawing a distinction between married couples who should not departing from each other and a situation where it is possible to separate more easily (contrast 7:11 with 7:15).

b. Living together relationships would indeed be in the Corinthian church if there was one of the partners unwilling to marry, because the partner as an unbeliever does not accept the Christian doctrine of marriage. This fits the situation Paul seems to be addressing

c. The teaching about the children makes sense also if Paul has a living together relationship in mind (7:14), because of the curse of illegitimacy. There would be no such issue in a married relationship even when one partner is an unbeliever.

d. 7:13 makes sense where the woman can send the man away – something which a woman in a living together relationship could do, but what she could not do if in a married relationship.

I am the source not the Lord. If any brother has an unbelieving wife, and she is pleased to live with him, do not send her away.

The significance of "unbelieving" is that such a person refuses to obey Christian values or walk God's way. We are mainly dealing with living together relationships here where one partner refuses the Christian way of marriage. (There is however the possibility that there is also included the couples who are married in law where the Christian is so unhappy with the partner being not a Christian, that they want a divorce. The advice Paul states here does not exclude the latter scenario).

The teaching is whenever there is someone who refuses to adopt Christian values and wants a separation (divorce).

Unmarried living together relationships would be common practice where there was a divided ethic in the relationship. Not everyone has been brought up with the idea of getting married, and marriage was not always possible in a pagan society. Paul is saying here that the same rule applies to living together partnerships between a man and a woman as with marriage, i.e. that they should stay together. If this is the case, the next verse about children being sanctified makes more sense if he is referring to living together relationships as the curse of illegitimacy is ended through faith of one parent.

The standing of the relationship does not bring sanctification to the children but the faith of one of the parents.

Unmarried living together relationships have been dubbed by society as "living in sin" and adultery or fornication is at the foundation of such relationships. Paul says that when someone turns to Christ they might be in a relationship that started this way, but he says in such circumstances they should stay as you are. It is the same principle as for the married, divorced or single. Stay in the same way that you were in when you were called (i.e. first became a Christian). Paul also addresses the concerns about the children from a unmarried living together relationship, for there is a curse of illegitimacy (e.g. Deuteronomy 23:2; Exodus 34:7)). But Paul says here that there are effects on the children for good when just one parent turns to faith. Presumably if both turned to faith they would then be married in compliance with the wishes of Jesus. The only ones in church who are in living together relationships are those who have non believing partners. Paul affirms them to stay as they are without guilt. Our faith breaks every curse.

13. And in the same way a wife who has an unbelieving husband and he is pleased to live with her, she should not send her husband away.

A wife could not send her husband away, but a woman in a living together relationship could. If Paul were referring to a marriage relationship he would have spoken about the woman being loosed from (as he does later in the chapter) rather than sending away the man.

14. For the unbelieving man sanctifies in the wife and the unbelieving woman is sanctified in the brother.

Greek word here is "brother" not husband. In addition in the first clause re the unbelieving man the word used is not sister but "wife". If all Paul was saying was that sanctification happens through the believing partner whether husband or wife, why make distinctions in the words he uses? Paul must be saying something further. I think Paul is revealing the means of grace which brings about the sanctification and it is all to do with the source within the relationship through which the sanctification flows. When he mentions "brother" he is referencing the relationship in the church which is defining the avenue of sanctification for the man to his unbelieving wife. The way this works however is different for the woman with the unbelieving husband. What impacts the unbelieving husband is not the relationship of his wife in the church but it is as wife and home builder (rather than as sister in the church) that the unbelieving man is sanctified. This power of sanctification will affect the home including the partner and the children.

So - what will impact the unbelieving wife is that her husband is part of the church and specifically the quality of his relationship ("brother") in the church (not so much what he does in the church) whereas for the unbelieving man, her relationships in the church make little difference. It is rather how the woman behaves in the home and with him that makes the impact. Peter makes the same point in I Peter 3:1.

Before we move on, just a note about Sanctification. Sanctification is not a royal decree that stays in the throne room of heaven. This is something which makes a difference in mind and heart now on the earth which bring blessing to their home and offspring. Sanctification is a necessary precursor to impartation of blessing. Sanctification means a setting apart from the darkness which once ruled hearts and minds; it changes destinies and renders powerless curses and past decrees. It aligns us to the blessing of God so that promises are fulfilled for good, destinies bear fruit and hearts and minds enter the rest of God.

> **Since if this was not the case** (*this is not in the Greek but does accurately take account of the* $\varepsilon\pi\varepsilon\iota$ $\alpha\rho\alpha...\nu\upsilon\nu$ $\delta\varepsilon$ *reflecting the Greek idiom of the sentence*) **your children are unclean, whereas they are (in fact) holy.**

There is a difference between unclean and holy. It shows in the mind-set, behaviour and demeanour, in speech and in deed. Unclean means your conscience is defiled (Hebrews 9:14) which affects judgements that are made. The unclean are unable to relate appropriately in word or deed, and in addition defile others by what they do or say. They lack the sensitivities that the conscience gives so they are unaware of their own needs, operating out of a self-formed world where most are an enemy to ignore or defeat and friendships lack feeling or understanding. If the conscience does not develop the person does not see what is dangerous to be avoided in a social context and what is good to pursue. Uncleanness defiles its environments without concern. The lack of sensitivity the conscience affects the ability to build good nourishing relationships which build others up in confidence and joy whether in home or work; whether in private or national life.

Sanctified children behave differently from those who are not. Children being sanctified is not just words. It is life changing. There are different outcomes both in their social skills and achievements for them.

Whether children are clean/holy is directly linked by Paul to the faith of a parent - not to upbringing, resources, or community environment.

The more families growing in the faith of Jesus in the church, the more likely will be the wellbeing of teachers in schools and society as a whole. Where-ever children are present, whether they are holy or unholy will make a great difference to the environments they are in.

Faith imparts grace to a family which only gradually fades as one unbelieving generation follows another. When faith has impacted a culture as it has in the UK in generations past, the culture can still continue to impart good values and appropriate behaviour, but amidst renunciation of beliefs and Christian values, there will be a culture decline in holy living and relationships and a growth of unclean speech, destructive relationships or unhealthy lifestyle choices, as the culture of the present fights against the values of the past.

The alternative to holy is unclean. The unclean attract the enemy. Just as flies gather around rotten food, so demons gather around uncleanness. Some of these can be named perversion or trouble, anger or fear. Holiness does not mean we do not have to battle against such entities for we live in the world where they operate; but holiness does mean that there is no legal right of access for such. Within our gift of holiness we can have a confidence in our identity and clarity of the truth to see the right way and to keep these "flies" away.

> **15. If the unbeliever** *(this can be someone who is not a Christian believer or a "Christian" who does not hold to Christian values Matthew 18:17)* **separates, let there be a separation.**

χωρισθομαι is the usual verb Paul uses throughout this chapter when talking about separation or divorce. It was used at the time in legal documents for divorce, but only because of its normal meaning is to divide. The reference here is where one of the partners refuses to accept the Christian position on marriage and wants to separate. Paul does not give the same advice as to married couples (in v11), where they are to stay in a possible place for reconciliation. Here the teaching is to divide and be in a permanent place of separation. To reiterate, this is in my view, because we are dealing with a living together relationship or one where the values of the partner who wishes to separate is unwilling to submit to Christian values.

> **The brother or sister** *(they are described like this because they are part of God's family the church)* **has not been enslaved in such matters,**

The pain of separation and the shame can lead to slavery marked by an inability to move on from the past relationship which has ended or is ending. The slavery Paul refers could be made greater for a brother or sister because they can be enslaved by their "Christian" sense of duty to stay in the calling they were in when they became Christians. But Paul says to such "End it. Walk away from it without guilt" (whether they are man or woman). There are no adverse results for them in this case. They are really free.

The enslavery Paul refers to can happen in more than one way. It could come about through shame at agreeing to a separation because they know this is not God's perfect plan for humankind or the enslavery could be staying in a relationship that the other partner does not want. In either case they are slaves and the right course is to be divorced and know you are free and rejoice in it. In the next verse Paul encourages them to move boldly in peace by standing securely on the fact they are divorced. This brings real freedom.

Paul adds the next clause

> **but in peace God has called you.**

This phrase is all about moving on from this relationship post separation. Paul knows the call of God is there for the next phase of life beyond the divorce and even (as we shall see) during the divorce proceedings. Paul states that the person has to be at peace to recognise the call. Slavery will rob someone of the peace that they need to move in. Jesus is called the Prince of Peace. Peace is where His rule is known and His purpose outworked.

This is not called "to peace" but called "**in** peace". Unfortunately some translate this passage "to peace" which implies that Paul is saying in these circumstances getting a divorce was the right thing because we are troubled and God has called us to peace. But Paul is actually saying "in peace". He is defining the environment in which we can hear the call of God - a call which we need to hear if we are going to move on from the separation. The "in peace God calls" is not a passing statement. It is pivotal, casting light forwards onto the next verses explaining what follows. This phrase points forward to the next stage after the freedom which comes through the separation. God has a purpose for the future and we will hear it when we are in peace.

16. For, wife, do you know if you will save your husband. Or what does the husband know if you will save his wife.

If this were in a different part of the chapter we might read this "If you do not get divorced it might be that you might save your husband or wife. You do not know what God might do". But the verses do not come in that context. It follows the verses about getting divorced (separated). It talks about getting out of slavery through staying in the peace of God and moving into revelation of His purpose for the future. The Greek text looks like it follows on from the previous sentence. This verse follows the phrase "the call of God in peace". Paul is saying when you are at peace; it is the best place for your husband or wife to be saved. He is preventing that peace being disturbed by responsibility for the separated unbelieving partner. For a separation in its finality can seem like the end of everything, but Paul makes clear that the separated Christian at peace can still bring an influence to bear on the ex-partner which might lead to their salvation. Peace is the key for this to happen.

He is continuing to teach that everyone should remain in their calling, but for the moment he is dealing with the specific group of those who are separating at the desire of their unbelieving partner. In our context this is relevant for living together relationships where the partner does not want to continue the relationship and also for marriages where one side demands their partner renounce their Christian faith

The next verse has two contrasting sides of the same coin which is brought out as contrast in the Greek text. One side says in the division, God is doing the assigning. He assigns a portion to each of the parties (not just to the Christian partner in the relationship) and the other side is that there is a call of God in the new life brought about by the division and there is an obligation to walk according to that call. This latter point forms the foundation of the teaching in the next verse (18-24)

So I translate verse 17.

17. If not

The Greek sentence opens with these two words. This means that even if husband or wife are not saved, or there is no change in them, the Lord still is in charge of your life and the future.

Lord has divided to each their share

The Lord has given to them a lot, i.e. an assigned place in life. As we have seen, it is in the peace of God this assignment can be recognised and understood. This verse also means the Lord has a plan for a right divorce settlement which forms part of the positioning for the new life. Whatever you receive from the settlement of the divorce you should recognise it is from the Lord, and within the peace you have which comes with that territory discover the calling of God and walk according to that calling.

or as each is called of God so let him walk. And I command this in all the churches.

Paul's perception of the teaching to "stay as you are" which he is giving to singles, married, divorced, and living together may have started in the circumcision debate in the council of Jerusalem (Acts 15). For the circumcision issue is the first example where the same "Stay as you are" principle applies. He then applies it to status in society.

The world made distinctions between slaves and free; the Jews between circumcised and uncircumcised. You could never be both. You were either slave or free; circumcised or uncircumcised. Paul says here you should accept who you are, knowing that God loves you as you are and has a purpose as you are. If you long for being a slave when free or free when being a slave, those desires can find their fulfilment in Christ and for circumcised or uncircumcised, the real focus is obedience to God. So in fact though there are distinctions in life, those distinctions are no issue in Christ.

---

18. Is anyone circumcised, do not pull over *(the remainder of)* **the foreskin** *(to try to hide the circumcision,).* **Is anyone uncircumcised, do not be circumcised.**

19. Circumcision is nothing and uncircumcision is nothing, but (what matters) is keeping of

---

This word "keep" is used in the sense of "have custody of". This is a reminder that the commands from God are entrusted to us. We keep them by obedience. Jesus when talking about those who hear the word but does not obey as hard soil on which the seed makes no difference(Luke 8:12ff,15;) or as a person who could have built wisely with foundations instead building foolishly on sand (Matthew 7:24-27).

---

the commands of God.

20. Let each remain in this calling in which he has been called.

21 Are you called as a slave? Do not let it worry you *(verb means meditate or study in its active tense. In this tense it is where you worry thinking about something over and over again)* **But if you will be able**

---

to be made free, it is to be useful *(i.e. if you are made free, God has a plan for you as free, but you could easily remain a slave as a Christian and God has a plan for you as a slave.).*

22. For you who are called in the Lord as a slave, are a free man of Christ

Although you might be a slave in the world's eyes you are in reality a free person in Christ able to move freely as a citizen of heaven in the anointing of God. No-one needs to regret their position in life or feel God cannot use them as they are. The slave also does not need to prove anything. A slave is free in Christ.

Likewise he who is called as a freedman is a slave of Christ. *Those who are free in the world's eyes have to focus on their obligations to their master Jesus. They are not their own but bought with a price. There is a balance here. Just as a slave needs to look at being free in Christ, so the free person needs to look to being a slave of Christ not of men.*

23. You were bought with a price. Do not become slaves of men.

24. Each should remain in which he has been called, brethren, near God. *($\pi\alpha\rho\alpha$ plus the dative means nearness. Staying in our calling is the way we can stay near to God).*

25. Concerning virgins I have no command from the Lord. *(He does not include virgins in his general principle of remaining in this calling. The monastic movements and Christian tradition made virginity a calling. Paul does not do so.)* **I am giving my thought as in the mercy from God I am trustworthy.**

26. I consider this good to live through the present age demands because it is good for a man to be so

i.e. being a virgin helps him in the demands of this present age. Notice this is not so he can get closer to God or fulfil the demands of the kingdom. It is interesting how celibacy is not because of the kingdom call but to help in coping with this world's demands. Celibacy is not so we can be "married to Christ" but so we can be helped to live life to the full here on earth with fewer demands. The world uses the good care for one another, the listening and fusion of values between a married couple to pressurize us, to stop us or hinder us in our calling from God. These pressures we can sidestep more easily if unmarried. This theme is brought out in v32, and in verse 25.

27. Have you been given a wife? Do not seek to be free. Have you been loosed from a wife, Do not seek a wife.

28. If also you marry you do not sin.

Paul states categorically it is alright for divorced to remarry. **You can remarry after divorce and not sin**.

The Church has made the mistake of taking the words of Jesus and stating that remarriage of divorcees are wrong. Paul says that whilst divorcees should remain as they are if they can (1 Corinthians 7: 27), if they marry they do not sin. This is the advice Paul gives the divorced. The advice he gives to the married is "do not divorce" (7:10, 11) but if there is a falling out to not rush off to get a divorce or to remarry. But if a divorce does occur he does not exclude remarriage.

And if a virgin marries she has not sinned.

Paul wants to make sure that they understand his teaching on the value of singleness does not mean it is sinful to marry. This verse is also relevant to anyone who might think sex defiles. Sex does not defile, immorality does. Where there is marriage, sex blesses.

These things which have trouble in the flesh, I would spare you.

Paul is making the point that his only reason for saying don't get married is just so they are spared from trouble in the world which family life can bring. If Paul were speaking in our era, "troubles in the flesh" might mean balancing family obligations against work pressures , paying university fees with perhaps increased worries over housing or schooling, and the providing for the family and not just oneself.

Paul also says to get married is good and is not at all a second best option to remaining single. Paul explains this explicitly in v32. The verses 29-31 must be connected with this.

> **29. I say this, brethren, for the opportune time** (καιρος) **is shortened** *(verb to make short. The current season of life will not last)* **In the period that follows this** *(λοιπον can mean henceforth and refers to the time after the "opportune time")*

In the past, this would be one of the verses used to show that Paul was expecting the imminent return of Christ. The theory used to be made that the early Church including Paul were expecting the second coming of Christ to happen immediately and were therefore encouraging the Christians to live in the light of this imminent return (including not getting married). The difficulties with this view is that it makes various verses of the bible to be based on a false hypothesis (as Jesus did not return within the lifetime of these first and second generation Christians) and not relevant for everyone for all time It also fails to show the teaching Paul is teaching here for there is no explicit mention here of the second coming of Jesus. It can make perfect sense without putting these verses into an eschatological setting. The advice given is to do with life in this world which brings trouble for humankind of all generations including the present one.

> **those having wives will be as not having them**
>
> **30. and those weeping as not weeping and those rejoicing as not rejoicing and those who buy as not possessing**
>
> **31. and those using the world** *(profiting from the way the world is)* **as not making full use of it**

What is Paul referring to? He is not saying that married couples should live as if they are not married for that would contradict all he has been saying at the

135

start of the chapter, and so he is not also saying that people should deny their emotional sorrows or joys, the possessions they have, or the opportunities and influence they have in the world order. Rather what he is saying is all these things will be superseded.

In life there is no stay. There is an opportune time when things seem to be fine but then a time following that time when it is not so. Paul has advice here for the difficult times v28 living in the flesh when times have changed v29. Paul is saying is about the experience of living life in this world. Whether it be marriage, business, emotional ups and downs, they are all passing. There will come a time for all when those present fine things will matter little as life moves on for each one. This is true for a married woman in a residential home, or a widow visiting the shops or a politician caring for an ill relative, or a business person in hospital. Each can find life that once was experienced as irrelevant in their current situation and to act as things used to be would be inappropriate for them as life has moved on. This is the point Paul is making here.

> **For the cultural shape** *(σχημα = present form)* **of this world passes away.**
>
> **32. I want you to be without anxiety. The unmarried man worries about the things of the Lord; how he may please the Lord.**
>
> **33. But the one who has married worries about the things of the world: how he may please his wife.**
>
> **There is a difference between the woman and the girl** *(virgin).*

The Greek word translated "woman" is not the primary word for wife but the word for woman. This verse is not drawing the distinction between married and unmarried. (That follows in the next verse where different words are used in the Greek). Paul is here making a significant point that his teaching that follows is age related. He is referring to the adult woman.

34. And the woman who is unmarried or the virgin cares for *("cares for" is singular as Paul is thinking of an individual whether it be an unmarried woman or a virgin).*

Paul says it is the same for the virgin as for the unmarried woman. The unmarried woman is a term used for the widow or divorcee or the single parent or someone who is unmarried but not a virgin.

the things of the Lord in order that she may be holy in body and spirit.

A woman who loses her virginity even through immorality can still pursue holiness of body and spirit and be on an equal footing with those who have not been immoral. This might come as a surprise to those who think that immorality forces you into a lifestyle devoid of holiness. In Christ it does not.

but she who is married worries about the things of the world, how she may please her husband

35. I say this for your own advantage and not so I can put any restraint on you, but towards the goal of that which is proper and being a good attendant to the Lord without distraction.

36. If anyone thinks that he is bringing shame *(because he is delaying marrying his intended wife)* **to his virgin, if she is past the bloom (of youth)**

This is not "oversexed" so should surrender to his feelings and marry as Barrett[2] translates this. This is not a man who has shame because he cannot control himself. It is rather that he is acting shamefully delaying the marriage (through possibly the best of motives- which could be possibly extending the kingdom of God, being involved in church planting or mission work; or it could be getting a house ready, the finances in place or promotion in his job). There is an obligation on the betrothed to enter marriage and not delay this, for there is a possible shame in delay. Paul explains his possible causes of shame. 1. The bridegroom perceives it is shaming his future wife not to marry immediately 2. The bride is getting to an age where she ought to be married. The second reason is a sub clause explaining why the bride may feel shame, as the Greek is all one sentence. Paul is making the point he does not want the bride to feel shame and the husband should marry. He should do the right thing not just necessarily on the grounds of her age. There may be other reasons which make it right to marry where there is no shame attached, e.g. they want to start a family whilst they are young.

> **and so ought to be (married), he should do what he wishes** *(which is he should marry as he intends to do).* **He does not sin.**

Paul has to say they do not sin, because they might feel they should have waited. This can happen in the region of kingdom work and also in the region of getting things right in life outlines above. It is relevant for both situations.

> **Let them marry.**
>
> **37. But who stands firm in his heart not having any compulsion** *(within like feeling shame because he thinks he is doing the wrong thing. Paul is now outlining the inner life of someone untroubled in his conscience and for whom he knows the time is not right for him to be married. So he says)* **but has authority concerning his own will** *(he is not being pressurised by anyone else,)* **and this has been decided in his own heart to keep his virgin** *(i.e. not marry her but keep her as his betrothed),* **he will do well.**

Note: the verb is about keeping his virgin; still being responsible for her, still protecting her. There is no suggestion of ending the relationship. It is of keeping not losing his intended. It is just he feels he should not proceed from betrothal to marriage that is being mentioned here.)

> **38. So as both he who marries his virgin does well and the one who does not marry will do better**

Because he is operating out of faith and conviction to obey God. God is a debtor to no one so he will be rewarded for this. Note the man who does better is not finishing the relationship with his betrothed but delaying it under God's guidance. What Paul is saying here has nothing to do with choosing path of celibacy rather than a married life.

Paul here has valuable comments on the inner life of the person obeying God. His decisions are not influenced by any external obligation rooted in expectation of others; he rules his own will and has decided in his heart. The heart covers the area of his soul where his mind and self-esteem meet. It is the place of conscience and vulnerability. His self-esteem is settled with this, his mind is at rest with this.

Paul now changes his teaching from virgins to widows.

39. A wife has been bound for as long as her husband lives, but if her husband has died, she is free to be married to whom she wishes only in the Lord.

This might mean she should marry only be Christian. It does not have to be that though. Paul is saying her only obligation is to what the Lord wants, not her family, her husband's family or her friends or church. She marries who she wants to marry; the only proviso is that she stays in relationship with the Lord'.

40. She is happier if she has stayed as she is

ουτως refers to what precedes. Paul is talking about remarriage in the Lord. Is this what he is referring to which makes the widow happier or is it that she should remain as she is (a widow and not get married). I think it probable means the latter.

according to my opinion and I think I also have the Spirit of God.

Paul is saying she will be happier if she does not marry and says this is just his opinion, but he also witnesses in his heart that the Holy Spirit is agreeing with his opinion in this.

A Dream

In what seemed like twilight, Paul could make out some large pillars of a hall similar to those in the temple of Artemis, yet the light was strange. As his eyes became accustomed to the dark he saw various figures moving around in what seemed like a palace court. He recognised there was a Jew present because he recognised the high priestly garments, and when he turned towards Paul, he looked straight beyond him as if Paul was not there. Paul knew him. He was Alexander the coppersmith. He was talking with Demetrius the silversmith who had a tattoo of Artemis around his neck in some odd way. There were others with him whom Paul recognised were part of the wealthy silversmith guild. Paul turned to look further across the room. The covered courtyard he was in was larger than it first seemed and there were a lot of people there. It was a mixed group of all ages, each dressed in distinctive ways which seemed to define them and to impress others. Some he did not know, but he had had direct dealings with others. Over in a far corner of the room were some of the guards he had met in prison who had openly mocked him. In another group lit by a torch secured to the wall were others he knew from the city who had sought to mislead the church. Paul looked around and all the people he recognised had opposed him or the gospel in one way or another. Paul was at first startled by this, and yet he was not afraid for he knew instinctively that he was safe. He also took great comfort that no-one seemed to recognise him or know he was there. It was as if he was looking at a moving picture yet he was in it at the same time.

The atmosphere was heavy with smoke from the torches on the walls and the air was stale, but this seemed normal to the people as they talked together and moved from group to group. Paul in the dim light could make out that there were some figures sitting alone down one of the walls with vacant looks on their faces and around each were what looked like charms and crystal balls. Occasionally in the room there would be raised voices and some obscenities exchanged, which caused the vacant faces to look up but no more. They quickly returned to their vacant pose. Paul looked away to survey the full scene before him. There was an air of seriousness about the place. It seemed like a drinks party before a big event.

He started to walk through the hall by one of the rows of pillars. There were plans on some of the pillars which resembled battle plans, but Paul only thought about that later. He dismissed the thought at the time because planning for war were men only affairs at the start at least, and there were plenty of women present dressed in their finery. Some of the women had an entourage of slaves and Paul felt the competition and rivalry between different groups. They seemed to move as royalty from one place to another seeking to speak to and to be spoken to by the more influential in the gathering. The men also had their attendants, and had different dress defined by job or culture. There were military uniforms from different nations. There were also religious garments, from different eras and there were even theatrical costumes some of which were bizarre. There was everyone from barbarian warriors to peaceful politicians. Paul recognised some of the soldiers from his prison days and also one of the leaders of the new gladiatorial schools opening with the recent ongoing reconstruction of the stadium under Nero, but most were unfamiliar to him. Paul noted there was every culture represented in Ephesus, and the predominant dress was from Asia though he noticed that there were quite a few from Egypt and Alexandria behaving in the distinctive way of lawyers and scribes. Some of the styles of dress were familiar but not all. Some were dressed very bizarrely indeed. Some exercised authority and others did the bidding of their master. The military men and political leaders of Asia were not there in large numbers and the main representation seemed to be from the business community and the ones directly affected in their families or in their jobs by the growth of the church. Paul would revisit this memory in days to come when a battle raged around him which would cause him to despair of life, and which would bring about his hasty exit from Ephesus. He walked through the pillars trying to get to the far side of the room from which he had entered. The atmosphere seemed to thicken like treacle as he walked. He recognised past symbols from ancient Persia, and Babylon, idols from Mesopotamia and scripts from ancient Akkadian and Sumerian empires and some markings which if Paul had known went back even before that. If he paused at any symbol, pictures of blood sacrifice and horrors filled his mind, so he quickly learnt not to take too much notice of what was on the pillars as he passed by them. He left the people he knew behind at the drinks party and he walked on towards the wall at the opposite end to the entrance. The pillared hall became more open with pillars around the edges creating a large open space which was deserted. He noticed the plain stone flags on the floor had changed to various mosaics arranged in some pattern which resembled the dress he had seen of the Artemis image in Ephesus, but there was a large crack along the floor which had not been repaired and the movement in the floor had dislodged a plinth pushing up the stone at an angle from the floor. On this heavy stone was a chair which looked like a throne. Once it would have been straight but now with the plinth at an angle the chair had slid and was resting at a strange angle upon it. "No wonder it is empty" thought Paul "It would be impossible to sit on that chair now". He approached the steps which led to the empty chair. Under the chair a river bubbled out and flowed westwards. It looked red in the glow of the lamps, and seemed more like treacle than a river. As he looked he could see the river as if the walls of the room were not there. He could see the red water going out from the harbour but he also saw a great wind blowing from the west which stopped the red flow westwards to Greece and causing it instead to change direction and go northwards towards the black sea or backwards towards the Ephesian coast. He instinctively knew as he saw it that this was one of the ancient rivers of idolatry which brought death wherever it was allowed to flow , and he also knew in that same instance that he was witnessing a work of God coming against its influence and power, which was effective, destroying its power. Paul instinctively prayed, but as he did so, those in the other part of the room far away turned to him and then suddenly he was aware of the room folding up and away from him. He knew he had been in a place of supernatural darkness, and then he woke up. It was a dream.

Erastus

E rastus was young and ambitious. He was already the treasurer of the major city of Corinth a newish city of just over 100 years built by the Romans on the site of the one destroyed 100 years before. Ephesus felt familiar to him because he was used to a city with a large mixed population of Romans, Greeks, and Jews, and there was Roman influence in Ephesus as there was in Corinth. Below the surface, however, this city was very different from Corinth. Erastus was a Corinthian and was seeking election for one of the top jobs of procurator and aedile in Corinth. He as treasurer had already done the job of the aedile, but he was aiming higher. He had not been idle whilst in Ephesus. He was already planning to introduce to Corinth the Marble Street he had seen in Ephesus if he was successful in the elections that were proposed next year.

Paul and Erastus had spent some time together on Sunday at first walking around the civic agora, and from there they and their companions had walked northwards to the temple over a mile from the centre of Ephesus. The temple of Artemis was regarded as one of the seven wonders of the ancient world. After the death of Alexander the Great it had been rebuilt and enlarged so it now stood 450' long by 225' wide and 60 feet high, with more than 127 columns each rising over 16 feet .Its marble platform and elevated position meant it formed part of the Ephesus skyline from the sea and could be seen from some miles away. Shops were on both sides of the road to the temple and also around the temple itself. Now that winter was over, and trade was beginning again in earnest, there was also the resumption of large numbers of pilgrims visiting the shrine of Artemis of the Ephesians. Some shops sold little replicas of the temple or of the image of Artemis for visitors to take home.

The town of Ephesus welcomed visitors from all over the Roman Empire and it brought in much wealth for the metal workers who forged the idols that were sold there. In Ephesus the images of Artemis were the old Phrygian mother goddess Cybele images, in preference to the female hunter images of the Artemis of Greece. This mother goddess of fertility with its occultist and sex rites had originated in ancient Mesopotamia long ago. Thousands of years before her followers had brought her worship to the shores of the Mediterranean. It was now well entrenched in the minds and culture of the region.

It took some time for the group of friends to reach the temple area. By the time Paul, Erastus and the others had arrived, their conversation was no longer on buildings or the traditions of Ephesus but on the wonderful things Jesus had done. Paul had recounted to the Corinthians some of the recent history of revival in the city and the scores that had turned to Jesus from the occult, even burning their spells and occult teaching publicly in the agora in the wake of the revival. Paul's arrival in Ephesus had from the start been marked by remarkable miracles and healing, and the conversions had affected other cities in Asia. Paul knew there were still waves of anger and dismay at the changes to lives that the revival had brought especially amongst those who profited from the local interest in the occult. Paul was speaking in Greek because no-one in the group easily understood Aramaic or Hebrew, and Greek was the common language throughout the eastern trading nations of the Empire, Paul spoke quietly because he did not want to be overheard by those who were passing by in earshot of their conversation. Ephesus could still be a dangerous place for him.

Idolatry was part of life wherever you were in the Roman Empire and Corinth was no different in that respect even though the culture was so different. "When did you start your travels Paul? Erastus asked, and Paul began to explain about Barnabas and the first mission to Cyprus and then also about his mission to Galatia and the work at Antioch and the commission he received from the Jerusalem church at the start of his missionary journeys over 10 years before when he had been told the things he needed to teach so that the Gentile church could still relate as one with the Jewish Church. At that time the council at Jerusalem had agreed that circumcision was not the sign of being a Christian. The promise of forgiveness of sin was for all who turned to Jesus whether circumcised or not. They had affirmed that this forgiveness was not through obeying the law or doing good. It had been purchased through the death of Jesus and all those whether Jew or non-Jew could enter new life through belief in Jesus, the Son of God.

The Council of the church at Jerusalem did however give some extra guidelines about the teaching that needed to be given to Gentile converts which was to include that they should reject idolatry, not tolerate sexual immorality and have a compassion for the poor. Paul turned to Erastus as he reminded him that he had adopted these three tenets in his teaching to the Christians in all the churches he went. Erastus knew first-hand that this was indeed what Paul taught. The letter he and his companions had brought with them had had concerns precisely because of the teaching Paul had given. He hoped Paul's letter to the Corinthians back home would answer all the questions that had been raised. Erastus looked up and saw in the distance a large crowd moving from the temple area towards the street they were walking. This was unexpected as it was normally on the 6th day of the week that festivals were held. But of course thought Paul more things happen at the temple at the arrival of spring. The quick thinking Erastus pulled Paul to the side of the street and then down a narrow alley away from the procession as it passed on its way back into the city. There was quite a crowd and it would take some time before they could resume their intended journey. They were now separated from their companions who had divided to the other side of the street and would find their own way back

Paul and Erastus for their part walked down this side alley and turned onto a track for sheep or goats beyond the close built houses and shops. Paul was grateful to be able to talk with Erastus alone, for he had a job for him to do on his return to Corinth. He continued to speak to Erastus about the commission from Jerusalem and the Corinthians and explained about the collection for the poor. Paul told him that this was one of the tasks Timothy and Erastus would have as they took his letter to the Corinthians. He hoped the church in Corinth and in Macedonia would make a collection to help the poor in Jerusalem who had suffered in the famine in Judaea during Claudius' reign 8 years or so earlier. Agabas the prophet had foretold these disasters before Paul had embarked on his missionary journeys and it had been the catalyst for the first help to the church in Judea from the Gentile world (albeit Antioch). Now Paul was asking for a collection from Macedonia and Greece. It was something he had not been able to mention when he was at Corinth before because as Agabas had in fact predicted other countries would also suffer from famine during Claudius' reign and indeed Corinth was just recovering from such a famine when Paul had arrived in the city for the first time. But now it was time for the Corinthians to be told about this. Erastus agreed to do this, and thought it would be possible to complete before Paul's arrival at Corinth later in the year so Paul could take the collection back with him to Jerusalem. They walked out of the city and then moved southwards to join a road which they could see weaved towards the gate in the wall from where it was only a few 100 yards to the place where Paul was staying. They walked together in conversation so unaware of the distance they walked, but as they arrived back, they knew they had walked many miles more than either had intended and so Erastus bid farewell to Paul at his house before travelling the few streets more back to his house and host. For now they would rest and early tomorrow Paul would continue the letter on the subject of idolatry.

1 Corinthians Chapter 8-10
Overview

Changing Cultures

Idols are not just in history books.

Changing cultures means confronting the idols behind the cultures.

Chapters 8-10 form a unity starting with the issue of idol worship in chapter 8 and explicitly dealing with the subject again in Chapter 10:14-33. All the teaching in these chapters is around the same subject.

All of us are influenced by the cultures we grow up in, and all cultures of the world are different from the Kingdom of God. When we are born again we enter into the new heavenly culture of the kingdom and have to change from one culture to another. This is not easy or immediate for all. The norms of the old culture still pervade our consciences in differing ways. We have to understand how to be not of the world and in the world at the same time so we can change the cultures for the better or at least bring the kingdom to some within a pagan culture setting. The danger is the Christian forms a culture where only believers can survive and the unbelievers cannot be near you. In such circumstances, the gospel will save no-one beyond you. The teaching he gives in these chapters is to those Christians who like Paul know idolatry is nothing, but unlike Paul have no concern about hurting the conscience of someone still troubled or drawn by the old cultures from which they have been redeemed. These are also lessons for us when we influence cultural change.

Paul faithfully followed his commission from the council of Jerusalem (Acts 15) at the start of his missionary activities and from that time wherever he went including Corinth he included teaching not just on sexual immorality, but also on idolatry. In these chapters he is responding to their questions as a result of his teaching and we are so grateful that we have Paul's reply so we can learn how we should operate when cultures are being impacted by the gospel of Jesus Christ. This is what makes these passages very important indeed. This holy writ is relevant to all even where there are no pagan sacrifices or Jewish food laws.

Idols are all about how we relate to God and the supernatural. They put something between us and God. If in Exodus 20 the first commandment is all about getting the right God. (There is only One – he who made the heavens and the earth) Then the second commandment is all about putting nothing in the way between the true God and ourselves. "Do not make a graven image". We are made in the image of God who is the creator. When people make images they also have creative power. Within the commandment in Exodus 20 there is the recognition that an idol can affect what happens to the third and fourth generation and because the word "generation" is used it is possible that changes to DNA can occur. The unseen realm can affect our environment and our bodies. We get this positively when Jesus speaks of the change the kingdom can bring. He speaks of the finger of the kingdom bringing deliverance to the demonised and the message of the kingdom bringing good news to the poor. Unfortunately idols can work also the unseen realm into our life experience or body health in a negative way. There is an unseen dimension to our health. Romans 8:11 where the Holy Spirit can well up into our mortal bodies and bring good to them. Idols can also affect the same areas. Images bring creative changes to cultures and bodies. Idol worship has an unseen demonic dimension and affects down to the third and fourth generation.

The Kingdom of God changes the world.

In Revelation 11:15 "The kingdoms of this world have become *the kingdoms* of our Lord and of his Christ" This happens during this age (see 11:18) just as the promises in Habakkuk (2:14) and Isaiah (11:9) "that the knowledge of the glory of the Lord would cover the earth as the waters cover the sea" also belong to this age which exists post Pentecost and prior to the second coming of God. One day there will be a new heavens and a new earth. This earth will vanish with the heavens and the kingdoms of the earth will be no more, but for now they exist (Daniel 7:12). The promise of Revelation 11:15 are whilst the kingdoms still exist; God's kingdom comes to reign. The change the Kingdom brings in cultures is evident in the first, second and third centuries when the Kingdom of God changed the Roman empire; it is there in the 5th, 11th & 16th centuries when the kingdom of God changed England and other countries of Europe and it is there in the 18th when the Kingdom of God changed USA and Britain. The Kingdom has changed countries in Africa in the 19th and the Soviet Union and South Africa amongst others during the 20th century. One day the kingdoms of this world will belong to Jesus but for now it is temporary and sporadic. When the kingdom of God is impacting an earthly kingdom it brings cultural change. God becomes central, prayer has a central place, morals and a stand against evil returns, and God's will is exercised through the nation to a greater extent.

The Kingdom of God is the antidote to idols

The Kingdom of God changes cultures to align with heaven so God can work more easily and His Kingdom advances more rapidly. Changing cultures changes the spiritual atmosphere making God's truth more easily heard and received, and evil has much greater difficulty to operate.

Paul in Ephesians 2, describes Satan as the prince of the power of the air. In other words he moves in spiritual atmospheres of which cultures are a part. God's Kingdom will change those cultures overthrowing the power of past idols. These changes prevent old evils from reigning as they once did. They also purify the traditions so they no longer draw from the old, but from the kingdom of God instead. We can cite as examples of this the agricultural feasts of Israel which were celebrations of God the creator not Baal the fertility god, or Christmas in the Christian church which replaces the old sun worship with the worship of the birth of Jesus. The genius of this is that traditions which are helpful to preserve community identity become vehicles for blessing rather than vehicles for sin and evil. The old Celtic church was a master of this, and facilitated a great move of God throughout Europe as a result. Despite the bible making clear that the plan of God is to rule everything under Christ (Ephesians 1:10, Rev 11:15, 1 Corinthians 15:25-28) not everyone in churches has recognised this. They have not seen that God wants to bring change to cultures, and that He redeems traditions and cultures. A community does not lose its identity by turning to Christ in the same way as an individual who turns to Christ remains the same person, and yet is transformed. When Christians have not seen God's intention is to change cultures, they have formed a church despising the cultures around them and forming instead a religious culture alien to those around them. Some Christians even condemn their own religious festivals because of what they once were before the Kingdom advanced into their culture. For example instead of rejoicing at the birth of Jesus at Christmas, they mourn because December 25th used to be a pagan festival. They see what is good as evil. We will discover in these chapters how Paul condemns such, but for the moment I want to continue to show some of the fruits of not understanding this. Church history has found such religious cultures which seek to impose their Christian culture on other societies and bring change by oppression rather than inner transformation brought about by the kingdom of God who resides in the hearts of Jesus' followers. Examples of such oppression is in the reformation (e.g. Calvin in Geneva), or The Anglican Church against some of the puritans in the reign of Elizabeth I or the Roman church in the Inquisition in Europe and the Americas. We have had to relearn primarily through revivals the truths Patrick and the first disciples of old had in their bringing the kingdom of God to a world ignorant of Him.

The teaching of 8-10
8:1-3 Knowledge is not the way but love is

Paul knew what it was like to reach into pagan cultures to find the lost sheep and bring them home. He knew he was "playing away from home". His home had been the Jewish world, but he was called as an apostle to the Gentiles. He has much to teach us

Chapter 8
The way to relate to believers who come from non-Christians backgrounds

Chapter 8 is about how we should operate with a fellow believer who has not fully developed a clear understanding of the kingdom and as a result is still unsure about his pagan past.

The key verse here is verse 7 of chapter 8 where Paul explains that a person who is accustomed to idolatry can be weak in conscience about this issue. He says such a person is someone who has been (and still is)

worried about idolatry. This is primarily someone who has been an idolater, who is not yet sure about the fact it is nothing and still is open to the belief it has supernatural effects both bad and good. The strong believer who knows idolatry is nothing persuades the weak in conscience person to eat. The "weak" in conscience does not share the same confidence and so eats with guilt or fear and that brings about his destruction (8: 7), or rather "his conscience is defiled". Paul wants to avoid situations where this happens.

What is a defiled conscience? It is a conscience which does not work properly. The conscience is our inner gyro of the soul designed to protect our confidence and to make us alert to danger or trouble. Defilement means we do not see danger as danger and may see good as bad so we run away rather towards the Lord. A defiled conscience might also means losing all inner guidance when idolatry or the old life surfaces and confusion results.

Our culture has beliefs and values which go deep and affect our conscience. Paul does not want to damage the conscience of a believer. He knows those who know their faith have the potential of hurting others who whilst also being believers still feel the pull from the old traditions and culture.

Chapter 9
The same attitude is essential for mission

His main point in Chapter 9 is that the way mission happens is through service. Standing on your rights is the exact opposite of being a servant. The same attitude which engenders sensitivity to the fellow believer engenders servant hood to the outsider. It is this which expands the Kingdom

Paul in Chapter 9 illustrates how to do this from his own lifestyle. In order to get to the main point he is wishing to make that he does not stand on his rights, he first of all states the rights he could have and then says he chooses not to do so. This is for the benefit of the Corinthians so they can receive the gospel without charge, but is also for his own benefit as it is his modus operandi enabling him to maintain a clear direction and focus not being obliged to anyone but able to serve whoever he meets so that the kingdom is extended.

Chapter 10
The danger of those who are not sensitive to their brother's conscience is you become insensitive to sin

This insensitivity can work both ways. We can be insensitive to our brother's conscience and be equally insensitive to the issues of sin within our own lives. Religious truths can make us proud in our freedom which then shows when insensitive to another's conscience Chapter 10:24, 12.

How many strong Christians, secure in their faith have then fallen into sin like the Israelites of old? The loss of sensitivity to the conscience of others can also lead to the loss of sensitivity to our own conscience.

Misuse of freedom can lead us into God's wrath and out of our destiny. All things may be available but not everything profits and our freedom we have in Christ is there so we can bless our brother

The danger of those who are not sensitive to their brother's conscience is that not only do they act foolishly with their "weaker" brother, but they do not act appropriately to evil

He never drifts far from Chapter 8 and especially the picture he paints of the weak in conscience stumbling because he sees someone who shares Paul's doctrine of idols not mattering and attending therefore an idol ceremony. So Paul then talks about the problems of doing this not just from a possibility of God's wrath like happened to the Israelites in the wilderness but because they would be partakers with demons that lie behind the images. His argument of the spiritual dimension linked to idol worship is drawn from the spiritual link of the communion service with one another and with God. This happens also in idol ceremonies except it is not the Lord but demons who are active.

Finally he returns to the point that while he is free to do whatever he needs to do, he should be guided by what profits others. Paul then illustrates this with the sharing of meat in a gentile home where conscience again is the main factor behind the decisions made. As conscience was the factor with the weak in conscience so they could go along with the expectations of family or society as their conscience would condemn them if they did not go; so in the same way with the so called strong like Paul. He is careful about the consciences of those around him so they do not stumble because he continues to eat idol meat after being told about its source. Protecting everyone's conscience and moving in peace seems to be the best way in such circumstances.

Some reflections from this section

1. Changing cultures happens not as result of all we know but rather in the love we show.
2. The culture is changed gradually – The conscience is where the values are held and it takes time to adjust
3. How a Christian relates to fellow believers who feel guilty or confused tells Pau (and us) whether that person is really able to reach out to others beyond the walls of the church and also tells Paul (and us) about whether their inner life with God is in good shape or not

Greek text commentary: 1 Corinthians Chapter 8

As we have seen from the summary, chapters 8-10 are a unit of teaching. Within this section there is a reference to the weak and strong in conscience. To help us I define the weak as Christians who are sincere but whose conscience is unable to stand clear of influence from the pagan practices around them whereas the strong are unaffected in their conscience by these cultures. The weak can be recognised by them still giving some credence to the idolatrous practices. Within the deepest recesses of the conscience of the weak there is a belief that there is something in idolatry. Whilst that exists, Paul counsels they should indeed avoid it, and the strong in conscience have a responsibility to protect the weak in conscience by their action and example. The freedom the strong know in Christ should not be used in such a way as to cause others to stumble. Paul is writing his letter here not to the weak but to the strong so they are clear about why they hold idolatry as nothing but also relate properly to their brothers who do not yet share their confidence and truth because their consciences still are influenced by their past beliefs and experience.

1. Concerning idol sacrifices,

Paul starts the sentence with this because this is the next area of concern the Corinthians have put in their letter to him to which he is replying. Ειδολοθυτος is an invented word from the Jewish Christian community. A word in common pagan use was ιεροθυτον, which refers to the sacrifices made at the pagan temples but means literally holy sacrifices. This was not a view shared by the Jews or Christians and so they replaced the part of the word which prefaced the word for sacrifice replacing holy with idol.

we know that we all have knowledge

Paul is making the point that his readers are well acquainted with the theme of idol sacrifices, but he still has something important to say even to the "experts" who may be hearing his letter read when it reaches Corinth

Knowledge makes someone arrogant, whereas love builds

The two Greek verbs here contrast the effect of knowledge with that of love. Knowledge puffs up with no beneficial result whereas love builds up. This is the principle undergirding the teaching of Paul through to the end of chapter ten. This is a key verse. The word "builds" is used because Paul is saying love makes a difference. It restores and strengthens. Love does bring about the real thing.

> **2. If anyone thinks he has known something, he does not know what is proper and good** *("proper and good" to draw out the sense of καθως (well) and δει (what is fitting))*.

This verse challenges our responses when we think we know what we are hearing. "I have heard it all before" means he does not know what is fitting and good. What is fitting and good does not reside in the education of the mind, but rather in the education of the soul and shows in appropriate action based on wisdom of what is appropriate or what is revealed from heaven.

The statements of someone moving out of love in contrast to those moving out of knowledge tend to be present tense with zeal and the Lord rather than mere principled "know it alls". Those moving out of love tend to be dynamic engendering hope rather than static in nature and those who move in love brings about a greater measure of God's power which does not happen for those who move out of knowledge.

> **3. If anyone loves God, such a man is known by Him.**

When we love God our focus is not so much of what one knows about God but what God knows about us. When we meet someone who loves God, God is never far away.

Our love of God is shown by our obedience (he who loves me keeps my commandments (John 14:12, see also 14:23) and our obedience brings about a recognition by God that we are His. He knows his sheep. So in the words of Jesus in John 10:27 "My sheep hear my voice and I know them and they follow me." The hearing of the shepherd's voice involves a response from us which will mean we are known by Him and also that we follow Him. Jesus only knows us as His own when we respond to His voice. (See for example Matthew 7:23)

---

4. Concerning the eating of *(the Greek word is Βρωσις which means eating and then by extension food. The normal word for food is Βρωμα.) This is one of the linked concerns in the letter to which Paul is replying* **what is sacrificed to idols, we know** *(again Paul is starting where they are all agreed)* **that idolatry in the world is nothing** *(i.e. idolatry belongs to the world and has no significance with God or His people or the Kingdom) This phrase and the next one are doctrines which I think Paul had taught the Corinthians previously* **and that no-one is God except One.** *(the demons which lie behind the images and benefit from the religious rites associated with the images are not gods (see 1 Corinthians Chapter 10:19,20))*

5. For if they are called gods either in the heaven or on the earth as if there are many gods and many lords,

6. but God is father to us, from whom come all things, and we are for Him and for the Lord Jesus Christ through who everything (was made) and we (are also created) through Him.

7. But this knowledge is not in all.

We have just read Paul's reason why idolatry is nothing - because God is one not many. The reason he holds to this is based on a creation argument. It is not that God is the only Saviour true as that is, but rather that God is the Maker of all things. There is one source of everything in creation including us and therefore there cannot be other uncreated beings. The pagans who call upon their gods are not calling upon gods at all. Idolatry is therefore given little credence by Paul, and is regarded as a waste of time for all on the earth (not just Jews) as idolatry is based on a lie. (Isaiah 44:12-20, Psalm 135:15-18. Deuteronomy 32:15-17)

The knowledge Paul has shared in verses 4-6, he also recognises is not known by everyone in the church. Paul focuses for a moment on those who do not know this in their conscience. These are called weak. Their lack of knowledge in their hearts about the position they have in Christ in creation. Although the truth of their position in Christ means there is no power in idolatry, because of their customs or traditions or past beliefs, they are not yet unconvinced in their conscience that idolatry is nothing and there is still a residue of belief that idolatry can affect them as Christians. This can show in anxiety or guilt around being involved in any way with idolatrous practices.

They are genuine believers but in this verse 7, he says some **in their custom or usage** up to now are idolatrous. Paul is referring to those brought up to idolatry (Gentiles). It is their past custom that is the cause of why their conscience is weak It is not defiled because they keep away from the old practices.

They know this with their minds; however, in their heart they give credence to the power of idolatry so when they eat food sacrificed to idols they feel guilty, and lose confidence. It is an issue of conscience.

> **Some accustomed** *(in their custom τη συνηθεια)* **until now** *(αρτι εως)* **to idolatry they eat as an idol sacrifice, and their conscience being weak (powerless) is defiled.**

Conscience is our radar working closely with our self-esteem in a relational context. God designed us to commune with ourselves (reflection) as well as commune with God. Our conscience has an effect on both of these activities. Our values and beliefs inform our conscience. Our conscience is part of the human soul which links heart and mind together. A defiled conscience lacks boldness and perception in the kingdom of God. It can make important what is not so, and can ignore what is important. It can malfunction making us feel guilty or anxious over things we should not feel so, and at ease when there is danger afoot. A defiled conscience is a blinded conscience. Confusion or uncertainty reign and makes the person vulnerable to stumble in their faith...some perhaps even thinking idolatrous practice is good (v10), others unable to raise their head to God or respond to his call through guilt. A Clear conscience is perceptive and confident.

> **8. But food will not bring us before God** *(The verb used here can be*

> *used in a sacrificial context. Perhaps Paul is choosing this because of the theme of eating the offerings made in sacrifice to idols. The basic meaning here, however, is being brought into God's presence.)*

The point he is making here is that all food is neutral – neither good nor evil in spiritual terms. He makes the same observation in Romans 14:6. We can operate spiritually with the Lord whether we eat or not.

> **If we do not eat, we have not been excluded** *(as refraining from food does not make us belong more to God or in the church)* **nor if we eat are we any better** *(because eating food does not bring us nearer God, character transformation or revelation or any other spiritual benefit)*

Paul is teaching a further truth which he may not have mentioned when he was in Corinth – that idolatry is not just a lie because God alone is God, but also the practice of eating food to get a blessing. Paul points out that eating food does not make any spiritual benefit and refusing to eat food does not exclude us from spiritual blessing.

The warning to those strong in conscience

> ## 9. Be careful lest your authority brings an hindrance (which is a cause of stumbling) to the weak

Understanding Paul's teaching here centres around understanding who he means by weak. The key verse is v 10, which shows the weak in conscience are worried about eating food which has been sacrificed to idols because (v7) he cannot forget that it has been sacrificed. His conscience is giving the fact credence. The weak feels guilty and this assault on his conscience destroys his inner balance which is important for the life of faith.

The weak in conscience are those who worry about possible spiritual results from idolatry because they have been in the culture which involves eating food sacrificed to idols as a means of devotion to pagan gods. He explains that food eaten in this way and even idolatry itself are non-issues, but the weak do not see it this way and they could stumble in their faith if they went against their conscience because of the knowledge of others in the church. It could even be because their conscience still has a concern about the possible spiritual results of eating food from idols that they are at risk. The "faith" they hold in their conscience can attract the very things they fear.

Paul is saying the strong in conscience need to respect and protect the weak in conscience. They should not ignore their conscience .The conscience is that part of our created being which links our mind and heart together. The conscience has thoughts and feelings. In the conscience are values, memories linked to our self-worth and esteem, and feelings of wellbeing, peace, guilt or dread. The conscience is part of our fallen nature so it can malfunction like any other part of us. We can feel guilty when we are righteous and feel well-being when in sin. We can feel obligations from our conscience to traditions and lifestyle which we no longer need to be obliged to because we are Christians. Gradually our conscience becomes aligned to God's thoughts and heart.

When consciences are wounded, we lose confidence (assurance). This is the crucial commodity for moving in spiritual gifts and moving with God. It dictates the effectiveness of our prayer life (1 John 5:14). The conscience influences our response to the word of God whereby faith is birthed within our hearts. Faith is a partnership between God speaking and we responding (Romans 10:19). We need to protect consciences. Assurance is hindered through conflict and is impossible when grappling with inner fears and doubts brought about by the words and behaviour of the strong in conscience Christian, and as a result many have stumbled in their ability to have faith.

The strong in conscience can be free of guilt feeling when they attend idol ceremonies or eat food which had been dedicated to idols, because they know in their conscience that idolatry is nothing. Paul says though he agrees with their doctrine, they (and he) have a responsibility in how they behave not to cause a brother to stumble. They should not visit the idolatrous places not because they are anything, but because it will affect the "weak in conscience".

The person with the weak conscience may know in his mind that he is free from the old ways of family or society, but because his conscience is not yet formed around the truth, he is powerless to stand in the same way as the strong in conscience. The weak in conscience has inherited and been educated in the idolatrous customs around him, and the weak are not yet free of its teachings. The same thing might happen when someone comes out of the occult and finds it difficult to act in a play like Macbeth which has spells or witches in it; or a church attendee who feels guilty praying in a group without incense or candles. There are numerous examples of people who find their conscience is not yet in the same place as the doctrine they are taught. In this example the strong by their behaviour can destroy the weak in conscience by insisting the ex-occultist should recite the spells or that the corporate prayer should be held without candles. Candles, a play or meat given to idols are not more important than the conscience of a believer.

Paul cites an example of a person weak in conscience seeing the "strong" in conscience in the idolatrous places which have been condemned as wrong. He pictures as a result the weak dismissing the words spoken by the strong about God being one and that idolatry is nothing, and his conscience reverts to what it was before he became a Christian. He would lose his rest, form a different set of precepts and operate from an unredeemed conscience, thus destroying his spiritual life. It is this to which Paul now refers...

> **10. If someone sees you who have knowledge who is sitting to eat in an idolatrous place, his conscience being weak** *(because it is not able to stand on the truth and is therefore able to be moulded by what it sees or hears)* **is made confident to the eating of idolatrous food?**

At first reading you would think this was good being emboldened to eat idolatrous food in the same as the strong in conscience which was after all based on truth (v5-7). But Paul says this destroys the weak in conscience. How?

1. He is affected in his heart. Our conscience and our heart are closely linked to our self-esteem. Real faith comes from an inner knowing in the heart. This emboldening does not come from faith. He is emboldened in the fears he has that there is something about

idolatry, and his doctrine changes as a result from God is One to there are many gods; from idol rituals and eating food is nothing to a belief that it makes a difference good or bad.

2. The weak can also be affected in his thinking. He thinks of all the rules that has been said, the reasons in doctrine and then compares the teaching received with the practice seen by the "strong "in conscience, and the weak in conscience is destroyed. He becomes a cynic and unbelieving and operates in this issue with a blind unredeemed conscience.

This is important because without this understanding chapters 8,9,10 fall apart into different teaching sections without any mainstream argument, whereas the reality is that the way the so called strong in conscience (as opposed to weak in conscience) behave is the platform and the reason for what Paul teaches.

> **11. For the weak are destroyed in your knowledge, a brother for whom Christ died.**
>
> **12. But so falling short of your rightful attitude** (*the verb to sin is used here and it could be translated" sinned against" and is the same verb used later in the sentence to reference their sin against Christ. Because the root of the verb means to fall short, this emphasis within the verb is brought out here)* **to your brethren and in wounding his weak conscience, you sin against Christ.**
>
> **13. If food causes my brother to stumble, I will not eat meat for life in order that I do not offend my brother.**

In modern days church Christians have caused their fellow Christians to stumble over issues which have no consequence with God. For example - rules about drinking tea or coffee, beer or wine; rules about dress or attendance at certain meetings - all of which bring unnecessary hindrances to brothers and sisters in the faith.

The destruction which comes on the weak is that he rejects the Lord in the area of his family or society customs because he thinks the words of the strong in conscience do not match their behaviour. The Christian who is strong in conscience has to adopt a lifestyle which is considerate to those who are weak in conscience. They are to operate out of love rather than their knowledge. Paul concludes by saying it would be better to be a vegetarian than to eat meat and cause the brother to stumble.

Chapter 9

Paul has only just started on his advice to the Strong in conscience, but he now hammers home the theme of responsibility towards our brother and not to use our freedom in an unhelpful way. He is going to use himself as an example. He spends the first few verses establishing the fact he had rights which he chose not to exercise because of concern for the Corinthians. He knows when he starts to mention his rights as a Christian servant (in his case apostle) it may be less convincing for some hearers so he spends time expanding on the rights he could have used but chose not to.

1. Am I not free?

The Greek text starts with this as this is the main point of the section. NKJV inexplicably places this second after "am I an apostle", But the main point is not about apostleship but freedom. Freedom with responsibility to love is Paul's focus as he continues to teach the strong in conscience. The rights they have through their knowledge should not be used to cause the weak to stumble. Paul illustrates this from the refusal he has to use his rights as an apostle, and the way he enables mission as a result. The order of the Greek validates this.

Am I not an apostle? Have I not seen Jesus our Lord? Are you not my work in the Lord?

2. If I am not an apostle to others, I am to you. For my stamp of approval of apostleship is you in the Lord.

3. My defence to those who would answer me is this.

4. Do we not have the right to eat and drink?

5. Do we not have the right to travel with our wife if she is a sister (in Christ) as the rest of the apostles and the brothers of the Lord and Peter?

6. Or is it only me and Barnabas who do not have the right not to work for a living?

7. Whoever works as a soldier at his own expense? Who plants a vineyard and does not eat its fruit? Or who shepherds a flock and does not eat the milk of the flock. *(Paul uses the same verb to eat rather than the verb to drink. It probably reflects the fact they did not drink the milk from sheep but were more likely to make cheese from the milk)*

8. I do not speak these things from a human point of view *(Greek "according to man")*, **for does not the law say these things?**

9. For in the Law of Moses it is written "Do not muzzle the ox as it threshes the grain". It is not for the oxen that concerns God,

10. but it is written altogether for us, for because of us it written. For he who ploughs ought to plough in hope and he who threshes in the hope of partaking (in the harvest).

11. If we sowed spiritual things to you, is it a great thing if we reap fleshly things of you.

12. If others benefit from the decisions you make and the responsibilities you have *(εξουσιας is to do with the influence and activity someone is able to exercise which I have translated as decisions and responsibilities)*, **does that not mean us as well if not more so?** *(The Greek meaning of ου μαλλον ημεις)*

Now this is the crucial point coming up which he has been leading up to...

But we did not use these rights. But we put up with all things lest we should give any obstacle to the gospel of Christ.

Now he continues the theme of his rights. He has mentioned the practice of the other apostles, normal behaviour that you get benefit from your labours, the law of Moses with its teaching on the right to rewards from the labour, now he mentions temple practice and the Lord's command to live out of the gospel (paid for by others). He then finishes with verse 15 "I have not used any of these rights"

13. Do you not know that those who work with the sacred things eat from the temple and those attending the altar share in (the offerings made on) the altar.

14. Indeed the Lord also commanded to those who were proclaiming the gospel that they should live out of the gospel.

15. But I have not used any of these (rights). I have not written this in order that the same can happen to me.

Paul does not want them distracted into thinking he is writing this because he wants them to change and start to contribute towards him. Paul knows sometimes what we hear can be filtered through self-interest, shame or guilt and so we do not receive accurately what is being said. Paul is wanting them to see the way he operates so they will be sensitive to others rather than assert their own rights. He continues...

For it is good for me rather to die than someone should make my boast empty

The boast that he has is that he can preach the gospel free of charge. It cost the Corinthians nothing. We will find the reason behind this is that Paul did not want the Corinthians to get the wrong idea about the gospel being free. If he had made money out of it, they might have failed to hear the message. We also will find that Paul liked the freedom this unpaid status gave him as he was not under any obligation to fulfil anyone's personal agenda. Paul is being very open here so they can have the best opportunity of seeing the main point he is making.

16. For whenever I preach the gospel. I have nothing to boast of, for the necessity (to preach) is laid on me. Woe is me if I do not preach the gospel.

17. If I do this as a volunteer (Greek word is willingly) **I have a reward. If I do this unwillingly**

Paul like us, knew days when he wanted to serve and days when he was not as keen. The reward he knows and which blesses him only comes as a result of him being a willing volunteer. There were times when he was unwilling, as for example when he exorcised the slave girl at Philippi Acts 16.The focus then is on what has been entrusted to him which needs to be shared.

I have been entrusted with the stewardship

I.e. I operate as an employed manager. Paul elsewhere talks about being a steward of the mysteries of God and being entrusted with the gospel, but this is not his point here. He is saying his overriding motive is preaching the gospel. If he does it at his expense he looks to the reward from God, which is at least in part his personal satisfaction that he has been able to preach the gospel without putting any demands on anyone else to help with his material needs. It is this he finds rewarding. If he gets paid for it, he views himself as entrusted as a steward with the gospel so discharging his duty, and he does not have the same satisfaction.

18. What is my reward? That when I preach the gospel I may place the gospel without charge. And so for this reason I do not assert my rights in the gospel.

19. For being free from all, I make myself a slave to all in order that I may gain the more.

Paul's giving up of his rights means he is free to serve whoever he wishes. He recognises that effective mission comes on the back of real service. He shows in detail how he does this, in each case showing he is not standing on his rights but rather serving the people groups. He knows he cannot serve from a distance, and standing on his rights would distance himself. He has to be like them to serve them

20. And I become to the Jews as a Jew in order to gain Jews (for the Kingdom). To those under the law as under the law, though I am not under the law, in order to gain those under the law.

21. To those who are outside the law (I relate) as one outside the law, not outside the law of God but within the law of Christ

When relating to Gentiles, he does not abide by the strict rules of the Jew, but he will operate within the will of God defined by obedience to the anointing and within the law of God. He might not obey all the Jewish rules, but he would not steal, be immoral or lie etc. He is not outside the law of God. He is also within the law of Christ. The anointing puts obligations upon you which the law of God does not, but Paul obeys the leading of the Spirit because he is within the law of Christ

22. I become weak to the weak in order that I may gain the weak. I become all things to all men in order that I might save some in every way.

23. I do all things through the gospel in order that I may make connections with him *("make Connections" is translating the Greek συγκοινωνος which means joining together The Greek says "with him", not "with you" as NKJV).*

Paul is talking about mission and the outsider; of making connections not with the Corinthian church but with those who were outsiders. Through the gospel Paul can leave behind the old distinctions which would stop these connections being made. Because of the gospel he a Jew can make connections with Gentiles; he as a man of 50 years old can make connections with children and the young, he as a single man can make connections with the married and he as a man can make connections with women. Age, Culture, Education, Responsibilities and worldly status all form their barriers to others. In the gospel none of these should prevent bringing the gospel to the world. An old man can serve the teenagers to bring them to faith; a man from a drug culture can bring bankers to faith. Service can break down traditional defensive walls and bring about connections which change the face of society. The old distinctions that existed before the gospel came are no longer relevant. Relevant service combined with true trustworthy character brings relationship connections which form pathways along which the gospel can be transmitted and transferred these connections bring nourishment to both parties and the kingdom of God grows. This is one of the main ways joints and ligaments in the body of Christ are formed. (Col 2:19; Ephesians 4:16) These latter verses in Colossians and Ephesians remind us of the importance of these connections for God invests His Spirit into these connections and as a result growth happens. You cannot grow churches without connections being made.

We can illustrate this from Paul himself. Paul as a new convert had been served by Barnabas (Acts 9:27, 11:25) and this brought about a connection where God could invest His Spirit into forming the first mission team (Acts 13:24.)

---

24. Do you not know that all runners in a race run, but only one receives the prize? Run so you can receive it.

25. He who fights *(the verb αγωνιζομαι can refer to running in an athletic context but it is also used for wrestling and fighting. I think this is the meaning here. Paul has referred to the athletics in the previous verse, now he is focusing on the boxing ring. He will have the same two athletic disciplines in verse 26)* **must master everything.** *The verb is middle. He must master not just his opponent but himself and his life.* **These do it to obtain a crown which perishes, but we for an imperishable (crown). For this imperishable crown** *(τοινυν "accordingly" refers back to the last phrase hence this translation)*

26. I so run not with uncertainty *(Paul is clear in what direction he is to go)*; **and similarly** *(ουτω)* **I fight as one who does not beat the air.**

Paul is making sure his actions are effective and make a difference. These are the inner reasons for his serving others and not standing on his rights.

Paul still has his boxing match in mind. He makes the same connection here as he did in verse 25 when mastery of your opponent also involves self-mastery. Here Paul makes the same point. Effective mission comes from disciplined lives. Strategies and tactics that win come from those who win inwardly. Right decisions need the right perspectives which come from such inner victories.

> **27. But I give myself a black eye** *(the meaning of the Greek word)* **and bring my body into slavery so that I having preached to others may not be found unfit.**

1 Corinthians 9:27 could be taken to mean we should be self-disciplined and torment ourselves to stop God declaring us unfit. This is a mistaken view. This verse is still set in the wrestling ring .A contestant's unfitness would be shown by defeat. So Paul's unfitness is that having preached to others, the enemy wins. It is not God which declares him unfit. Paul recognises he needs to keep in the right place and his emphasis on being a servant and accepting some of the blows that come with this servant hood (we remember the blows he received from Jews because he was willing to serve Gentiles for example); it is these very blows which help him to stay on course. This is not some introverted self-discipline in the hope of making a difference in the world. Paul is someone all out to win souls. This is why he cannot move to accept his rights but prefers to stay as a servant. It is the place he can be effective and win; it is the clear direction he has to run so that the enemy loses and God's purpose and calling for Paul wins.

Chapter 10

Paul now wants to make clear it is possible for a Christian to miss out on his calling and destiny. He will illustrate this from the experience of the Israelites coming out of Egypt. Paul does not want to be like these. The purpose of this is to show a further motivation for giving up one's rights to serve.

> **1. I want you to know brethren that our fathers all were under the cloud and all went through the sea**
>
> **2. and all were baptised into Moses in the cloud and in the sea,**

The Israelites were slaves in Egypt until they passed through the Red sea and then they became a nation. The cloud of God's presence separated them from the pursuing Egyptian army and thus allowed them the space to go through the Red Sea. The cloud also continued to lead them through the wilderness. Paul says they are under the cloud before the sea is mentioned. The baptism into Moses happened not just in the sea but also in the cloud. Baptism means being immersed, and certainly the Church of England baptism service links the Red Sea imagery with going through the waters of baptism, but it might be that Paul talks about the cloud as well. It might be that baptism involves immersed into the presence of God (Cloud) as well as immersed into water (Red Sea). Baptism in water and the spirit are the ingredients for becoming part of the people of God. (See Acts 10:47, I John 5:8)

Paul is showing there was an unseen dimension to the historical narrative, and it is this he focuses on here.

> **3. and all ate the same spiritual meat**
>
> **4. they all drank the same spiritual drink. For they drank from the spiritual rock which followed them, the rock was Christ.**
>
> **5. But on most of them God was not pleased for they were ruined in the wilderness.**

> **6. These things were our models so that we are not desirous of evil; as they desired.**

He then defines these evil desires introducing each one with μηδε.

Remember throughout the previous section on immorality, Paul has linked the sin of idolatry, and here they follow closely on each other, but his focus in this section seems to be more with the history of the Israelites in the wilderness as described in the book of Numbers.

> **7. Not idolaters as some of them were: as it is written "the people sat down to eat and drink and they rose up to play"** *("rose up to play" was the phrase used for the sexual orgy which followed the worship of the golden calf in Exodus)*
>
> **8. Not being immoral as some of them were immoral and fell in a single day twenty three thousand,**
>
> **9. Not putting the Lord** *(some Greek versions have Christ)* **to the test as some of them tested (the Lord) and were destroyed by snakes.**
>
> **10. Not complaining even as some of them complained and were destroyed by the destroyer** *(a spiritual demonic entity)*
>
> **11. These things happened to them in ways that give us lessons** *("in ways that gives us lessons is translating the word τυπικως which is the word for model or pattern but in a descriptive form and I have expanded the text to try to bring out its meaning).* **It was written for our warning on whom the ends of the ages** *(not the end of the age but ends. Paul mentions this as the age of the Kingdom from Pentecost to the second coming is also a conclusion of every age that went before and as such includes the ingredients and fulfilment of every age.)* **have come.**
>
> **12. So that he who thinks he stands should watch so he does not fall.**

> **13. There is no temptation that has been received which is common to man, but God is faithful who will not let you be tempted above what you are able, but will make with the temptation also a way out so that you are able to bear it.**
>
> **14. Wherefore my beloved, flee from idolatry**

Remember Paul is still talking to the Corinthian Christian strong in conscience who knows idols are nothing but causes his brother to stumble because he attends an idol sacrifice. He is now going to talk to them in depth about the foolishness of attending idolatry although they know God is One and that idolatry is nothing. The way out to avoid the temptation/trial is to flee idolatry. This is the same advice given with regard to immorality (6:18). There will be a door open somewhere within the trial which allows you to flee.

Reasons for the strong in conscience to avoid idolatry

Paul argues from the practice of communion and the Old Testament sacrifices. He makes the point that there is a spiritual connection between the earthly rituals and the supernatural. Idolatry should therefore be avoided.

> **15. As I speak to those who can think for themselves, you judge what I say.**
>
> **16. The cup of blessing which we bless, is it not a sharing of the blood of Christ; the bread which we break is it not a sharing of the body of Christ.**
>
> **17. Because the bread is one we who are many are one body, for all share in the one bread**

Together we form the body of Christ. This is what the grace of Communion affirms, builds up and creates. God's Spirit dwells corporately in the church. This must be the main spiritual dimension of communion for it is being used to show there is a connection between eating in a worship context and the spiritual realm in the same way as Old Testament sacrifices did. This has implications for how we view communion but we return to this subject when we reach 1 Corinthians 11

18. Look at historic Israel *(Greek is Israel after the flesh)*: **Are not those who eat of the sacrifices those who share in the altar.**

19. What is the point that I am making? That there is something about idol sacrifice and something about idolatry?

20. (No) but that which the Gentiles sacrifice, is sacrificed to demons and not to God. I do not want you to be sharers with demons. *Paul wants the "strong" in conscience to know that although idolatry cannot do anything one way or another, there are demons involved in the lie of idolatry.*

21. You are not able to drink the cup of the Lord and also the cup of demons. You are not able to share the table of the Lord and the table of demons. *(as the people of Israel tried to do at the time of worship of the golden calf).*

22. Or do we make the Lord angry (especially when) we are not stronger than He.

23. All things are possible but not all things are beneficial. All things are possible but not everything builds up. *Love builds up (8:3) and Paul is here in verse 23 emphasising his underlying principle on which the whole of chapter 8-10 depend, so he continues*

24. Let no-one seek his own (benefit) but that of the other.

25. You eat everything that is sold in the meat market not asking (any questions about the meat's origin) for conscience.

26. for the earth and its fullness (and everything in the earth) is the Lord's. *This is the doctrinal anchor point for the eating everything sold in the meat market.*

27. If someone of those who do not believe invite you (to dinner) and you want to go, eat whatever is put before you

not asking (any questions) for the sake of your conscience.

28. If anyone says to you "This was a temple sacrifice" *Paul is using the colloquial expression for idol sacrifice though it actually says holy sacrifice and is not the explicit term for idol sacrifice that Paul uses elsewhere. Paul here is quoting the very phrase which would be used by Gentiles when they refer to idol sacrifice.* **Do not eat it, for the sake of the one who informed you and the conscience.**

29. I mean not your own conscience but the conscience of the other person. *Paul explains why. He will have no trouble in his conscience eating anything for all is the Lords, and he has given thanks, but he does not want to offend or allow the judgements of others (which come from the values and beliefs held in the conscience)to fall on him. Why make extra hassle. It is easier and good to refrain from eating if someone points out the source was an idol sacrifice. It stops them being offended and him being slandered. So he continues...* **For why should I be judged by another's conscience?**

30. If I share with grace, *(which I think refers to manners at the table and courteous in relationship)* **why am I slandered on behalf of which I give thanks.**

31. Whether you eat or drink or whatever you do, do all things to the glory of God.

32. Do not give offense either to Jews or to Greeks or to the church of God.

33. As I please all men in all things, do not seek profit for yourself, but for the many in order that they may be saved. *(11:1 Be imitators of me as I am of Christ.)*

This is part of this section rather than belonging to the rest of the following chapter. The chapter divisions were not made by Paul and can sometimes be in the wrong place. This is one of those times.

Paul the Jew

It was now later than either Paul or Sosthenes had realised. They had risen early and eaten breakfast in haste, and had hoped to continue after lunch, but it was now early afternoon, and the letter had reached a natural break the end of what would be known as Chapter 10. So the synagogue leader of Corinth sat back in his chair and turned his head to Paul. "What was Gamaliel like?" he asked. Gamaliel was the grandson of the great rabbi Hillel the Elder and a high authority in the Sanhedrin, and Paul's old teacher in Jerusalem. Paul reminisced about his time as a disciple within the Pharisees of Jerusalem where he had been a top student excelling beyond the others in his group. Gamaliel was a wise man at the height of his influence just before Paul's conversion, and central too much of what happened amongst the Jewish elite at that time as the Christian church rapidly expanded in Jerusalem during the first years of its existence. Things had changed in Jerusalem now, and Gamaliel had died about the time he had first come to Ephesus and Gamaliel's son Shimon ben Gamaliel was rumoured to be fiercely patriotic. Paul paused as he recounted the old days in Jerusalem. Paul spoke about how he had held the clothes of those who stoned Stephen, and then of the dramatic moment in his life when Jesus met him and talked with him when Paul was on his way to Damascus. Sosthenes already knew about Paul's conversion and his meeting with Ananias, but knew what a profound moment that was not just for Paul but for all those who had been converted through his ministry including him. He did not interrupt but listened with great interest. Paul spoke about his time in Arabia coming to terms with the implications of his encounter with Jesus. He explained to Sosthenes that before he could speak to others he needed to know what was what and to get a true foundation for his new found faith and spiritual zeal. For two years Paul had looked again through the Old Testament seeing these scriptures afresh as he saw how they spoke about Jesus. He wondered how he and his fellow Jews could have missed all this about the Christ and made such a mistake as to oppose the Christian faith? "What we think dictates what we see", thought Paul. The encounter with Jesus had changed the direction of his life and changed his thinking. He knew now that the law he valued as a Jew could not meet his need of forgiveness and salvation, and he stood vehemently against those in the churches who tried to turn all converts back into Jews by circumcision. Paul knew this to be wrong because it denied the importance and significance of Jesus' death on the cross. If obeying the law could give life, Jesus would not have had to come to die so that we could have life. This invitation was on a different basis to the old covenant agreement of the law which offered life for the perfect. In fact everyone knew it was impossible to be perfect and therefore the law only could condemn rather than give life. Paul knew all were on equal footing before God needing that forgiveness and salvation that only Jesus could bring.

Sosthenes had not believed this when Paul first came to Corinth, though Crispus and some other important people in the synagogue had become believers. When there was a split in the synagogue, he had replaced Crispus as leader and had remained convinced in his views that Christians were wrong until some time after Paul had gone from Corinth. He remembered how he and other opposing members of the synagogue had thought with Gallia's arrival as the new proconsul in Corinth they could get rid of Paul, but it all backfired and Sosthenes remembered the beating he got instead as from a different time and place from his present life experience. He now knew that Jesus had died so that all sin need no longer stand between people and God. He had long ago accepted the invitation to belong to the Christian church and to Jesus Christ.

Paul spoke gently as He told Sosthenes story after story of the wonderful things He had seen Jesus do. Whilst still being a Jew, Paul had been free to act like a Gentile ignoring food laws and special rituals. He had found lots of friends within every place he had visited who were non Jews. Jews however always had a special place in his heart and he longed that all of them could find Jesus as he had done. Sosthenes shared this same view. God had brought them together. They paused and then they prayed together.

Aquila & Priscilla

Sosthenes moved from his desk and poured out some wine into clay cups and brought them over to where Paul was now sitting. They were getting ready to write the next section of the letter about church life. Aquila and Priscilla were busy downstairs arranging something, but they were too far out of earshot to hear exactly what it was. They used to live in the complex that Paul and Sosthenes were now occupying but they had recently bought a farm just outside the city. Aquila still had his tannery leather working business, and he exported his wares all over the Mediterranean. He still owned the shops at the edge of the complex of buildings near the butchers down the street. Priscilla his wife was from a privileged background and she was excellent at organising life at home and in business. In fact wherever she was there was always a plan. She had a perceptive gift and interest in people which made her an excellent hostess for the many and varied diversities of people that travelled through Ephesus. Both Aquila and Priscilla were Romans at heart and hankered to return to their roots, where they had many friends. Now with the recent changes in Rome following the arrival of Nero as Emperor, they hoped the situation in Rome might be less dangerous for them to return, but though hopeful, they were waiting to see what happened. They had no wish to return to the troubles from which they had fled nearly ten years before when Claudius was emperor. Paul had first met them during his early days in Corinth when he had worked for Aquila's tannery making tents. Paul's financial support had grown since then and his energy was fully focused on helping the Ephesian church and other churches in the region through the current outpouring of God's spirit. So many were being saved that it was affecting the whole culture of the region. Paul has suffered with this too, spending a short time in the prison by the harbour with a possible death sentence. But that was now behind them. Paul talked with Aquila and Priscilla about Rome. He had long discovered Priscilla's heart was always in Rome. Few could tell for she was an excellent hostess and leader in the church wherever she was, but those who knew her a long time could tell for the hope before her was always of returning there. It was a city Paul had never visited but it was inevitable that the city they talked about so much would eventually form part of Paul's places that he wanted to bring the gospel of Jesus Christ and build up the church there. The gospel had already reached Rome fairly quickly from its birth at Pentecost through the effective communication and travel which the Roman Empire afforded. It really was true that all roads lead to Rome and the gospel had travelled those roads and the church had been securely established there. Nothing could dislodge it. The apostle John was there at the moment and it was probable that Peter also was there. Priscilla and Aquila had met John when they first came to Ephesus but neither of them had yet met Peter who had visited Corinth after she and Aquila had left there, but she hoped to meet him one day when they returned to Rome. Paul also hoped one day to visit Rome, but for now he was in Ephesus. Paul looked around the large upper room which had windows out into the courtyard below which made the room seem even bigger than it was. Priscilla's influence was everywhere, for she was the brains behind the furnishings, decor and contemporary design. Each room had simplicity with items of great beauty and great taste. There was an atmosphere of peace and welcome in each of the public rooms on the ground floor which pervaded the whole house. Paul had noticed with Aquila and Priscilla both in Ephesus and Corinth that they did everything well. Priscilla cared for her servants and they were well organised in their tasks. Everything ran so smoothly. The new farm they had purchased had some cows as well as vineyards and Aquila had many servants looking after his varied business interests. The new house was large with figs and olive groves overlooking several acres of grazing land just outside the city walls. They had bought this house within the year and it provided a place away from the hubbub of Ephesus life and had easy access to the work place in the complex next to the old house they still owned where Paul was staying.. This house was still a major hub for the church as well and they met frequently in the lower rooms and often when there was a large number expanded into the courtyard. It was a perfect venue for a church within walking distance for everyone in the area.

Priscilla had organised as usual the supper the church had had together last week, and Paul noticed wherever she went she commanded respect because of the way she spoke and acted with them. She continued to have an important ministry in the church. She was not the only woman who ministered in the church. Paul knew many women who were leaders in the church of God. There was Mary who was one of the family of Epaenetus who was Paul's first convert to Christ in Asia. He had since then in the last 2 years now moved to Rome but was still going on with God. It was great that he had watched his daughter rise in her leadership gifts which were benefiting the whole region. Ephesus and the province of Asia had many women in leadership.. Apphia hosted the church in Colossae 120 miles away to the east, and Nympha hosted the church in Laodicea, 11 miles from Colossae. Corinth too had a wide range of leaders who were women. There was always movement between Rome and Corinth and some of the women leaders he had first met in Corinth were now leading in the church at Rome. Paul recalled Tryosa and also the sister of Nereus plus Julia.. Paul worked out that of all those he knew personally as leaders who were now in the large Roman church at least 5% were women. Chloe who was still in Corinth, and Phoebe from Cenchreae (Corinth's east port 6 miles east of the city) who was a minister and overseer in that church. He remembered also Lydia one of the first converts in Macedonia who had helped Paul find contacts in Colossae. It was not unusual to find women in leadership and influential positions anywhere in the global church; after all there was Junia member of Paul's own family who now lived in Rome and was a lady recognised as an apostle. Paul reflected how important the ministry of women was. They had an important role in bringing God's Kingdom to the world.

Paul turned to Sosthenes and said It is time to start and so he wrote…

1 Corinthians Chapter 11
Overview

Church Life

This is a new section. The old theme of idol worship has ended and the new theme is about the people of God meeting the true and living God.

The Christian life is a new life rooted in heaven and directional towards the Father in heaven. We come from heaven and return to heaven. Church gatherings are means of engaging in that heavenly realm whilst here on the earth.

Real Christians have a special relationship with God. He is first to them and they are first to Him. Love for God and one another is the mark of this life from heaven on the earth. Corporate worship where we meet with God and him with us is at the heart of this relationship. The meeting together of Christians we call church is at the heart of the vibrant spiritual life which comes from knowing God. Without this Christians lose energy, hope and direction. In addition without genuine life in the community of which worship is central, any work Christians do for the community beyond the church seems like charity and is at best worthy only of a nod of respect. It is the quality of this spiritual life which can make the difference in lives and communities, in society and national life, and without which Christianity is reduced to just words.

The spiritual life of a church is manifest relationally. It is our love for one another rather than our love for the outsider which impacts the world. (*John 13:35 "By this shall all men know you are my disciples, if you have love one for another*). Involved in this encounter with Him is the manifestation of the Holy Spirit through Christians when they gather, especially tongues and prophecy, and Holy Communion. How we relate with each other in these gathered moments can either welcome God's presence dwelling with us or grieve Him and bring about missed opportunities.

It is the inconsiderate relationships and bad behaviour at the heart of the church at worship that Paul seeks to change.

The themes Paul teaches in these chapters 11-14 are women in ministry, Holy Communion and Spiritual gifts in the church. In this section we will look at the first two and the next section spiritual gifts

The Holy Communion Service

The Communion service is first mentioned in the earlier section (Chapter 10: 16-21) in which he makes the point that there are real supernatural connections between those taking communion and the Lord. These are summarised as,

10:18. In the Old Testament Eating the sacrificed food connected the person to the altar, so taking Holy Communion connects the believer back to the cross. Jesus referred to this when he instituted Holy Communion at the Last Supper when he said "This do in remembrance of me". It is not that Holy Communion is a sacrifice. It is rather the connecting us back to the sacrifice of Jesus on the cross for our sins, and in so doing receiving grace.

1. "When we bless the cup at the Lord's Table, aren't we sharing in the blood of Christ? When we break the bread, are we not sharing in the body of Christ" 10:16. The blessing of the bread and wine is what many would know as the prayer of consecration. Paul here establishes how the connection between the participant and the sacrifice of Jesus happens. Holy Communion is not a re-sacrifice of Jesus, but a connection with the one-time event in history when Jesus was crucified but which has eternal consequence. The blessing of the cup and the breaking of the bread declares the way open to the blessings from that sacrifice. There is also no mention of transubstantiation. The blessing does not change the bread or the wine in their nature. Rather, it is the declaration which makes the connection with the sacrifice (share in the blood,) and with the rest of the church who are one with Christ in every generation and geographical location. (Share in the body). Both the sacrifice at the cross and the Church have an eternal spiritual dimension. It is this which makes Holy Communion important as a means of bringing grace into the church and life of the Christian soul.

2. "Though we are many we eat from one loaf of bread" 10:17. The togetherness of believers was strongly symbolised by the

communion service. They had no individual wafers; it was one loaf broken. The bread they ate connects them to the ones of the church in the same way that the wine connects them to the cross. This is different from the liturgy of the communion service in the Church of England which connects the eating of the bread with the physical body of Jesus on the cross. The consecration prayer in 1662 has "may be partakers of his most blessed body and blood", and the prayer of humble access "grant us therefore gracious Lord so to eat the flesh of thy dear son Jesus Christ and to drink His blood". In such a context the breaking of the bread is all about the suffering of Jesus on the cross, but Paul does not make that connection. He connects it instead with the church as the body of Christ (1 Corinthians 10:16 a, 17 "The bread which we break is it not the communion of the body of Christ? For us being many are one body: for we are all partakers of that one bread" – see also 11:29). Though this verse is included in the liturgy of more recent communion, there has been little mind set change from the bread symbolising not the church but the broken body of Jesus on the cross. We need to do a paradigm shift in our subliminal understanding of communion in order to embrace what Paul is saying here. The connection of communion with the cross should remain but we need to make a deeper connection between the communion service and the belonging life of a church. Our understanding of the connection between communion and church life needs to grow. The church through its oneness with God occupies a unique place in the created order. These supernatural links to the cross and the church are real and if we "operate unworthily we become guilty of the body and blood of the Lord" (11:27). Both the cross and the church are a blessing, but operating unworthily causes both to rise up as witnesses against us making us vulnerable to the enemy who afflicts and destroys. (11:29-30). This had already occurred because the church which was not in a good shape relationally. (11:21-22.) You cannot be part of the new life of heaven and remain distant from your brother. How can we say "I love God and hate our brother" (I John

4:20). The new life in Christ is marked by love. "We know that we have passed from death unto life, because we love the brethren. He that loves not his brother abides in death." 1 John 3:14. The law had two commands love God with all your heart soul mind and strength and a second one Love your neighbour as yourself. In the new place we have in the Godhead, both these commands merge into a new commandment "love one another as I have loved you". John 13:34, John 15:12 1, John 2:7-8 1, John 3:23, 1 John 4:21

3. The church is where the anointing of Jesus dwells (Ephesians 2:22) and we are part of that body where Jesus is the head exalted as He is in the heavenly places (Colossians 1:16-20). The church brings heaven and earth together. Ephesians 1:10 onwards introduces the church as the first fruits of what is the global plan of God to reconcile all things under the Lordship of Jesus- all things in heaven and all things on the earth. The church has an earthly and a heavenly existence at the same time and comes from heaven to bring life to the earth. This is the significance of the bread broken for you. At Jesus' baptism the heavens were rent open so the Spirit could descend upon Him. That same spirit He imparted to the first disciples at Pentecost and then was received by the converts who followed them. The Church had the same call and same empowering as Jesus during His earthly ministry. They could now do the same and greater works than He could (there were after all more of them!). There is a unity of the Spirit which is affirmed by communion. In the Corinthian church however there was no such opportunity for that unity. Their practice was hurry (because of their own hunger) and they ignored the needs and desires of others, even though it might have been unintentional. The most tender heart towards others can become hard when need of self predominates. It was not just at the beginning of the meal. It was also at the end. Some misused what they brought so they were too full or drunk (alcohol was not forbidden, but drunkenness was) whilst others remained hungry. Sharing what they had got would have been better all round. Both the events at

the beginning and the end disgraces the church (bad behaviour) and shames the poor (because they cannot afford to eat what others are eating and feel therefore not as good or excluded). Thus the communion is no communion at all. There is no oneness in relationship in the gathering and no awe at the cross because it is subjugated by selfish desire.

The unity which the communion is designed to engender is also important in the area of spiritual gifts. Paul returns to this in the latter part of Chapter 12 and then the famous passage on love. The Holy Spirit life is marked by manifestation of the Kingdom of God through spiritual gifts, but it is love, so heaven life as it breaks through the church to the world must have both.

Women in ministry

The overriding theme of chapters 11-14 are instructions for the gathered church, and it is no surprise that within that theme unity should be a key factor and love mentioned in a whole chapter to itself (Chapter 13). It is however not the only theme. Spiritual Gifts and women in ministry are also important themes within these chapters.

In the twentieth century there has been a gradual emphasis from those whose cultures have adopted Christian truth in the past for women to be treated better in marriage and society as a whole, and so the rightful position of women alongside men has been gradually affirmed in the workplace and the home. This has been in Christian circles seen by some as a rightful message bringing freedom to women in society in a similar way to the freedom given to slaves by the abolition of slavery (which was also from a Christian principle). On the other hand there have been Christians who have quoted verses from Paul to affirm (so they think) a position where the woman should not take ultimate responsibility in the home or church and possibly other places of society, because a man should always "rule" (in the nicest possible way) over a woman. This has meant that often society and the church have been alienated from each other on this issue and it has brought a gulf between the two, with ongoing debate and introspection on the church's behalf, whilst lack of relationship with society as a whole gets deeper and deeper. This is a misunderstanding of Paul who is often not understood by both sides of the argument.

Within this book, you will find the message of women being equal with men and able to exercise fully their callings. The verses Paul writes are not because he is a misogynist – for he says many good things about women, nor is it because these verses were written in the 1st century AD and reflect the age or environment in which the church and Paul lived. The Bible is true for all time and these verses do contain truths no church serious about women moving in power should ignore.

What I will attempt to show in this chapter is that Paul far from restricting women in ministry is giving guidelines for the best way to operate in their anointing. Men and women have a different sexual identity but can do the same job. They can both pray and prophesy. The Church needs the ministry from women and it needs it from men. If women ignore what Paul writes here, the anointing that flows through them will be unaffected. They can still minister powerfully. What will be affected are the men in the church, who will withdraw from their ministries, and their anointing will not be manifest. If, on the other hand, men ignore what Paul writes about how they should move in power, women will still minister, but the anointing will be affected. Women need to read Chapter 11 for the sake of the church body – its fullness; men for the sake of the church body – its life.

Paul starts by saying in Chapter 11 that their current practice is good, and this involves women in ministry. He is happy about this whereas he is deeply upset about what happens at the communion services (11:17ff). In this first section (11:1-16) he is giving further guidelines on the way men and women minister in the supernatural ministry of prayer and prophecy.

Women are therefore prophesying and praying alongside men. Paul has advice as to how they should operate spiritual gifts within their sexual identities. The rest of the teaching they had already heard and were practising so he does not need to expand on that. We can infer therefore that,

1. Paul expected women to minister as well as men.

2. Gathering together was an important part of the practice of the first Christians.
3. He had taught about prophecy and prayer and this was not the issue.

Greek text commentary 1 Corinthians Chapter 11

This is a new section. There is no more reference to idols or advice to the "strong in conscience". The verse which propels us from the previous section into the new subject is verse 1. The previous section concludes with command to imitate Paul. It is the conclusion of the advice Paul has given in chapter 10. This verse also provides the gateway for the next section. In verse 2 Paul praises them because they have faithfully kept what he had given them.

This next section (Chapter 11 to Chapter 14) is about spiritual life and the gathered church of Corinth which is where spiritual gifts manifest and so Paul teaches on how they should be used in the assembled church.

His first subject is the way to operate under anointing as a man or as a woman. The teaching is for both sexes, for all can move in spiritual gifts, but occasionally both here and in chapter 14, he gives specific teaching with church order and gender in mind which are in the context of prophecy .In Chapter 11 the teaching about men and woman is in the context of prayer and prophecy, and in chapter 14 the context is tongues and prophecy. The teaching is about the exercise of anointed ministry in the church. Whether a man or a woman it should not prevent moving in the anointing - for both men and women are in Christ. Our gender does however affect how we should exercise the anointed ministry for the maximum benefit of all.

This is not a restrictive passage about men or women in ministry. Paul envisages both men and women being free to exercise their gifts in the church.

Chapter 11:2-16 - Re. Men & Women who pray and prophesy

Here are a few rhetorical questions which are relevant only to those who have read other interpretations of 1 Corinthians 11. If this is the first time you have come across a commentary on this chapter, skip the questions.

1. Where in this passage does it say that men are the covering for a woman? It does not.

   Since when has the covering been the same as the head?

We will see how this passage is not about men regulating for women, but rather women self-regulating in order that the anointing they have can prosper

2. Why do some Christian churches state that women should attend church wearing a veil or equivalent on their heads, when there is no mention of veils in the text?

3. Why do some think that Paul is making some obscure cultural point related to the apparent uncovering of the head by prostitutes in the first century in Corinth region? This means the passage can be ignored in cultures where men have long hair or where women do not wear veils. This empties this passage of relevance for many today (as it would have done for many living in other regions of the world in Paul's day also). God must be saying something important for all here, so any cultural argument must be false (see point 5)

4. Why do some think there is a link between what you wear and the anointing you exercise? Paul cannot be talking about what you wear or do not wear when prophesying or praying because there is no link anywhere else in the Bible between anointing and what you wear. God responds to the heart not appearance!

5. Why do some think this passage about women is cultural and therefore just for the 1st century? Is it not true that scripture is for everyone for all time? This passage cannot be relegated to being only relevant to the culture of the time because then its content becomes "less accessible" to the modern era. Let me explain: - To argue any part of scripture is cultural makes those parts of scripture either irrelevant for us modern Christians or only accessible after understanding what the culture was at the time. This means we believe a lie that intellect has an important role in accessing revelation, making the truths of this scripture inaccessible to those who through ignorance do not first know the culture of Paul's day. "All scripture is God breathed and useful" (2 Tim 3:16) for all generations whether they are students of history of not; and whether

they are part of Paul's first century culture or not. We therefore have to reject any cultural argument. There have to be truths here which matter for every generation, culture and church.

The approach to this passage

The approach to this passage is based on the attitude that Paul is writing something simple and down to earth. It is only made complicated by men. We need to take what he is saying at face value and interpret the passage accordingly.

Key Words

To help us, let us pause to look at some of the central expressions Paul uses in this passage.

The key words which are mentioned are "head", "authority" "because of the angels" "covered" "uncovered" "ashamed".

Head: the source of existence and basis therefore of authority exercised in prayer or prophecy. Like English the Greek can use the word head to mean not just part of our body but also the head of a firm, head of a river or the top of a mountain. In verse 3 head of the man is defined as Christ (the word "Christ" means anointing and also refers to Jesus – which, in turn, reminds us that the anointing is personal!) When interacting with the anointing of God, you interact with the person of the Holy Spirit.

In verse 3 the head of man is Christ whereas with woman the head is man. The physical head as part of the body is not the first meaning of the word κεφαλα (head) in this passage, it is rather the source from whence something comes. Paul with explain this difference in source from the order of creation. The differing ways of creation dictate how the same anointing works best in the different contexts of manhood and womanhood.

Authority (v10) is linked to this. The covering is to do with the authority a woman exercises in prayer and prophecy and similarly the uncovering is an important ingredient in the authority a man can exercise. Both require humility in the realm of their sexual identity. The woman acknowledging a covering which means she cannot step forward without circumspection whilst the man acknowledging something within which is not within his strength or pride and requires his obedience.

Because of the angels (v10) shows prayer and prophecy has authority which affects the angelic realm. Prayer and prophecy both activate and provide environments for the ministry of angels.

Angels are either messengers from God fulfilling His purpose or fallen angels (demons) promoting the schemes of Satan.

The "Covering or Uncovering teaching" of this passage is because of this. Therefore we draw a conclusion that when we moving in the anointing our sexuality as male or female is a feature of whether the angelic realm can respond fully and whether the demonic realm can have ground to stand against the prayers/prophecies being answered/fulfilled or to weaken us or perhaps to use the prayers for its own ends.

Covered and uncovered and shame. Both these terms could refer to the physical covering or uncovering of the head of the body, but does it? Paul say in every verse from v4-6 the uncovering of the head by a woman and the covering by a man shames his/her head. It is the same verb throughout the passage which is translated sometimes as shame and other times as dishonour. It is all about bringing shame.

Shame is a feeling. It originates in a deep relational understanding of receiving a lack of recognition, proper respect, and causes a withdrawal which does not argue, for shame empties the soul of strength and hope so the soul has no cause it can see, or if it has, no zeal to defend it. Shame destroys confidence and makes a faith response impossible. Shame is how the head (Christ or man v3)) feels, not the man or woman doing the praying or prophesying.

Paul illustrates shame by stating it is the same sort of shame a woman feels were she is shaved or shorn. A woman can have her hair cut off or lose her hair. She can still carry on and is still a woman, but there is something not being stated about her femininity in a way that does not happen with the male. He can assert his manhood bald or not. Similarly, a woman can put her hair into all sorts of styles and can project her femininity, whereas manhood is not projected through his hair style.

Paul then says to the reader now look how you if you are a woman would feel if you had to go through this process of being shorn or shaved. That feeling is how the man (in the case of a woman) or Christ (in the case of a man) feels.

Covered, Uncovered and glory This is making the positive point. Getting this right not only avoids shame (withdrawal, dishonour etc.) but it brings glory. Glory is linked to honour but also truth and reality. Glory is the word made manifest. Glory shows up good purpose, good ways and good character and produces encouragement, faith, righteousness and further revelation. Glory flows in good deeds (Matthew 5:13). Prayer and Prophecy are good deeds and will therefore have glory with them. Prayer and Prophecy are designed to make a difference. This glory is powerful and will be beneficial to the church if the covering/ uncovering is right. We are designed to be glory carriers and this teaching helps us carry the glory corporately in the church.

Now for the text itself...

---

2. I praise you, because you have kept in mind everything of mine and you hold fast what I have passed onto you just as I delivered to you

---

They have not changed or put a different view on what Paul said or did. He is not happy about what they have introduced into the church life as a result of what they have heard from him when he was first in Corinth. This he deals with in verse 17 onwards. For the moment Paul focuses on what he is happy about to give guidance to men or women prophesying or praying in church.

Paul does not revisit what he taught them in the 18 months he was in Corinth previously but what he spoke about then has tremendous relevance for the church of his day (and ours!). We cannot be fully sure what this is, but as Paul talks about men and women, prayer and prophecy, it is reasonable to assume that the teaching had given which they were adhering to was that women can pray and prophesy in the church where men also are present. The Church did not take on the Jewish distinctions in the synagogue where men prayed and women listened or in the temple where the female was even more separated from the male. In verse 11 when Paul writes "in God there is no such thing as independence from the other sex", he is probably reflecting something of his teaching that he had said before. Paul wrote in a letter he probably wrote whilst at Corinth and teaching the church at that time how "there is neither male nor female in Christ" and "we are all one in Christ Jesus" (Galatians 3:28).

Such is the teaching he has given previously. There is more he wants them to know that lies behind a right approach to prayer and prophesying which Paul had not taught before, so he starts "I want you to know."

3. I want you to know that Christ (the anointing is personal!) is the head of every man, but the man is the head of the woman but God is the head of Christ.

Paul here is defining what he is about to refer to throughout the passage when he uses the word head. He will return to man being the source of woman in verse 8, 12.

4. Every man who prays or prophesies putting his head down

κατα plus genitive is used of down from a certain place- here "down from the head". This is an expression meaning none asserting his source when he prays or prophesies. It could mean something in addition to the head or the source, but it could also be not being bold in his anointing and call. The anointing needs no addition, but it does require faith and boldness; it needs authentic character. The man is to focus on authenticity, who stands in a real relationship with Jesus and prays and prophesies from that standpoint.

shames his head. (His prayers may be effective. It is just the anointing. (Christ (anointing) is his head). Shaming his head means the anointing is not seen or despised. The authority of Jesus is not there. The woman has a different focus.

> **5. But every woman who prays of prophesies** *(both sexes therefore can be involved. Paul is not against women in anointed ministry)* **with head uncovered has shamed her head**

Here is a reminder that this is a teaching about how to pray and how to prophesy. It has relevance to this only. There is a link between covering and anointing for the woman and uncovering and anointing for the man. This is what Paul is talking about. He has started this passage by defining what he means by "head" (man for the woman; Christ for the man). Head in Greek is used in the same way as in English. The head of a stream means its source; the head of a firm focuses on authority, and like the Greek it also means part of the body. The teaching is on the right way to pray and prophesy so there are no detrimental effects anywhere.

What does shame her head refer to? Shame is a hiding or a withdrawal of what could be; a falling short of what is. Shame is the opposite of manifesting glory. The rightful authority (head) is shamed – not seen in a way that brings that "head" respect

She does not shame herself, but her head which cannot mean husband but must mean man or else only married women could prophesy. We will be looking more closely at what it means to be covered and uncovered but for the time being we note that this behaviour brings shame to men, who because of the shame will withdraw, lose confidence, and be absent. Churches who operate without reference to the teaching of Paul here, will find women active and men absent.

If a woman operates as a man, some women instinctively react against this, but Paul says it is the men who suffer.

I chose one example of this in my generation from the Church of England. I welcome women being ordained but without guidelines that this passage lays down being listened to, ordained women can accelerate a decline in male applicants for ordination. Here are the results of the survey produced by the Evangelical Alliance and compiled by Peter Brierley, who used church statistics from the United Kingdom dating back until 2005.

Official records from the Church of England showed that in 2010 there were 290 women compared with only 273 men ordained in priesthood marking the first time the number of women ordained outnumbered that of their male counterparts.

The survey also showed that in 2011 there were 1,763 women in full time parochial appointments. That is a 50 percent increase from the last set of figures which were published in back in 2000. The number of women priests translates into one out of every five paid parish clergy in the Church of England, which are now female.

It would seem that positions within churches are being filled predominantly by women and that in years to come, if current trends continue, women would comprise the majority of spiritual leaders in England.

"It's obvious that over time the priesthood will become increasingly a female profession. As far as the church has a future it will include a predominant ministry of women and they will get to the top."[3]

For it is even the same as being shaved.

6. For if a woman is not to be covered,

This is not clothing .It is rather saying If she operates with only the anointing (or calling in mind) she will operate as a man and will shame her head. A woman is free to minister but must remain under a covering. This will become clearer, but for the moment take the point that a woman has to look to the way she relates to the permissions, culture of the church and the men within it).

---

let her be shorn *(verb used of Paul having his head shorn to fulfil a vow after he had left Corinth Acts 18:18 before arriving in Ephesus for the first time to drop off Aquila and Priscilla before moving quickly onto Palestine)* **If it is shameful for a woman to be have her head shorn or (her cheeks and chin) shaved** *(The verbs relate to men having head shorn and the beard shaved)*

---

7. For a man should not cover the head,

This cannot also be to do with clothing for the same reasons as for the women. This requires an understanding on anointing (for this is the context of the teaching before us). Anointing is wedded to who we are. Its manifestation will be in accordance with this. The anointed man should push forward, be bold, and be strong. Joshua received this advice to move in the anointing of Moses. Elisha pushed through to receive the possibility of the anointing of Elijah. David to conquer Goliath. This is what men should do, but women should operate differently. The lessons are contained in the way the women of the bible operate in their anointing and call. Deborah goes to Barak before embarking on her anointed task, Esther looks to Mordecai whilst bringing deliverance to the Jews from the schemes of Haman and King Xerxes of Persia.

---

as he is the likeness and glory of God: The woman is the glory of man. *Glory is goodness and truth made manifest at the same time: when the unseen is seen. To shine with glory you must align to the source.*

8. Man is not from the woman but woman from man. *This is then explained more introduced by* καὶ γαρ,

9. for also man was not created through woman but woman through man.

διά plus accusative is used here in verse 8 which means the reason "why" something exists, i.e. the cause. διά plus genitive is used in verse 12 to denote the "how" it happens. So man is the origin of woman but in verse 12 woman is the means by which man is made. This is referencing sperm as the source of life and the womb as the means of formation of that life. This is the way God created things to be. There is no need to think that Paul is making some point here from the Genesis passages of creation. He is rather making his point from biology. It has in my view been misleading to connect this verse with 1 Timothy 1:13 where Paul is saying a different point about some women being silent. In this passage he is talking about men and women speaking in prayer and prophecy. Unlike the I Timothy passage there is no mention of Adam and Eve here. The normal biological facts are what Paul is referring to which lies behind the straightforward interpretation of these verses.

---

10. Because of this, *(i.e. that man is the source of woman, and so the way she operates in anointing honours and reflects this)* **a woman has authority** *(no mention of veil here)* **with reference to her head** *επι with the genitive. "On her head" as in NKJV and others not only does not make obvious sense but would be επι plus dative which answers the question where is it based or going towards. The genitive means it is "in reference to" or "in relationship to" answering the question where does her authority lie. The point is that a woman needs to exercise authority with reference to man because of the angelic dimensions of creation* **because of the angels.**

11. It is neither woman without man nor man without woman in the Lord

12 Just as woman came from man *(the sperm from man)* **so also man through woman** *(from the womb of woman)* **but all things are from God.** *Whether you are a woman from man or a man through woman the ultimate source is from God. Paul says the fact we are different does not mean there is any difference in our position in God. Male and female are equal.*

13. Judge among yourselves. Is it fitting for a woman to be unveiled when she prays to God?

14. Does not nature itself teach us because if a man wears his hair long it is without honour to him,

15. But if a woman wears her hair long it is a glory to her, because long hair is given to her in place of a cloak *Paul is referring to the physical covering of hair and cloak. περιβολαιου the word used for cloak or covering is the only reference to an actual garment in this passage.*

---

16. But if anyone wishes to be contentious, we have no such custom nor do the churches of God.

The glory of manhood is not in long hair. Man's glory lies in his zeal and relationship to God; in what He stands for and seeks to achieve. A woman's glory lies in her womanhood of which her hair is integral. Glory for both sexes' lies in deeds done and character displayed, but that does not come from what sex we are, but from the obedience and the achieving of the deed.

Remember the teaching Paul is giving is all about how prayer and prophesy should happen in the church.

The anointed servants of God should be authentic all the way through including our sexual identity and so the way we move according to the anointing will be different for the male as for the female.

This teaching is about man and woman not husband and wife, because Paul has left far behind the teaching on marriage; and prayer or prophecy is open to all men and women whether married or single.

Paul is saying the man is not better than the woman. It is simply male and female are different. The woman is designed to exercise authority in relation to her head. (v10)

Paul is therefore **not** saying the following statements....

1. Man is better than woman; more intelligent than woman or in a better place than woman. He says the exact opposite (v11,12)
2. Woman should not exercise authority. He says the exact opposite (v10)
3. Woman should wear veils in church services. The covering is not about clothing. Anointing and effective prayer or prophecy is not dependent on our dress code.

So ...What is Paul saying? Some things are clear...

1. Prayer and prophesy are open to both men and women.

2. Woman should make sure they are under a covering. This means she steps back in her womanhood to pray or to prophesy and focuses on the covering. This will show in her attitude, demeanour and obedience. She will seek to pray or prophesy within the limits set by the church culture or rules but also keeping in mind that she is wife or daughter.

3. The man also has this same attitude as the woman in the Lord, remembering church rules and his family, but when he is exercising prayer or prophecy it is his walk with God alone that is his focus as he speaks.

4. The woman does not assert their womanhood without a covering (whereas men are to make sure their inner life with God comes on display). Prayer and prophesy is spiritual power at work in the service of Christ. Covering for the woman is important because of this.

5. There is a parallel between man with Christ, and woman with man. There may be a further reason for operating correctly in covering. Just as Christ responds to the inner life of man when he is moving in anointing, a woman has to be wary of the same approach because man can be attracted to the inner life of woman as Christ is attracted by the inner life of man. Man is however not perfect like Jesus is and some women can suffer unnecessary attention from men attracted by the anointing on them. Covering helps the woman in such cases.

1 Corinthians 11:17-34: Holy Communion

Now Paul turns to what he does not praise about them (v17)

17. In giving of my instructions I do not praise you (whilst they were great in receiving his teaching they had not ordered their church life well in this case) **you come together not for the better but towards the worse.**

18. First Paul has many reasons why they meet for worse rather than better.

First reason: there are divisions when they come together **when you**

> **come together in the church** *"Church" is not used of the people but of the building where the gathering happens in a similar way that we would talk about going to church. This usage accords much more with the idea of εκκλησια being equivalent to synagogue than to an inner meaning of called out ones and this usage tends to put a counter argument to the view that the early church was all about the people not the building. In my view church was all about the gathering more than the people per se or the building.* **I hear that divisions exist among you. And in part I believe it.**
>
> **19. For it is necessary that there be dissensions among you in order that the worthy ones may appear among you.**

Controversy is God's way of bringing to the forefront both the truth which is made clear in the testing of controversy, and also bring to the forefront his servants for the action needed for the hour.

Without Goliath David would not have been noticed; without the arguments about entry to the promised land Joshua and Caleb would have been just part of the crowd; without the controversy at the time of Ahab Elijah and Elisha would not have brought a testimony which stood down the centuries and without the controversy surrounding Nebuchadnezzar's dream Daniel would not have emerged onto the world stage.

> ***Second Reason:*** *their bad behaviour which* **demonstrates the meetings are for worse rather than for better**
>
> **20. When you come together and are together** *(επι το αυτο emphasises the coming together which is the meaning of the verb συνερχομενοων)* **to eat it is not the Lord's Supper.**

So the Corinthians were gathering together for what they called the Lord's Supper but because of what was going on, Paul says it is not the Lord's Supper. There was food and gathering at both so how could one be not the Lord's Supper. The answer is that their bad behaviour meant that Jesus was not there. Relationships directly affect the presence of the Spirit.

21. For each takes his own meal to eat at it and one hungers whilst another is drunk.

22. Do you not have homes for eating and drinking or do you despise the church of God and shame those who do not have (food). *Shaming the poor and despising the church are two wrongs of which they were guilty.* **What shall I say to you: Should I praise you in this? I do not praise you.**

23. For I received from the Lord *I think Jesus directly told Paul this, though those at the last supper would have known already. If the apostles had told Paul I think he would have said so here. Paul defines his sources accurately (see 1 Corinthians 7:10, 12, 40);* **what I passed on to you that the Lord Jesus in the night in which he was betrayed took bread,**

24. and giving thanks, he broke it, and said "This is my body which is for you *(on your behalf)***. Do this in my memory.**

25. In the same way (he took), the cup after the meal saying This is the cup is the new covenant in my blood. Do this, as often as you drink, to my memory.

26. As often as you eat this bread and drink the cup, you proclaim the death of the Lord until he should come.

Through the blessing over the bread and wine there is a link made with the death of Jesus. The blessing makes the eating of the bread and the drinking of the wine linked to the sacrifice (see Chapter 10) and through this brings a supernatural blessing to the participant. The new kingdom age made available by the cross but ushered in through resurrection with ascension and marked by the sending of the Spirit, still has a central place for the proclamation of the cross until the complete kingdom age brings a new heaven and a new earth. Jesus expected this at the last supper "I will not drink again of the fruit of the vine until I drink it new in the kingdom (post resurrection). That same perception of the coming kingdom therefore is part of the focus of communion.

There is also the important response of memory - holding Jesus in remembrance whenever we eat and drink the cup. Memory accesses the past and brings it to the present. We can feel what it was like through memory recall as well as reflect on something past in a detached way. Recall must have a spiritual dimension to it similar to prayer. Both access through our choice something of the unseen in that present and we enter a journey which is within distant from our present surroundings. Jesus is asking us to remember him as we would remember someone who has blessed us and from whom we have given life. This is done not just because it is the right thing to do in acknowledging Jesus, but is also the way we receive spiritual strength.

---

27. Whoever eats the bread or drinks the cup of the Lord unworthily, is guilty of the body and blood of the Lord.

How we relate to each other affects the whole blessing of communion which affirms in the eating of the bread the church as the body of Christ and through the drinking of the wine avails the blessing of the cross.

---

28. Let each man examine himself and so eat from the bread and drink from the cup.

29. For he who eats and drinks, eats and drinks judgement on himself because he has not discerned the body. *("Of the Lord "occurs in some manuscripts. Whether it is "body" or "body of the Lord" it refers to recognising the church for what it really is.)*

30. Because of this many among you are weak and sickly and a large number have died.

31. If we *(this is a principle including the Corinthians as well as Paul)* judge our own behaviour, *(bringing out the meaning of the Greek words εαυτους διεκρινομεν)* we would not be judged (by God).

32. When we are judged by the Lord, we are being disciplined in order that we might not be judged with the world.

Paul is saying two things about the infirmity and death which has afflicted the Corinthians as a result of the wrongs they were making at the Lord's Supper:-

1. That if they were to look to their behaviour, there would be no judgement. The spiritual discipline of examining oneself can avoid opening us to judgements. Hence v28

2. The motive God has in allowing judgements in the church is to stop the church being denied its separation from the world status as the people of God, and instead becoming just part of the world it inhabits. We are designed to be in the world but not of the world (John 15:18, 17:14) as Jesus was (John 8:23). God's special people (I Peter 2:9). Judgements will come to the special people of God to prevent the church losing its special status in its relationship with God.

So Christians are more likely to experience God's judgements than the worldly person. This is even more of an incentive to continue to be discerning examining our own ways so we avoid any judgements at all.

---

33. So that my brothers, when you come together to eat, wait for the others.

34. If anyone is hungry *(so finds it difficult to wait)*, **let him eat at home in order that you do not assemble to judgement.** *The waiting will resolve the issues here as they will be in a better position to share food with the poor.* **But the rest** *(there were some lesser issues probably raised by the Corinthians which Paul will speak about when he comes)* **I will instruct when I come.**

The Lost Manuscript

At this point there was a sudden interruption. Some of the church who met at Aquila's house all suddenly arrived downstairs. They called up for Paul to join them and Sosthenes put down his quill and joined Paul as they descended the wooden stairs into the rear courtyard and then into the cool downstairs room. Just inside the entrance was a decorated delicate glass vase with spring flowers which added the finishing touch to what was already a well-furnished room. Priscilla was a woman of great taste and organisation and every house she owned reflected this. Paul stepped quickly over the coloured marble floors looked up at the tasteful paintings on the walls and turned into the main hallway. This was a large room in the central part of the downstairs from which most of the downstairs rooms could be accessed. In the middle of the hallway was a group of about 15 people, of all ages. Paul was curious at this unexpected arrival. Amongst the group were some he knew well Tychicus, Demas and Luke as well as others he had seen in the church meetings, but there were some he had never met before. Tychicus was beaming. Paul was still surprised because such a large group without Priscilla or Aquila was unusual and was not what he had expected at all. As Paul approached, the group parted to reveal a family Paul had passed most days when he had walked to the hall of Tyrannus. The man introduced himself to Paul. Cerinthus was his Roman name though he was a local man born in a village about 3 miles to the north of Ephesus. He and his family ran a successful market stall in the agora selling cheese, butter, dried figs and nuts, as well as seasonal fruit and wine that they got from their small holding. Paul knew this for he had become a customer. They sold the juiciest oranges in Ephesus and all the rest of their produce was good. He was surprised because although he knew them, they had to his knowledge never heard him speak and until now had not been within the company of the church folk that he knew. Paul welcomed them and they sat down whilst Cerinthus told them his story. About lunchtime a man had bought some milk from him and as he was leaving a precious manuscript had dropped out of the shoulder satchel the man was carrying. Cerinthus began to explain how he had learnt to read both Greek and Latin but was interrupted by other members of the family who steered him back to the point of his story. Cerinthus continued "I picked up the manuscript he had dropped, looked around and he had gone. This was at the height of the day when less people brave the bright heat of the sun, and so with few customers I read what had fallen from the man's hand. It was in common Greek and contained a series of stories about Jesus. I knew right away that this was something to do with Paul because people who heard Paul would speak about Jesus near my stall. The manuscript was not complete. It started with some teaching about a sower and finished with a story about a blind man being healed. I thought this manuscript was important. My wife said should make sure I returned it. We both agreed we did not want to be accused of theft. I thought you Paul would know who owned it. I was not sure where you lived but I knew some neighbours – the parents of Tychicus - and they have come with me as well as those who were living with them in their house to ensure we arrived here safe and sound". Paul reached out his hand to take the offered manuscripts. He said. "I have seen these before. They belong to a man called Mark who used to live in Jerusalem and knew Jesus and the disciples". Paul then explained about Jesus, and as he spoke, a peace descended. It was clear to the whole group that the story of Jesus was having a profound effect on Cerinthus and his family. They listened attentively, and then Paul invited them to become followers of Jesus. They paused, bowed their heads and accepted Jesus into their hearts quietly but profoundly. The whole group was moved as Cerinthus prayed to Jesus aloud to come into his life and guide him and his family, followed by his wife who also prayed with her head bowed. Paul than prayed for them and both Cerinthus and his wife felt the power of God as he prayed. The silence was then broken by rejoicing Christians and there was soon some refreshments brought in to the rooms by an invitation to stay to the meal which was being made ready. This was a good day.

Some hours later Cerinthus and his family left. They left in good spirits with warm goodbyes sounding in their ears as they started their long walk back to their home. Paul turned back into the house with Luke and Demas who had remained behind. He mentioned Mark to them, for he was surprised that he was back from his travels so quickly. Mark had lived in Ephesus since joining up with the small group of believers who had come from Jerusalem, which included Mark's mother. She had hosted one of the churches in Jerusalem where Peter had been a member, but after the murder of his brother James, John and the mother of Jesus decided to move to Ephesus from Jerusalem, and other members of the group including Mark 's mother had come too. Most of those who had arrived then had now either died or moved away. It was twelve years since there had been a steady stream of arrivals to Ephesus from the Jerusalem church first beginning just before King Agrippa died, but many more had arrived in Ephesus after Agrippa's sudden death. Mark had not come to Ephesus with the others. He had chosen instead to travel with Barnabas to Antioch where he had joined the large church where Paul and Barnabas both taught and were part of the leadership team. It was there that Mark had been first introduced to a travelling ministry as he accompanied his cousin Barnabas and Paul. He later travelled with Barnabas to Cyprus where Lazarus and Martha had gone to live. Lazarus was now one of the leaders in the church there. The first Christians who had known Jesus were well dispersed around the known world and beyond. Mark had joined John in Ephesus where he had lived now for some years. He had been on a trip to Hierapolis visiting Phillip and the church with Tychicus and the team. As expected Mark had stayed there whilst Tychicus and the others travelled onto the opposite side of the Lycus valley to Laodicea and then further up the valley to Colossae. Tychicus had returned without Mark. He had been back over a week now from the mission trip, but Mark was not expected for another few days. Demas said he must have just arrived and dropped the manuscript as he was returning to his house in the west of the city. He would have passed through the agora to reach it. Mark had started to write down the ministry of Jesus at the request of

Peter. Peter had visited John in Ephesus some years back and Mark had spent some time listening to Peter as he talked about the old days with Jesus. This is where the majority of the future gospel had been written, though Mark had travelled to Rome twice to see Peter since. The scrolls he had written were already in great demand and it meant Peter and his wife did not have to travel so much for the church to hear first-hand about the life and teaching of Jesus. Mark's scrolls could tell the story. He had read some of them to the church at Hierapolis and it had been well received. Paul expected Mark to be at church at the end of the week. As they left the hall, Luke whispered to Paul, and asked if he could look at the manuscript. For Luke had been for some time engaged in research for his own story about Jesus. He had already got a lot of notes. He had met Mary in Ephesus a few years before when Paul had left him there with the team whilst Paul had gone on to Syria. Mary had told Luke about the birth of Jesus and he had several other stories already written after listening to many other followers of Jesus who had known Jesus during his ministry on earth. He said "I intend to write it all down in order when the time is right". He had been approached already by a Roman by the name of Theophilus who was willing to sponsor him in the task, but nothing was certain yet. Luke was always thorough in his research, and he needed space to write, space which the demands of revival in Ephesus and Paul's ministry did not allow. He was also keeping a diary of the present events in case there was also a need to show how the church developed after Jesus ascension into heaven. This he would call the Acts of the Apostles. Paul showed him a quiet place in the downstairs complex where he could read the manuscript undisturbed and asked him to bring it up to his room when he had finished. Paul stayed downstairs for a while before climbing the stairs to his room.

Apollos and Aristarchus

Paul looked over the table at his companion Apollos. They were seated in the main lower room of Priscilla's house where she had as usual laid out fruit and drink in copious quantity. Apollos was younger than Paul, intelligent and gifted. He was like others from Alexandria often in the company of others from Alexandrian background. Alexandria had new technologies which produced glass ware unrivalled by anywhere else in the world and was also an exporter of the riches of Africa to Ephesus, Corinth and other major centres in the Mediterranean. In addition it was a centre of learning in the world and so Alexandria did not just send goods but also people who were experts resourcing the communication , administration and legal duties of the empire. Most people who came from Alexandria to Ephesus were either lawyers or librarians. One of his closest friends was Zenas the lawyer. Alexandria had the foremost library in the world - not as old as the one at Pergamum – but the most influential encouraging both the development of lawyers as well as librarians. It also had inspired Augustus Caesar to build a library in Rome within the last 40 years and there was now talk that Ephesus ought to have a library too. None at the table knew that within 40 years Celsius would build one in Ephesus, but if they had done, they would not have been surprised. Documents relating to trade purchases as well as military movements, pay, taxation and many other documents including some of antiquity were already stored in the city.

His Alexandrian upbringing meant Apollos from his earliest years had met people from all over the known world. He had learnt how to communicate with people of differing cultures. Apollos had been one of many to make the trip from Alexandria to Ephesus, but he had quickly made his mark in the smaller church as it was before Paul arrived, and thanks to Priscilla and Aquila he had had opportunity to bring the gospel to Corinth after Paul had been there. Corinth was a Roman colony built as a Greek city but because of its position on the trade routed diverse in culture and society. Alexandria also, although in North Africa, had been built as a Greek city, and so Corinth was not too strange a place for Apollos. He had spent some months there, been effective in the gospel and helped to build up the church. He was now back amongst his Alexandrian friends in Ephesus.

Apollos was from the large Jewish community which existed in Alexandria, and he lived amongst the Egyptians in a part of Ephesus where Paul seldom went since his imprisonment. The first Jew Paul had met from Alexandria was Clement who he knew from his days at Philippi. But whereas Clement was a pastor and a writer, a problem solver and a diplomat, Apollos was a passionate preacher who communicated well, loved debate and got the message across with utter clarity. Not everyone liked him, but he understood the Greeks well and was ideally suited to go to Corinth.

Apollos had had a very different education to the one Paul had received under Gamaliel in Jerusalem. The large Jewish community in Alexandria had Christians in it, some of whom had been converted in Jerusalem on the day of Pentecost. Through these Apollos had found faith in Jesus before he had come to Ephesus. Paul had found out first hand some of Apollos' earlier results of his teaching when he first arrived in Ephesus. He had found some believers who only knew what Apollos had told them before Aquila and Priscilla had spoken to him. As a result all they knew was the baptism of John the Baptist and nothing about the Holy Spirit moving in power. Fortunately when Aquila and Priscilla explained the truths of the gospel more fully, Apollos had a teachable spirit and had been a great help in Corinth. He had done a lot of good helping the Corinthian converts in their faith. Apollos had returned just under 2 years ago to Ephesus and Apollos now seemed very much at home. Ephesus was a large city and the church also was large and diverse and it met in different places of the city so their paths had not often crossed. The last time Paul had met Apollos was when they had met in Aquila's house during which Paul had discussed returning to Corinth. He had invited Apollos to join the trip to Corinth either with Erastus and Timothy or later when Paul was to go, but he had declined both offers. Apollos may visit Corinth again but it was clear that he had decided not to go currently and he was sticking to his decision. Paul and probably Apollos knew that it might be easier if Apollos was not part of his team this time with the partisan divisions that existed at Corinth at the time. Apollos having made up his mind not to go to Corinth, was at least open to the suggestion of travelling with his friend Zenas to help Titus for a short time in Crete to build up the work there. Apollos was a man God had raised up to preach and nurture Christians in different countries and cultures; and there was much to do both in Crete and other parts of the Mediterranean. Paul was pleased that Apollos was considering Crete as definitely somewhere he should visit. Paul and Apollos discussed this for some time.

Their discussions were interrupted as appearing through the doorway was Aristarchus the Macedonian. He was known to Apollos, but Paul had first met Aristarchus as a young man in the synagogue at Thessalonica nearly 10 years earlier. Paul and Apollos broke off their discussion and stood up to welcome him. Aristarchus had accompanied Paul on most of his travels since combining his kingdom work with his business for the trading company he worked for. This was based in Thessalonica, and was seeking to broaden its markets into the province of Asia and beyond. The company was already trading with Alexandrian glass, Spanish olive oil, and Italian wine and North African pottery. Aristarchus' job was to provide new sales for these products in Asia. Ephesus was the hub centre for this with strong immediate links to Alexandria, Philippi and Corinth. Around that table Apollos, Paul and Aristarchus knew a great amount about those cities and the people in them.

Aristarchus had been very successful in life and business. As a youth he had been introduced to trading and business contacts in Neapolis, the town where he lived which was also the main port for Philippi. His father had worked on the ships and through family contacts Aristarchus had got to know successful traders who had employed him to expand the business which he had done beyond all expectations. He had been converted to Christ when he first met Paul and had managed to travel with Paul from time to time combining his work and mission. This had sometimes led him into danger. He had recently been arrested with Paul and spent time in prison with him. Paul valued Aristarchus who alongside Mark and Justus had encouraged Paul in affirming his Jewish roots amidst what was a very non Jewish culture in Ephesus. Together they had brought reminders of home to Paul which he had valued much. Aristarchus and Paul had lived in the same apartment in Ephesus until the arrest, and now Aquila had thought it safer for them to be not in the same place. Aristarchus was staying with Aquila in his new house just outside the walls of the city near the olive groves and fig plantations which grew in the neighbourhood.

It was only a few days since he and Paul had waved goodbye to Epaphroditus, a friend of Aristarchus' from Macedonia who had been sent by the church when they knew Paul was in prison. Epaphroditus had now journeyed back to Macedonia with Paul's letter to the Philippians preparing for Timothy's arrival in just over a week's time.

As Aristarchus entered the room it was soon apparent he was not on his own. Behind him came an older man who Paul also knew from Philippi - Gaius the Macedonian. Gaius had arrived on a ship very early that day. It had been delayed and had had to wait until well after first light before being allowed to dock in the harbour because there had been some ships unloading provisions and resources to help resource the military as they moved towards far off Parthia. There was little surprise at this. There had been increased military activity throughout the autumn and winter through Ephesus. Preparations had begun for what was now starting to take place in the eastern edge of the Empire, and there were rumours that a war with Parthia far away to the east was beginning.

Gaius was staying with Aristarchus at Aquila's house until Paul was to depart with them for Philippi (and Corinth). Paul quickly arranged some more refreshment for them and they sat together and ate whilst Paul asked about any more news from the church at Philippi, and then Paul explained the plans he had for his visits to Macedonia and Corinth. He would send Timothy to Philippi and then onto Corinth whilst he planned with these companions to travel to Corinth meeting Timothy there and then onto Macedonia. Paul explained to Gaius that his plan was delayed by a few weeks because during his time in prison there had been some conversions amongst some relatives of Caesar and he wanted to pursue what God was doing there. Gaius and Aristarchus could still prepare for the coming voyage and overland trip. There was a lot involved in preparing for the next few weeks, yet little did they realise how much activity it would involve. Gaius and Aristarchus would be caught up in a riot and they would flee the city travelling with Paul instead to Troas to escape Ephesus immediately and then from there onto Macedonia and Corinth in just a few days' time...but for now all seemed well.

1 Corinthians Chapter 12-14

Overview

Spiritual Gifts at work

Background:-

Jesus was a real man. Matthew tells us he was born before King Herod died in 4b.c. and all the gospels tell us Jesus died on a cross and rose again from the dead after 26 AD - the year Pontius Pilate became procurator of Judea.

Jesus started his earthly ministry aged about thirty when the Spirit of God came on him in power after his baptism in the Jordan river. From that day on, for three years Jesus did miracles he had not done before. These included words of knowledge and wisdom, many types of healing, and raising the dead to life. There were also other supernatural miracles (e.g. feeding the 5,000) as well as teaching and prophecy from revelation direct from heaven (John 14:10).To do this Jesus operated in spiritual gifts.

Jesus said although He was the son of God "the Son could do nothing of himself" (John 5:19), because Jesus did not do things because he was God (though He is), but rather operated as a spirit filled man. This is why he could say to his disciples that they would do the same works he had done and indeed greater works. (John 14:12), and they could be sent in the same way as He was (John 20:21).

When Jesus died on the cross he paid the price for our sin and when He rose from the dead he demonstrated he had removed forever the old barrier of sin from our lives. He had cleansed our history. There was no barrier between us and the Holy Spirit once sin had gone. Humankind could still choose to receive this or reject it. Receiving the offer Jesus gives, means a change in us. With the old barrier gone and our hearts turned towards Him, there is nothing stopping the Holy Spirit filling our lives. One of the results of this is spiritual power manifested through spiritual gifts. No wonder Paul does not want the Corinthians to be ignorant about the gifts of the Spirit, and devotes some verses on this theme.

It was through the Holy Spirit that Jesus brought teaching that confounded and amazed .It was through the Holy Spirit he did miracles demonstrating the reality of the kingdom of God. Spiritual gifts are everywhere in the ministry of Jesus. Here are just a few: He "knew their thoughts "(Matthew 12:25; Luke 6:8) – words of knowledge abound. He knows how many husbands the woman of Samaria has had and her current status in life (John 4:17). He knows when Lazarus has died though he is far away (John 11:11). Jesus also used prophecy accurately predicting the future (Luke 18:13, 19:43; 22:10; 31:61), as well as bringing God's word for the present to multitudes "No-one spoke like this man" (John 7:46). Jesus spoke what he heard from the Father (John 14:10) and confounded those who tried to trap him with words of wisdom (e.g. Render unto Caesar the things that are Caesar's and unto God the things that are God's "Matthew 22:21).

Because his healing and miracles were spiritual gifts, his followers who receive the Holy Spirit can do the same works Jesus did (John 14:12; see also John 7:38, Acts 2:1; Acts 1:8, 5). Jesus expected his followers to move in spiritual gifts also. Jesus told his disciples to wait until the Holy Spirit should come. This happened at Pentecost a few days after Jesus ascension. From that day on the church also moved in the same power that Jesus had shown, because the Holy Spirit was now in the church in the same way He had been in Jesus during his earthly ministry

Spiritual Gifts in 1 Corinthians 12-14

These next chapters are all about the Holy Spirit who gives gifts. Elsewhere (Galatians 5:22) Paul gives the definitive lists of the fruits of the Holy Spirit; in this chapter Paul gives the definitive list of the gifts of the Holy Spirit.

12:1-3 Getting spiritual gifts clear so we can move in them

Some of the Corinthians had had bad experiences of the supernatural. The occult was part of life alongside pagan worship. They knew the occult was not good, and it made some wary of the supernatural whatever its source.

We are spiritual beings designed to connect with God, but not everything is as God intended in our hearts or in our world seen and unseen. This means we can be led astray in life by our hearts as well as by the world. This is true also in the area of the supernatural. The Corinthians knew this and it had left a lens of fear so when they experienced the Lord at work they would not respond in faith but rather fear. They treated the Holy Spirit as if He is the same as the pagan experiences they had had and so run away from, rather than welcome and move with, the Holy Spirit. Paul therefore states the difference between the old way of life in the occult and the new way of life in the Holy Spirit. The new life has a new environment. If Jesus is Lord in declaration or in agreement, the Holy Spirit will be there. Recognising this dispels fear and gives us the confidence to trust in what we are receiving or experiencing without always rationally being able to understand or emotionally feel anything. This is important because the Holy Spirit will engage with our human spirit (Romans 8:16) and therefore we will not always rationally understand what is happening (1 Corinthians 14:14) for the spirit engages us at a level deeper than mind, will or emotions.

12:4-7 getting Spiritual gifts clear so we can recognise them.

There are different gifts. God's Spirit is not monochrome. In addition the way they operate and manifest can also be different (different ministries) and will have different results (workings).

An illustration of different ministries: There were 3 prophets in David's court (1Chron 25:2-4) who operated in 3 different ways in their prophetic gift. All had the gift of prophecy but they had different ministries. Asaph (though musical himself) operated prophetically at the direction of the king. The trigger for prophecy in his case was an authentic request or need. When David asked or there was a need, prophetic revelation was given. Jeduthun, on the other hand prophesied through the trigger of music. This was the way he accessed the relationship with the Lord so he could hear revelation. The third prophet mentioned in 1 Chronicles 25 is Haman. He was different again as he was a seer moving as revelation stirred him regardless of request or music. He seemed stirred by what he saw within rather than anything else. Daniel moved in the latter (see his diaries recorded in Daniel 8 onwards). It is noteworthy that Daniel also moved prophetically in the Asaph type (see his dream interpretation of Nebuchadnezzar in Daniel 2). This is a reminder that the same person can have a prophetic gift which works in different ways. Some may have just one "trigger" whilst others might have several. Elisha is also an example of this. When he was emotionally not in a good place with the king, he used music in order to access revelation (2 Kings 3:14, 15)

Different workings

"Ministries" is all about how they work, "workings" is all about the results which can also differ. For example the gift of evangelism in Billy Graham or John Wesley had brought thousands to faith at the same time, but there are many others who have brought people to faith one by one. They show God at work in each case. It is the source not the different results which count.

12:7-10 the basic spiritual gifts are defined.

Summary: - Paul wants them not to be ignorant about spiritual gifts. The Holy Spirit works in more ways than Paul defines here. There is no reference here to hospitality, teaching, or helping he mentions in Romans 12:6-8 as spiritual gifts , or leadership /administration which Paul refers to later in this same chapter 12 v28, or even evangelism, worship leading and pastoring just to name a few where God works through his spirit. Why not these in this list? It cannot be a random list because of Paul's intention to teach about the gifts yet it does not contain all the ways God's Spirit moves. The answer lies in recognising Paul is listing what I have called the primary gifts from which every manifestation of spiritual gift comes.

All works of the kingdom are a combination of these gifts

Although Paul has other lists of gifts and anointing (Romans 12, Ephesians 4, and later in 1 Corinthians 12), because he starts the chapter here by stating his intention to teach on spiritual gifts, the list at the start of this chapter must be definitive on spiritual gifts. It cannot be random.

My contention is that this list contains the primary colours from which all spiritual gift manifestation comes. Most gifts if not all when they manifest are a combination of the primary gifts mentioned here. For example exorcism can be a combination of healing and prophecy and probably words of knowledge and words of wisdom; Worship leading can be a combination of words of wisdom, prophecy and faith; Teaching can be a combination of word of wisdom and knowledge with prophecy; Evangelism can be a combination of prophecy, discernment and word of wisdom; Leadership a combination of words of knowledge and wisdom and faith - to name just a few examples.

We are in a church context. Wherever the church is the gifts will be there. The church does not just occupy a building on a Sunday but is present wherever there are obedient Christians in the world. He first teaches about spiritual gifts in the church wherever the church is as the body of Christ. In Chapter 14 he will teach on how to operate with these gifts in a gathered context for worship. For these gifts are manifested in the church as it meets together and is for the common good. Paul teaches in chapter 14 how to steward the gifts so they can be of greatest blessing to the church.

If they are not in the church, there is something amiss in the church. In fact Spiritual gifts have been in the church since Pentecost, but in many churches today remain unrecognised and unheralded because of ignorance of how to recognise the source of what they see combined with a theology which excludes in their mind the possibility of the gifts of the Spirit in the modern age.

Spiritual Gifts in the Human Spirit.

We act like a prism to light.

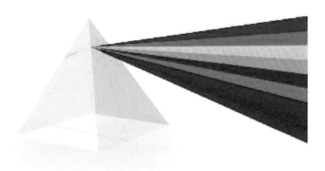

We know from Romans 8 that the Holy Spirit relates to our spirit (Romans 8:16). The Light of God accesses our spirit and shines through us in spiritual gifts. Spiritual fruit is as a result of exposure to the light. Our inner being changes to become more like Jesus. However the light of God can shine through our life long before we have character change. It is possible to move in evangelism (for example) and still have a character and lifestyle very different from Jesus. Do not trust someone just because they move in gifts of power; you trust them according to character, honesty and integrity. But we also know that God Spirit can breathe through people with unsuitable characters (remember God prophesying through Nebuchadnezzar (Daniel 4:10-18) or Caiaphas John 11:51) or Balaam (Numbers 24:17) to name just a few. Just because they prophesy accurately from God does not mean you trust them.

We know from Romans 8:16 that God's Holy Spirit will access our human spirit rather than our soul. We can speak in a tongue inspired by the spirit and our mind is uneducated (1 Corinthians 14:14). We can also experience things our will has not chosen (Paul on the Damascus road or Jesus healing the woman of bleeding before he knew it) and we can be in the things of the Holy Spirit and not know it because we do not feel a thing (Jacob in revelation Gen 28:16 "Surely the Lord is in this place and I knew it not"). All this is because the Holy Spirit accesses our spirit rather than our soul. It is below our mind, will and emotions.

People are eternal spiritual beings encased in an animal mortal body.1 Thessalonians 5:23 describes us as spirit, soul and body. We know from Hebrews 4:12 that the soul and spirit in people are closely connected. The areas of the soul we define as mind (not the human brain but the place of values, memories, values), the will (place of choice and decisions and vows) and emotions (the place of feeling and well-being).

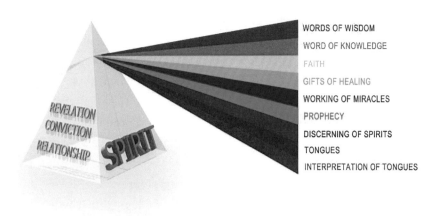

This has echoes of our human spirit for they are related. Whilst both our souls and spirit are eternal and part of our human frame, they are not the same (Hebrews 4:12). The human spirit is connected to but distinct from our soul. Our soul bridges the gap between our human spirit and our human body. The soul is the part of us which is best described as made up of mind, will and emotions – mind the place where we hold our memories and priorities; will the place of our choices and vows; emotions the place of our feelings and our self-awareness. The human spirit engages with the human soul in these places. The will of the soul relates to conviction in the human spirit; the emotions of the soul to the arena of relationship in the human spirit and the mind of the soul to revelation in the human spirit.

The spirit has echoes of what is the soul, but it is different.
In the human spirit it is
Revelation rather than mind
Conviction rather than will;
Relationship rather than emotions.

The order of the gifts in 1 Corinthians 12 explained

WORDS OF WISDOM

WORD OF KNOWLEDGE

FAITH

GIFTS OF HEALING

WORKING OF MIRACLES

PROPHECY

DISCERNING OF SPIRITS

TONGUES

INTERPRETATION OF TONGUES

We can see there is a connection between the gifts without needing to understand about the human spirit. For example the word of wisdom and word of knowledge seem to go together well as does healing and works of miracles or power, and speaking in tongues and interpretation of tongues. But there are also seeming anomalies. Why for example is prophecy so far away from words of knowledge and wisdom? They are all speaking gifts of the Spirit, each one speaking revelation from God.

The way Paul arranges the list is because of the order they have as the Holy Spirit shines through our spirit.

Now we are ready to return to the list which follows revelation, conviction and relationship. As the list progresses they move gradually from revelation which grows less as conviction grows more and then conviction grows less and relationship grows more. As relationship grows less revelation grows more and so on. As we read this list we can begin to recognise the way the gifts interact with our spirit and can understand better the one operating the gift.

Revelation words of wisdom & knowledge have little to do with conviction though words of knowledge may tend more towards conviction than words of wisdom. Revelation can come through thoughts, supernatural phenomena or bible verses explained, physical sensations in body or awareness of atmospheres.

Conviction is where you are more personally attached to the revelation or activity. Your well-being in your soul may sometimes feel it, but conviction is a noticeable spiritual force or drive.

Faith needs both revelation and conviction whereas **gifts of miracles** just operate out of conviction. Notice the conviction of David before he operates in God's power to bring the miraculous defeat of Goliath (I Sam 17:37, 45-47) or of Jesus when he is to raise Lazarus from the dead (John 11:1139-430 or the feeding of the 5,000 (John 6:6).

Prophecy also operates out of conviction but will have a relationship angle to it.

Relationship is with God or the people or the situation.

Discernment (Discerning of spirits) has a conviction element to it, but it is primarily relational. Discernment brings effects of well-being or foreboding, peace or agitation. It is not supernatural facts but relationship.

Tongues also does not need supernatural facts or conviction to operate. Those who speak in tongues do so at any time. It enhances relationship with God (1 Corinthians 14:2), which strengthens us (1 Corinthians 14:4)

Interpretation of tongues approaches from relationship back into revelation. The rainbow spectrum is actually circular and there is transition from relationship to revelation.

Spiritual gifts and the Church
1 Corinthians 12: 11-26 Spiritual gifts at work in the Body of Christ

The different gifts, ministries and workings are the basis for the teaching in this section about the body of Christ. Where people fail to recognise that the different gifts are the same spirit or that the different ministries are the same Lord or the workings are through the same God so that they say they do not belong or that they have no need of someone exercising a different ministry or a working which brings a different outcome from others. This all comes from comparing different parts of the "body" as opposed to looking at the source.

1 Corinthians 12:28-31 The order of working in the church

Paul is referring to the process the gifts manifest in the church happens. "First apostles" does not mean that they are pre-eminent above the other gifts because Paul has said there is not a pecking order of gifts. They are of equal value. 1 Corinthians 12:1-4; 12-26. "First" must refer time. The apostle starts the work going. He speaks elsewhere (Ephesians 2:20) of apostles and prophets providing the foundation with Christ as the cornerstone. It is this to which "first refers". This foundational work is followed by prophets who also are engaged in that same work. Structures are then built on those foundations and so it is ", then teachers", and into these structures are poured various works and signs of the Kingdom – "miracles, healing, helping, administration (or more likely leadership) and tongues. Church is formed this way and Paul is outlining the different stages of formation and the primary spiritual gifts manifest at each stage.

The Apostles are sent and form the foundation alongside the prophets (Ephesians 2:20), followed by teachers. We pause and think of the Celtic church Patrick and then Columba as apostles with many prophets and teachers like Aidan. There were many wonders in evangelism and supernatural grace during this time which helped the extension of the kingdom. The next layer in Paul's list is miracles which are the wonders which authenticate the foundation and framework and enable a framework of further gifts. The same process occurs at a local or denominational or global level. It happened in the Reformation. The pioneers of Wycliffe and Huss started a movement which brought the

English reformation into being through Cranmer and raised up teachers like Tyndale and the Puritans .This was followed by the establishing of the English church, which not only successfully abolished the influence of witchcraft and other occult practices though they had been exercised by all from monarchy to peasant up to the reign of Henry VII. This in turn led to helps and leadership in the English Church. We find same process in the book of Acts. The apostles with the prophetic Peter speaking into the situation at the birth of the church with a word of wisdom and prophetic interpretation of scripture at Pentecost (Acts 2) followed by the teaching (2:42) followed by the miracle in Acts 3:1-10 and miracle of the church life Acts 4:32-34 (note also Acts 5:1-10) This was followed by healings Acts 5:16 and helps(Acts 6) and leadership development (Acts 6-15). Paul adopted the same model establishing leaders (elders) in the churches once the churches had been formed had been formed (see Titus 1:5). Apostleship anointing is not the same as leadership. Leadership steers a church life which the apostles have brought, and which with the prophets have founded.

In conclusion

This section (as is all the chapter of 1 Corinthians 12, especially from verse 11) is about the working of God in the church. This has a list starting first apostles etc. Paul has been keen in the earlier section to stress the diversity yet equal value (as each is essential in the body) of each part, so this is not saying apostles are better than the others.

This is all to do with the way church life emerges, and describes the order in which they are used for that purpose.

Apostles bring the shape to the church through spiritual life and values which the teachers build on. Into that environment further works of power and miracles expands the domain of the church and tongues has its part in interaction with God and in revelation to the church (when there is interpretation) - but this happens on the foundation and ongoing development built through the other gifts. So to conclude:- a work is started by an apostle, history does not call many of these "apostles" for the term apostle tends to refer to the first shapers of the church – the disciples of Jesus – but there are many others down the centuries who were apostles. They can be described as a missionary or a founder of a monastic order or someone who pioneered a work of God which inspired others. St Bernard of Clairvaux, St Francis, St Patrick, St Columba, John Wesley, Luther, Basilea Schlink, John Wimber to name but a few. Apostles are far more frequent than we often think. In the fourfold anointing of Ephesians 4, it is reasonable to surmise that about a quarter of the total people of God move in this anointing.

Prophets also are part of this foundational process. Paul described the household of God as founded upon the "apostles and prophets" (Ephesians 2; 20)

Teachers then arise to affirm and make clear the revelation which has appeared in the apostolic and prophetic ministry and which forms the foundation of the work. This brings understanding for the many and so others can join and the work grows. Next in the list are those who do miracles. Some things occur which cause amazement. These are victories which bring the work onto a new level. It can be radical new works of the Spirit, or strange phenomena; or simply a work achieving something that no-one thought possible or would work. This is a necessary stage of a work development of God. Healing follows, which gifts can be in many different ways. Helps then form which look like creation of teams of infrastructure or projects. And then from those teams and helping comes leadership which establishes a work. It is then that the supernatural tongues can be released as we shall see from 1 Corinthians 14, leadership provides the important order which allows tongues (and other manifestations) to be profitable to the body of Christ and through this to the world.

Verses 29-31 reminds us that no one occupies every stage of a development of a work, but we are all responsible for seeking gifts which are the most helpful at the stage the church is at. I think that it is in this sense Paul means seek the "greater" gifts. Chapter 14 v1 about prophecy has often been linked to the end of Chapter 12 with chapter 13 as an intrusion on the teaching about gifts. This is a mistake. Chapter 14 Paul says we should seek prophecy because it builds up the church and contrasts this gift with tongues, but here Paul is talking about "best gifts" NKJV (plural) which is not just prophecy. The context is the formation of the church and therefore the explanation that fits best is that the "best" or "higher" or "greater" gifts are only greater when they are the best to build the church. The actual gifts that are best may vary from season to season. This also reminds us that it is feasible for the Christian to move in any gift that is required, but it will be a team effort because "are all apostles?" to "do all speak in tongues, do all interpret"v29 means it is never just one person who has all the gifts required.

Anointing and Spiritual Gifts

The Holy Spirit breathes through our spirits and can manifest spiritual gifts. The Holy Spirit in action is what "in Christ" all is about. We move in the anointing which is in fact far more than the manifestation of gifts through us at particular moments of our days that we live. We are in Christ all the time, we abide in Him and He is us. This all the time aspect to our spiritual experience in the Holy Spirit is called anointing. This is evidenced by the church when the Holy Spirit manifests through us for a specific purpose all the time. This is called anointing

Different Anointing's through which the gifts flow

Apostles and teachers are not in the list of primary gifts in the early verses of Chapter 12. They are part of the list of anointing in Ephesians 4:11 (KJV) "And he gave some, apostles (to build the church); and some, prophets (to speak revelation to the church); and some, evangelists (to make manifest the good news and bring people into faith); and some, pastors and teachers (to build frameworks of community providing care, teaching and understanding for those in the community and beyond)"

In this same passage Ephesians 4:7 (KJV) "But unto every one of us is given grace according to the measure of the gift of Christ." This means every Christians moves in one of these anointing.

Paul is defining the distinct spiritual environments within the Christ anointing that Christians will move in. They can exercise all the gifts outlined in 1 Corinthians but will do so within distinct and differing anointing.

The Holy Spirit is sent. He has a lot to do with focus and motivation and so the anointing differs in focus and motivations. I want to try to point out the differences so you can begin to assess the anointing under which you operate. None is any better than any other. They are just different.

Apostle The focus for apostle is to build foundations and to remain outside any framework that is built so it can be foundational for the next level.

Prophet. The prophet is focused on what God is saying and to speak that at foundational levels for church, people or current events in any strata of life whether it be church or family or business or national life.

Evangelist The evangelist has a people focus and is an encourager. He/she creates an environment where a pastor/teacher can operate. The good news is the shoots appearing above the soil, the signs of growth from the life laid down by the apostles and prophets.

Pastor/Teacher. This is the same anointing but one is directed towards care (pastoring) whilst the other is directed towards content (teaching). The pastor/teacher can now get to work. His focus is problem solving, making framework for care or teaching (depending on whether pastor or teacher). Without the pastor teacher there would be nothing tangible for the next generation to receive. The framework the teacher/pastor brings provides the opportunity for increasing work of the kingdom outlined in these verses.

What is your focus? We can understand our anointing by the normal focus we operate with. Apostles love to build, but flourish outside not inside the frameworks they build; prophets focus is what God is saying and do not respond to structures, the evangelist responds to people not structures and hates problems; the pastor teacher loves problems (for loves solving them) but is a framework builder to resolve problems or to bring increased strength, and is less people focused.

Whatever out anointing, because it is from the Spirit of Life, it will show up in every aspect of our life – not just in the "spiritual" aspect of it.

The anointing has nothing to do with the gifts you operate with. You can be a pastor teacher by anointing and move in the gift of revelation (e.g. John Stott) or an evangelist and move in the gift of prophecy (e.g. Hudson Taylor) or an apostle and move in the gift of worship leading (e.g. Wimber)

Ephesians 4 mentions how every Christian moves in one of four (or possibly five) anointing: Apostolic, Prophetic, Pastor/Teacher, Evangelistic. If we think the apostolic is restricted to the twelve or the 1st century we are not seeing the value of 25% of the church, and if we see this but restrict it to men only we are not allowing or recognising 12.5%. This is important for in Ephesians 4 it is the church which recognises the gifts (Acts 13:1). These anointing will manifest and bless the church the more the church recognises them.

Ephesians 4:7 But unto every one of us is given grace according to the measure of the gift of Christ.

Ephesians 4:8 he gave gifts unto men

Ephesians 4:11 and he gave some, apostles; and some, prophets; and some, evangelists; and some, pastors and teachers.

Ephesians 4:12 for the perfecting of the saints, for the work of the ministry, for the edifying of the body of Christ.

Chapters 13-14

1 Corinthians 13 The right environment for gifts to operate in is Love

Love is the characteristic of the new life from heaven. When we love one another we demonstrate says the apostle John that we have moved from death to life. In Jesus the old commandments love God with all heart soul mind and strength and love your neighbour as yourself become merged into a new command love one another. (John 13:34, I John 2:7) For now this new life is heaven on earth. The love of God has filled our hearts by the Holy Spirit. (Romans 5:5). We are in the love of God (Romans 8:35) and the love of God in us. This is the atmosphere of heaven, the presence of God in his people who dwells in love. This is what knits us together (Colossians 2; 2). We are no longer sinners looking at a smoking mountain called Sinai holding back in fear, but rather are in the throne room of the Lord drawn into the close relationship with Father Son and Holy Spirit. The Spirit lives and dwells in us but the relationship with the Holy Spirit has not changed with the Father and the Son, rather it is us who have changed; we have been transformed to be in as close a fellowship as the Son is with the Father.

This is not Paul cautioning those who move in spiritual gifts to make sure they hold back and not upset anyone. He is saying to those who operate in spiritual gifts to remember love provides the atmosphere through which the purpose of God can be furthered. In a vacuum a voice cannot pass for there is nothing for the sound waves to travel. Similarly without love, spiritual gifts are clanging gongs without meaning, and the one who exercises them nothing and is ineffective despite moving in the gifts.

1 Corinthians 14 Practical advice for operating in spiritual gifts when the church gathers

The main principle behind the teaching is the importance of building up the church. This is done through encouraging the faith and prophecy has a major role in this.

Greek text commentary: 1 Corinthians Chapter 12

> **1. Concerning spiritual gifts, brethren, I do not want you to be ignorant.**

Although Paul references spiritual gifts in other letters, this section is unique as Paul teaches specifically on the theme of spiritual gifts. The list he gives here is different from the one in Romans 12 or elsewhere. The reason for this list is that they are the primary gifts from which comes every other spiritual gift mentioned in the rest of the bible and others not mentioned in the bible as Jesus said we would do works that he would not do. This is explained further when we reach verse 8 onwards

> **2. Know that when you were pagans, you were led astray and carried away to the idols which are voiceless.**
>
> **3. Wherefore I reveal to you that no-one speaking in the Spirit of God says** "**Anathema Jesus**" *which means "No-one speaking in the Spirit of God curses Jesus (puts Jesus down). The Holy Spirit exalts Jesus as the Lord He is. This phrase could also mean those who claim to speak by the Spirit who say Jesus is bad for you (i.e. Jesus is a curse)* **and no-one is able to say** "**Lord Jesus**" *There may be people who say Lord Jesus in mockery of hypocrisy, but what Paul is talking about is the person who is moving in the supernatural and is genuine. When we say Jesus is Lord, we are saying Jesus is our master and our God.* **except by the Holy Spirit.** *The Holy Spirit is involved in such a response and it is not just us in our heart response. It is us plus the Holy Spirit. There is more interaction with the Holy Spirit than we often realise.*

Paul in these verses is addressing 3 common barriers to moving in Spiritual Gifts

We saw in 1:6 confidence is very important in moving in power. Paul addresses the three things that can undermine that confidence when it comes to moving in spiritual gits

- **How can I be sure this is not deception?** V1-3. The answer here is the obedience to truth; and this is shown by asking the question what is the attitude to Jesus and His Lordship.
- **"How can I be sure what I do really is the real thing"** v4-6 there are varieties of gifts but the same source; moreover the same gifts can look different and even if they look the same they will work differently Jesus healed all in a town on one day (Matthew 15:30, 31) and just one at Bethesda pool on another day. (John 5:3,5-8)
- **"People are getting upset. How can this be good"** Everyone can benefit but not everyone does v7 e.g. Jesus ministry amongst the Pharisees. The blessing of the spirit through spiritual gifts will be disputed and opposed.

---

4. There are diversities of gifts but the same spirit.

5. And diversities of ministries and the same Lord

6. and diversities of workings but the same God who works all things in all.

7. For to each one is given the manifestation of the Spirit for that which is advantageous *(there is no reference to "the common good" but the word means for the advantage which could be for the Kingdom, for self or for others)*

The list of spiritual gifts now is given.

These are the primary colours from which every expression of power by the Holy Spirit comes. For example exorcism is a combination of prophecy and healing, with possibly words of knowledge and wisdom, worship leading a combination of words of wisdom and prophecy and discernment, teaching a combination of words of knowledge and wisdom, of words. Ministry of healing is a combination of healing, faith and prophecy, prayer a combination of prophecy and faith. All gifts we see manifested in the church or world from the Spirit of God are a combination of these primary gifts. Paul is separating them out to show us their basic form because he wants us to not be ignorant about the gifts. This is not a seminar in how to move in these gifts. That is already assumed (1:4; 11:1, 4; 14:39) as the church was demonstrating these gifts daily, but he wanted them to recognise them for what they are. Paul's intention is that as a result they would be more effective in building up the church.

> **8. For one through the Spirit is given a word of wisdom, another, the word of knowledge according to the same Spirit,**
>
> **9. to someone else faith in the same Spirit,**
>
> **10. to another gifts of healings** *(Greek words are plural emphasising the diverse nature of the manifestations of healings. You can have a gift for healing one sort of illness but not another. We need to ask for further gifts of the spirit to move in other areas of healing.)* **In the one Spirit, to another works of powers, to another prophecy to another distinguishing of spirits, to someone else kinds** *tongues are of many kinds. They can seem like a human language but can also be of angelic tongue (13:1); can be spoken or sung (14:13,15)* **of tongues, to another the interpretation of tongues.**
>
> **11. All these things work in the one and same Spirit who apportions** *(divides what he has got)* **to each one according to what He purposes** *(The Spirit has a purpose behind the distribution of spiritual gifts*
>
> **12. Just as the body is one and has many parts, and all the parts of the body being many are one body, so also is Christ**

"Christ" means anointing and has a body which is made up of many parts. The many spiritual gifts and the diverse way they manifest even with differing results will nevertheless point to an oneness which is the body of Christ. The teaching here is first about anointing and second about church. The body is not brought about by organisation but by the unity of the spirit. The anointing of the Holy Spirit is manifest in all the activities of the spirit expressed through different people in different ways. This is what it means to be in Christ. The resultant body which links these various anointing together is the church. Real unity includes spiritual gifts and we must be wary of conclusions about the church from these verses if there is no inclusion of spiritual gifts.

13. For in one Spirit we all were baptised into one body *"The word "Baptism" means to immerse. We are immersed in the spirit. We walk in supernatural realms; we dwell in His presence and it is from this point we start to drink in the spirit to our own lives. When we abide in the Spirit, we can receive more within our lives as we drink of His Spirit (John 7:37),* **whether Jew or Greek; whether slave or free, and we all drank in the Spirit.**

14. For the body is not one part, but many. *Firstly Paul states that the identity of the body is not from just one part. In fact one part needs another part in order for the body to have all its functions*

15. If the foot should say "Because I am not a hand, I am not from the body, it is not a reason for it to be not from the body.

16. And if the ear should say because I am not an eye, I am not from the body; it is not a reason for it to be not from the body.

17. If the whole body were an eye, where would be the hearing? If it were all about hearing, where is the smelling?

18. But now God has put parts in each of them in the body as He wanted. *Secondly Paul states a body by its nature must be a combination of different parts*

19. But if everything was one part where would be the body.

20. But now there are many parts and one body.

21. It is not possible for the eye to say to the hand I have no need of you; or again for the head to say to the feet I have no need of you.

22. But rather more *(i.e. the opposite attitude is more accurate).*

Paul references 3 attitudes which could lie behind "I have no need of you"

a.   Recognise others as weaker compared to your strengths so think they are not needed for a task,

b.   See other parts which have seem unseemly so instead of recognising they need the covering of honour, reject them "I have no need of you" for you are unseemly – don't behave right, speak correctly, or know enough

c.   or do not look good which make us feel vulnerable/ ashamed

> **So those parts of the body which are considered weaker** *(e.g. stomach and other inner organs)* **it is imperative that they are there.**
>
> **23. And what we consider of the body to be more unseemly, we bestow much more honour.**

We clothe them, make them look good. This word translated "unseemly" is ατιμοτερα used here. The word ασχημονα is used in the next sentence and also means disgrace. Paul is saying two ways in which disgrace can be felt. In the first word it is to do with a lack of honour being given. Its cause is external. The second word is about disgrace coming because of the way it operates or looks. This is an inherent not external issue. The first word ατιμοτερα is more about the parts of our body that we make less of a fuss about their function but to which we give great attention (e.g. lungs, heart or eyes to name just a few) but there are other parts which are ασχημονα because they do give us shame if exposed. ασχημονα is talking about those parts which actively make us feel vulnerable. They are parts we do not talk about and are reluctant to put on open display, because to do so could bring shame.

> **And those shameful parts** *(Greek word in the Greek version of Old Testament LXX is in a sexual context Gen 34: 7; Deuteronomy 24:1)* **of us have much more decency.** *ευσχημονα. Is the word used here and is the exact opposite of ασχημονα.the word translated shameful. Paul says we make sure we are appropriate and decent with those parts we could easily find bring us shame. We are even careful to speak about these parts of the*

> body. We ensure they are protected and have concern when they are exposed, a concern we do not have with other parts of our body when they are exposed. **Those parts which have decency have no need (to be given decency),**
>
> **24. But God has blended** (verb literally means mix together) **the body together giving honour to the part lacking it most**
>
> **25. in order that there be no division in the body but that the parts may have the same care for one another.**

Honour provides the opportunity for no division and allows everyone to feel cared for. Division comes where there is lack of honour.

The first commandment to promise life of the famous 10 commandments (Exodus 20) is the commandment to honour father and mother (Ephesians 6:2). It has a promise of life because honour is the way we align to God's purpose and so receive life. Lack of honour stops the flow of life to that gift/ soul, and without nurture, it withers and then dies. Dry bones are dead bones and they become divided

> **26. And if one part suffers, every part suffers. If a part is glorified every part rejoices together.**
>
> **27. You are the body of Christ, and an (individual) part of the parts (which make up the body).** *The body exists through the many parts being one (see verse 19). If there were no different roles in the church there would be no church; and if there was no love/unity there would be no church either. The different roles are about church ministry and activity whereas the love/unity is all about the church life.*
>
> **28. God has put these (parts) in the church first apostles, second prophets, third teachers, then workers of power,** *the Greek seems to indicate that Paul has a fourfold foundation followed by other parts of the body following on the back of this fourfold foundation* **then gifts of healing, people who do helpful deeds, leaders** *This word is the word for steersman on a boat. It is sometimes translated*

administrator, but leader is a better translation because the leader steers what they lead. This could be as an administrator, but it could also be as a pastor or as an inspirer/vision caster, **and kinds of tongues.**

29. Not all are apostles, not all prophets, not all are teachers not all are workers of power

30. not all have gifts of healing, not all speak in tongues. Not all interpret.

31. Earnestly desire the greater gifts. *The verb used here Paul repeats in later verses (14:1; 12) as the right approach towards spiritual gifts. Paul is saying here that this right approach which the Corinthians have already (14:12), should be directed towards the "greater gifts".*

In general these are gifts which are greater because they are more effective in extending the kingdom. In such a context some spiritual gifts can be greater in two senses. Firstly from the many different gifts, pursue the gifts which have the greater help in the church. This theme Paul returns to in chapter 14 where the gift of prophecy or interpretation rather than tongues is to be earnestly desired so the church can have understanding and thus be built up. But in these verses there is no such reference to prophecy as a greater gift than tongues, and prophecy is not described as "first" but apostleship is. It would also be mistaken to draw the conclusion that desiring the greater gifts means to aim at apostolic anointing because he is talking about "gifts" listed in 1 Corinthians 12:4-7 where he uses the same word as here and he has also said that not all will manifest a particular gift or anointing, so he cannot be then saying to the Corinthians to all aim at being apostles. In the context of this verse where spiritual gifts form the church, Paul is saying to earnestly desire the gifts which will help the church at the time, and are in that sense "greater".

Secondly it can also be greater not because it primarily helps the church more at the stage it is at but because it is further extends the kingdom power and authority. In other words Paul is saying "Whatever gift you move in, earnestly desire to do more with it". They are greater in that they do more. For example if you have a gift of healing press in so you do more with it – for example from healing headaches to healing depression or schizophrenia; if you have a gift of words of knowledge sometimes, use it more frequently; if prophesying one to one; do it with more people at once. In other words seek for greater power in the gifts you have.

Paul is now writing to show a way that is even better in forming the church. He wants to outline the command to earnestly desire spiritual gifts and to pursue love (14:1) Chapter 13 is all about pursuing love.

Without spiritual gifts there are no ministries of the body of Christ to make it manifest; but there is also no manifestation of the body of Christ without the unity of the body. Love holds everything together and as such forms the life of the body of Christ.

Spiritual gifts are not made irrelevant by the more excellent way, but that the way of love exceeds in importance the gifts however great the gifts may be in effectiveness.

And still I will show you a more excellent way

The Greek words used here mean a way that is beyond limit in every way. 1 John also talks about love in terms of eternal life – a life without boundaries. This is the characteristic of the new life in Christ.

This introduces the chapter about love. In Ephesians 3:17-19 Paul describes knowing what is the breadth and length and height and depth and to know the love of God which surpasses knowledge. We can be rooted and grounded in love from where we discover more and more. Revelation and relationship go together. We were never intended to have a knowledge which has no implications for our relationship with God. Learning science should lead us to worship the creator, learning a language should lead us to love others more and acknowledge the breadth of the love of God. Learning our history also should lead us to the Lord of history. Unfortunately since the dawn of humankind we have chosen independent knowledge of good and evil and this has brought a division between us and God. But in moving in the love of God we start to make the connections again. Real knowledge is not found in the classroom but in the place of prayer. Real knowledge brings life to us and our relationship with God because this is not the old knowledge of good and evil but that which comes from the tree of life. We do not reject classroom knowledge but we have discovered something greater. At the tree of life we learn about God's love for us and we learn to love God. Because of our love for God, we honour our teachers, and learn much as Solomon learnt much about the world but we also seek God and walk in humility and as we do we learn more and more.

This new way is all about love. As the many parts form the body, it is no surprise to see that which applies centrally to the body (love). God's love is poured into our hearts by the Holy Spirit (Romans 5) so the characteristic of anointing is love.

Love also allows us to be together. The composite parts/ministries are of greater significance than any one part working better or being greater. The anointing which is the life comes from the body as whole not just one individual part. Love therefore is the key! It is in the togetherness that God's anointing flows (Psalm 133)

Chapter 13

Chapter 13 is not an interjected caveat in his teaching on spiritual gifts giving the message to hold back on the use of spiritual gifts in favour of love. It is rather saying pursue with all your effort on developing the gifts you have, and this will have a positive effect on the church but also recognise that love is the way to build the church. Gifts work best within the atmosphere of heaven which is where the presence of God abides in fullness. That presence has the characteristics of God embedded within and without. This is the very nature of God. This is described in the bible as the love of God.

> **1. If I speak with tongues of men and of angels but I have not love, I become a clanging gong or tinkling cymbal** *(sounds which have no meaning but which disturb according to the amount of sound (noisy Nχων) or to the pitch of the sound (shrill αλαλαζον).Love makes what we say profitable.*
>
> **2. If I have a prophecy and I know all mysteries and all that is known, and if I have all faith so as to move mountains, but I have not love I am nothing.** *Spiritual gifts can be present in your life but inside you can be empty, feel unrewarded and ignored, for it is love which attracts these precious responses which feed the identity of the soul.*
>
> **3. And if I give away all my possessions bit by bit (to do good)** *The verb is related to the word for a small piece and means to hand out bit by bit. The emphasis is therefore not on the giving away of possessions per se but the act of being intentional to help another.* **and if I hand over my body so I am burnt, but I have no love, I profit nothing.**

Both selling possessions to help or being burnt either in rescuing another or in the cause of duty are acts of great sacrifice for the benefit (presumably) of another. But if there is no love but only obligation or another motive there will be no benefit to the person. If there is no love the echo of a job well done never returns to bless through relationship where you are loved by another or valued by those around you. This is because there is no track of love along which it can travel. The great sacrifice reaps no reward in their life experience where there is no love.

The person who sacrifices much is not necessarily possessing love despite the good deeds. Such a person who tried to do good, even involving damage to themselves, but has no love, does much for little or no increase. This is true for vicars in churches, parents in families, and government leaders in nations. It is a global principle. We need love.

---

4. Love is long suffering, love is kind *(Greek word here means kind but also good, generous, upright).*

"Long suffering" is the necessary discipline to allow goodness to emerge. Love which causes us to be long suffering will show itself in goodness (kind). Love which causes us to be kind/good will show itself in long suffering. Love is the unseen link between the two and when the two are there, love is seen.

This verse defines love. Love is not created in a vacuum. It shows itself relationally. Long suffering and goodness (kind) are relational words. You cannot show these traits without others being there with you. How we behave with one another will show up love or lovelessness. Goodness is about being kind, relating appropriately or generously to our neighbour

In the next sentences Paul then begins to show what love is not. Again in a relational context (e.g. jealousy etc.)

It is not jealous, Love does not vaunt itself, is not puffed up,

5. does not bring shame, *(act disgracefully, would be a fair translation of this, but at root this verb means to bring suffering because of something disgraceful, or indecent, and it is the same verb used in 1 Corinthians 7:36. I have therefore translated it in such a way it can be the same meaning in both verses. This verse has significance for the teaching of 1 Corinthians 11:4 and 14:35)* **does not seek things for self, is not provoked, does not consider what is evil,** *This has massive implications. Considering what is pure and lovely (Philippians 4:8), not what is wrong is a mark of love. Church people who love do not talk about the negatives of their church or others and*

---

think they are being godly or responsible need to rethink. Love looks at the positives; it does not focus on what the enemy is doing but on what God is doing. Jesus did the same "I only do what I see the father doing" (John 5:19).

6. it does not rejoice where there is *(επι plus dative)* **injustice** *(αδικια. δικη is punishment or justice and αδικια means without justice,)* **but rejoices with the truth.**

The Greek word rejoice is slightly different from the basic word rejoice used in the first part of the verse re. Injustice. This time the verb rejoice is συγχαιρει which means to rejoice with. It is used like this in the parables of Jesus in Luke 15 where the shepherd who finds the lost sheep and the woman who finds the lost coin says to their friends and neighbours to rejoice with them. Here Paul is saying they are to rejoice with the truth. Truth is already rejoicing as the shepherd and woman were in the parable. You are being asked to rejoice with the truth. When you access God's truth, you should also access His joy. Rejoicing is not about winning or the defeat of our enemies but the vindication of the truth

Love enables us to respond in this way when we see God's truth. Without love we do not enter into joy, but into our prison of fear and doubt or into the law court of pride or legality. The joy of the Lord is present wherever the truth of the Lord is. Love enables us to access this!

7. Covers all things *(Greek word στεγει means "to cover" in the sense of confidentiality covers another or "enduring" in the sense a stiff upper lip covers desires to hit back or accuse or complain),* **believes all things, hopes all things, endures** *(in the sense of being willing to remain under the pressure or circumstances)* **all things.**

8. Love never falls*. it remains standing whatever the pressure. This leads onto the contrast of spiritual gifts which does not have the same enduring quality as love)* **Whether prophecy, they will be irrelevant** *The verb translated made irrelevant in these verses at root means to be made ineffective or powerless or abolished. The nearest meaning in this context in*

English is being made irrelevant. **or tongues they will cease; or knowledge it will be irrelevant.** *Paul explains why he has said this about prophecy and knowledge*

9. For we know in part and we prophesy in part.

10. When the complete has come, that which is in part will be irrelevant.

11. When I was an infant, *(the Greek word νηπιος sounds similar and has a similar meaning to the English "little nipper")*

I spoke as an infant, I thought as an infant, I reasoned as an infant. When I became a man I made the things of infancy irrelevant.

12. For we see now as through a mirror indistinctly *(word used in the Old Testament of riddles and unclear revelation - called dark sayings)* **but then face to face.**

This has been thought of to refer to heaven, but there is no direct reference to heaven. The theme is about love as the more excellent way (than purely spiritual gifts). Verse 9 is contrasting prophecy (and spiritual gifts) with the reality of the love of God. When perfect love is there it is described in verse 10 as "complete". In the love of God you see as a man, in contrast to however mature we are as a prophet, we can only see as an infant unless the love of God invades our world.

Now I recognise in part then I will know completely through and through *(verb επιγνωσομαι emphasises the completeness of the knowing)* **even as I am completely known through and through.** *Paul knows he and the Corinthian church have not yet reached perfect love, but when they do they will know as they are known.*

13. Now remains Faith Hope Love these three, but the greatest of these is love.

Everything changes when the complete comes except faith hope and love. Spiritual gifts are in part pointing forward to the complete picture. It is not "faith that vanishes into sight" to quote the old hymn but "prophecy which vanishes into sight". Faith defines the trust which undergirds our relationship with God and one another and that faith stays into eternity. Hope also "does not vanish in delight" but continues. Life does not end when the complete comes. There are future things to look forward to in heaven. Life in heaven is not sitting on a cloud just looking backwards over our life. There is a new heaven and a new earth. There is delight of further discovery, of friendships, of adventure, with fresh accomplishments to achieve, and promises to be even more fulfilled. Hope is an essential part of living and this continues into eternal life.

Paul mentions faith hope and love but not joy although as we have seen joy is mentioned alongside faith and hope when describing aspects of love (verses 6, 7). Paul in Romans 14:17 does have a trio of words like here with joy in them and these are joy, peace and righteousness in the Holy Spirit. The reason it is just faith, hope and love mentioned here and not joy is that they come about differently from joy. Faith hope and Love need a relational context whereas Joy does not. Joy, peace and righteousness come from inner choices within our relationship with the Lord and are created outside social contexts. This is not the same for faith, hope and love. There is no faith without relationship. Faith comes by hearing and hearing by the word of God and is expressed in a relational context for it is all about trust. There is no real relationship without trust at some level, and there is no trust possible without relationship. Hope is the same. You cannot have a fulfilling relationship without hope, but you cannot have hope without relationship. Perhaps some of you remember some of the images of hopelessness on the faces of orphans without real human contact in Romanian orphanages and other places, and contrast the camaraderie and togetherness in war camps which kept hope alive amongst brutal imprisonment. Hope is about possibilities and goals and is birthed in a relationship environment. Where there is poor relationship hopelessness comes. Hope comes on the encouragement of others. Love also is not created away from social contexts.

Paul started by saying how spiritual gifts come from what is in part and that the more excellent way is putting our main focus on what is with the whole.

We cannot leave this chapter without making just one more observation. The body of Christ manifest amongst believers is not shown by spiritual gifts though they will and should be present. But no one gift defines the body (just as one member does not equal the body. The foot is only part of the body not the whole body). The body however must display faith, hope and love for these remain when what is in part ceases. These are the relationship constants which must define the body of |Christ and help us find our place within this body.

Hope is all about belonging, faith is all about believing and love is all about behaving.(It is not proud, acts kindly etc.). Within this trio we have the secret of church growth.

First Belong, then Believe then Behave. The story of Zacchaeus might help us here. Jesus first comes and says I want to come to your house for tea (welcome of belonging), then Zacchaeus start to believe which then shows itself in behaviour when he says he will give away some of his wealth to the poor and defrauded and Jesus then states salvation has therefore come to this house (Luke 19). "But the greatest of these is love" because this lies over and breathes through everything.

Belonging has to be without any preconditions or love is not real love. Belonging is never what God intended if It has a precondition of either believing or behaving. Real love has no such preconditions.

Some Churches in UK especially in the 1950s could be described as BEHAVE BELONG BELIEVE. Many who attended felt they had to dress in a certain way or speak in an agreeable way to belong. If they believed in God it was fine as long as they behaved and belonged. There were other churches with the message of BELIEVE then BELONG and BEHAVE The 1960s evangelical churches especially post Billy Graham's crusades to the UK could be described as such. They stressed the need to believe, to join up in classes before being allowed to join the church. Believe to belong .Behaving was seen as good but not as essential as believing. Both these approaches put barriers between the church and the community and has affected the ability of the church to relate to the real people in this land, for it hindered the love of God being made known through the church. Millions today do not go to church because they feel they cannot belong. Why do they think that? Because they have been taught by the church over the years that they cannot belong unless they behave or unless they believe. Those who do not behave or those who do not believe are excluded. But Jesus does not put the same constraints on those he meets. Those who followed Jesus had the opportunity to grow in faith and behave (bring the kingdom). BELONG BELIEVE BEHAVE.

Belonging is the start so connections are made and then blessing are passed through those connections. Belief then starts to emerge and changes in behaviour comes gradually as the person hears from God and changes his lifestyle accordingly. Church leaders should encourage belonging and demonstrate the kingdom so faith can grow and model how to live so that others can hear from God for themselves and behave in ways that does not disappoint God.

Chapter 14

1. Follow love. Earnestly desire spiritual gifts *we are to earnestly desire the gifts (same verb used at the end of chapter 12) but to pursue love. Love is something we follow, love dictates our behaviour; love is what we are led by and what we choose; spiritual gifts, however, are what we have zeal for, and for which desire. This is different from the message we have received in a church life which has denied spiritual gifts. We are told to be zealous and desire love; whereas Paul says be zealous for spiritual gifts. Our inner desires should be for spiritual gifts not love. In such a context our sober choices and paths we adopt and ways we behave are dictated by love. This is what Paul means by pursue love.* **especially that you may prophesy.**

2. For he who speaks in a tongue does not speak to men, but to God. No-one hears, *ακουω the verb to hear used here is about hearing with the heart as well as the ears. Hearing with the heart is what Jesus refers to when he says "he who has ears to hear let him hear" (Mark 4:23) by which he means if you can hear me, hear the significance of what I am saying. As Jesus references in Matthew 13; 13 "hearing and not hearing". Paul is talking about not hearing in the sense of seeing the significance of, or understanding the spoken gift of tongues so the utterances remain mysteries hidden from our understanding* **for he speaks mysteries in his spirit.**

3. But he who prophesies to men, speaks edification *the prophecy builds us up making us stronger in our faith or confidence, (e.g. see Daniel 10:19 Daniel's testimony of the effect of prophecy in this case through an angel).* **and encouragement** *This is encouragement may be a stirring to action as for example the prophetess Deborah to Barak (Judges 4:6, 7) or encouragement through recognising God is with us in a situation. The word means being called alongside. We discover through prophecy that He stands with us and knows what has or is happening.(e.g. As with the prophet Azariah to king Asa in 2 Chronicles 15:7)*

and comfort. *Prophecy also brings comfort through consolation speaking tenderly, ministering grace, understanding the situation and calming the soul (e.g. Isaiah 37:33-35, Haggai 1:13, 14).*

4. He who speaks in a tongue edifies himself, but he who prophesies edifies the church.

5. I want all of you to speak in tongues, but especially in order that you should prophesy *Paul is not saying that only those who speak in tongues can prophesy, for there were many prophets in the old testament for example who never spoke in tongues. What Paul is saying is that if you speak in tongues you will develop your intimacy with God and you will exercise faith when launching into the experience of tongues with the accompanying revelation of vision or feelings. Both the intimacy with God and exercise of faith should equip you to begin to prophesy. He wants the tongue speakers to be prophets also for the benefit of the church.* **He who prophesies is greater than he who speaks in tongues, unless it is interpreted in order that the church might receive edification.**

6. But now, brethren, if I come to you speaking in tongues what shall I benefit you unless I shall speak to you either in revelation or in knowledge or in prophecy or in teaching *(In this verse Paul shows the four different ways the church is edified – 1. what is revealed to the spirit, 2. known to the soul 3. prophesied through spiritual gift or 4. taught after study or experience).*

7. Likewise a lifeless instruments which give sound (as for example) from a pipe or a harp. If there is not a distinction given to the sounds how can it known whether it is pipes being piped or a harp being strummed. *Distinctions in the sounds show up what source it is. Knowing the source also helps in hearing what response to make. A trumpet sound in war has one significance (battle orders) and the harp another.*

> **8. And if a trumpet gives an unclear sound who will prepare for war.** *Clarity imparted through revelation or knowledge or prophecy or teaching will also point forward to the required action.*

It is one thing to recognise the source; the actual content from that source is also important. If that is clear there is action. It is worth noting that when you recognise the actual message you will also recognise the gift that is bringing that message.

> **9. You also are (in the same position as this) through a tongue if you do not give an easily recognizable word** *Paul knows that some tongues may be recognisable in that it might be in a language known to someone in the church but most will not be.* **how can it be understood what you are saying? You will be speaking to the air.**

> **10. There are, as one finds in life** *(Greek ει Τυχοι means as may happen)* **so many types of sound in the world and nothing is without sound.** *"Sound" is the original Greek meaning of the words and is the most likely meaning here. Nothing is not referring to the speaker for it is neuter but to a general fact that nothing is without sound. The word can mean "language". Language is the primary focus for Paul here in verse 11 where he is talking about sounds spoken between people which is a language, but here in verse 10 it is more general. This fits in with the examples of music as sounds in verse 7 & 8.*

We can reflect that all sounds have significance wherever you are. From the sound of wind through trees or of sea on seashore or of the buzzing of wings of a bee to the cry of a baby and to the notes which make up music and language. Everything in creation has a sound.

> **11. If I do not know the significance** *(Greek word is "power ", and is about knowing the impact of what is said by understanding its meaning or relevance)*
>
> **of the language (used), I will be a foreigner to the one who**

speaks *Because Paul's response will not be appropriate (because he lacks understanding) there is no relationship. Understanding brings the opportunity for proper responses upon which relationships are formed and grow; when there is no such response we remain alienated from each other),* **and when he speaks he will be a foreigner to me** *The importance of this second clause is to show that it is the same attitude for both. There is little connection, a feeling of distance and not belonging for both parties. This comes about by talking unintelligible talk. How important it is that the church and the Christian speaks in such a way those who hear can understand what is being said. If it is unintelligible, it creates a relationship distance.*

12. So also you, since there is (among you) an earnest desire for spiritual things *the Corinthians have the right approach to spiritual gifts. The same verb as is used at the end of chapter 12 and beginning of chapter 14 where Paul encourages the Corinthians to desire spiritual gifts. This means,* **seek for the building up of the church in order that you may abound.** *The building up of the church is not so the church may abound but so "you may abound". The well-being of the church benefits everyone. Sometimes those who have sought spiritual things have left or weakened the church rather than built it up. This has not benefited anyone not even themselves. Building up the church is the way that all can be blessed. Some Christians do not make any significant contribution to the strengthening of the church in the nation or their locality and therefore their blessing is limited. Paul makes the point here to belong to the church is to be a blessing.*

13. Also he who speaks in a tongue should pray to interpret *The reminder here is that we grow in spiritual gifts by asking for them, rather than waiting to see what God might give us. Prayer is the way to ask and get spiritual gifts*

14. If I pray in a tongue, my spirit prays but my mind is unfruitful.

15. What then? I should pray in my spirit and I should pray also in my mind. I sing in the spirit but I also sing with my mind.

16. Since whenever you bless in the spirit, he who fills up the place of a person who is uninstructed *Ιδιοτης is used in classical Greek of the private soldier who is not privy to the strategic decisions of battle etc. Paul uses the word here to mean those who are out of the loop and are not in a position to know what is being said because there is no prophecy or interpretation* **how can he say the Amen upon your thanksgiving** *tongues can be expression of thanks or praise or blessing. All these words are meant by the Greek word used here and translated thanksgiving.* **since he does not know what you are saying.**

17. For you may give a great thanksgiving, but the other person is not built up.

18. I thank God, I speak more in tongues than you all,

19. but in the church I want to speak five words with my mind in order that I may instruct others than ten thousand words in a tongue.

20. Do not be children in your minds.

Paul explains what he means. In their character be childlike but in their minds be mature. He does not want people to lose their innocence. When this happens it affects our well-being. Life becomes empty for "know it all's outside their own world because relationship, intimacy and trust with others is negatively affected. Knowing evil spoils innocence, but innocence is not the same as foolishness. Paul also wants them to be childlike but not think like a child; not to be naïve in their mind like a child might be: i.e. unaware of possible dangers or undercover motives of others. He wants them mature so they cannot be conned, led astray or foolish in their relationships and wide in their ordering of their homes or lives.

But be childlike with evil, but be grown up (mature) in your thinking.

Paul is now bringing new revelation to their thinking. He is moving from the consequences of not being able to understand tongues and the benefits therefore of prophecy which build up the church to the spiritual effects of tongues and the spiritual effect of prophecy to those who are unbelievers. He illustrates his point first from scripture and then from a story of what can happen in church.

---

21. In the law it is written that "in other tongues and in lips of others I will speak to this people and they still will not pay attention to me says the Lord".

22. So that tongues are a sign not for the believing but for the unbelieving. Prophecy is not for the unbelieving but for the believing.

At first sight this passage can seem confusing. If prophecy is a sign for believers not for unbelievers, why does Paul then give an example of prophecy benefiting an unbeliever (verse 24), and if tongues are a sign for unbelievers why give an example of unbelievers not benefiting at all from tongues (verse 23). The answer is in the meaning of sign which shows up something. Tongues are a sign for unbelievers because they show up unbelief –"will they not think you are manic "verse 23. Prophecy likewise shows up faith "he proclaims that God is among you" verse 24.

---

23. If the whole church comes together at the same time and all speak in tongues, and uninformed people who are unbelievers come to the church, will they not say that you are manic.

24. But if all prophesy *Paul has rules later in this chapter for how all in the church congregation can prophesy in order. This could be the whole church gathered not just a few recognised prophets.*

and someone who does not believe and is uninstructed comes in, he is condemned by all, he is judged by all

25. and the hidden things of his heart are made known. And so falling on his face he worships God proclaiming that God is amongst you.

At first it might be strange to think of an unbeliever being condemned and judged in a church when God said to his disciples not to judge or condemn (Luke 6:37) But Paul is not saying about the church people's attitude to the unbeliever, but how the unbeliever feels in the church when prophecy is at work in the church. Prophecy is manifest through them all, so everyone has a part to play in the impact on the unbeliever – hence "by all" in verse 24.

Paul mentions three things occur when prophecy is in the church which results in the unbeliever worshipping God and stating God is amongst them. He mentions (a) inner conviction (that is what Paul refers to by "condemned"). The unbeliever feels he is not good enough; and he sees the people as better than he is (b) he also experiences God's view on his choices, beliefs and actions (that is what Paul means by judged) he might recognise his sin as a result. (c) There are direct words of knowledge about what is on his heart that others would not know. All this causes him to proclaim the statement of faith "God is among you". Prophecy evokes faith. This is in contrast to tongues which does not encourage faith to surface but rather unbelief. This is what Paul refers to when he says "prophecy is for the believing and tongues for the unbelieving".

---

26. What is it brethren whenever you come together, each has a psalm has a teaching has a revelation has a tongue has an interpretation. Let all things be for building up.

This is the key principle which he is now going to apply to both tongues and prophecy in their management within the gathering. The same "rules" apply to both. There are no more than two or three manifestations before a reaction in the body. In the case of tongues the looking to interpretation within the gathering; in the case of prophecy an evaluation from the body. The tongue speaker keeps silent if no interpreter, the prophet if there is someone else with more revelation. In both cases they are submitting their gift to the principle that the church is to be built up.

---

27. If someone speaks in a tongue twice or at most three times and in turn and let someone interpret.

28. If there is no-one who interprets. Let him be silent in the church, let him speak to himself and to God.

29. But two or three prophets may speak and the rest judge

I think that "rest" refers to the rest of the gathered community. It is not that the other prophets sit back and judge their brother's prophecy as good, bad or indifferent. It is rather the body respond to what they recognise is from God so they are all built up. People in the church speak out what they felt was right or helpful. This is not about testing the prophetic word as much as making clear what God is saying so there is a solid building up of faith and lives.

30. If something else has been revealed to someone sitting down, the first should keep silent.

31. For it is possible for all to prophecy one at a time in order that they may be instructed and all may be encouraged

32. and the spirits of the prophets are subject to the prophets *these verses reflect the difference between revelation and prophecy. Prophets can choose and control what they prophesy whereas revelation which comes unexpectedly- note "one sitting down" in verse 30- needs speaking out immediately or it can be lost.*

So....The reason Paul writes verse 30-31 is not so that prophecy is rightly evaluated. The primary reason is so revelation can be heard in the church. If it were for right evaluation of prophecy by others, there would be no need for verse 30 about revelation. Revelation comes in a feeling or a thought or an insight or a vision, and can be easily lost. It needs to be given straight away. Because a prophetic word is different and can be given out anytime at the prophet's choosing, they give way to allow the revelation. This is possible because prophecy is under the control of the prophet.

33. For God is not without a way of life *(καταστασις means character, state of being or a way of life). The Greek says God is not without these characteristics.*

This is not completely unconnected with what has preceded because he returns to the teaching of prophecy in v 37 "If anyone considers prophecy to be spiritual, let him recognise what I have written to you. We also cannot ignore the summary of the chapter in v39, 40 which makes no direct reference to women so I conclude this command for women keeping silence is within a teaching about prophecy in the gathered church. It does not, of course, refer to the women who want to prophesy as a command by Paul for them to be silent and that it is shameful for them to speak in church would contradict all that Paul said in Chapter 11 about how women should prophesy under a covering. No this must refer to the way the rest of the assembly should behave after the prophetic word has been given. It is to do with the discussion/ response to that word in terms of either interpretation or application.

It does not refer to inappropriate content in speaking in church. If it were so, why just the women and not the men? Also the Greek word λαλεω has been used throughout the letter without any reference to inappropriate content. Paul's command here to be silent is not linked to content but timing. (See verse 35 "ask their own husbands at home"). You recall Paul describes in v29 that the rest of the church are invited after 2 or 3 prophetic words to make comments or ask questions about what they have heard to help process what they are hearing. (To assume this is the leadership testing the prophetic word is to ignore the Greek text which says "the rest"). This general term used

255

without any accompanying detail does not refer to the prophets but rather the assembled church who test the prophetic word. It is with regard to the response to the prophetic word that Paul is seeking to put some order down providing peace so that the direction of the gathering and the receiving of God's truth is not distracted by additional questions which could be done outside the meeting (at home).

Just as tongue speakers keep silent if there is no interpreter present or the prophet keeps silent to allow another to speak or to allow response from the church meeting, so women also have a role to keep quiet to allow God's peace and order to be maintained. In such a context the men would be speaking or evaluating what was heard at the time. The command for women to be silent is at this time. It is worth pointing out in this context that Paul in the second half of verse 34 and in the second half of verse 35 seems to point back to the teaching about shame he was covering in the first part of chapter 11. Paul does say in verse 37 that this is a command from the Lord and so we must reject that this teaching is cultural relevant only to Paul's time in Corinth.

Paul is expecting church meetings when there is multiple input with congregational response. This is God's plan for all churches everywhere. The rediscovery of the prophetic gift by the church will lead to these characteristics becoming normal. These verses remind us of the lengths to which we need to go to release the spiritual gifts in the church meetings and at the same time to preserve peace.

The main point is that we should be providing an environment where contributions are given and response happens from the people in an orderly way and that all aim to build the church up.

For it is not permitted (or entrusted) for them to speak but they are to be under authority just as even the law says.

35. If they want to learn, they should ask their own husbands at home. For it is shameful *This is the same word used when women act inappropriately as chapter 11. There is a negative effect on the church* **for a woman to speak in church.**

This is not a leadership manual for leaders but a letter to the whole church. This then accounts for the following verse 36 which encourages the person to remember they are not the origin of the word (God and the prophet is!) and they are not only one who has heard the word. They do not have to own the word or be responsible for it. Others can ask the questions. The woman aims to preserve the peace and avoid shame coming on others.

36. Is it from you the word of the Lord has come? *The context is again affirmed that this is all about the response to the prophecy which the woman has heard so she is not God or the prophet. She bears no responsibility for it. She is concerned instead for God's way of operating for her and remain silent.* **Or has it reached only to you?** *It may be that others may cover what she has been thinking, so she can still remain silent.*

37. If someone thinks he is a prophet or spiritual, let him recognise what I have written to you, that it is a command of the Lord.

38. If anyone does not understand it, let him continue to be ignorant. *Paul states this is a command from the Lord (not a passing cultural norm) He is also telling his readers not to try to make people understand this. The reason is because as the earlier verse states it is perceived in the spirit. Arguing about it won't help.*

Certainly not understanding what Paul is fully getting at here regarding women being silent is true for us in the West and the modern society where we welcome women taking their place as equal citizens, rejoicing at the changes in society where women are now able to vote and own bank accounts and where women can make a proper contribution to society as they are. This passage is not teaching about the position of women in society or in the church in general. Paul is talking about when there is a manifestation of spiritual power and prophecy.

Within these verses is a command for the women and church. The anointing is the tree of life, the Holy Spirit relationally present in the church and the anointing is increased by women self -regulating themselves.

Now he summarises his main points. Pursue prophecy; don't stop speaking in tongues is his first area where he has established the priority is prophecy because it builds up the church. Then also, the way of peace is to be a reference point to working through the manifestation of spiritual gifts in the church.

39. Therefore my brethren, you should pursue prophecy and do not forbid (hinder) speaking in tongues. Let all things be done peacefully and in order

Ephesus in Revival

The prayer meeting had finished and the team were going back to their hosts. This was the last time everyone in the church that met in Aquila's house and the Corinthian delegation would meet together before they sailed. Erastus and Timothy left the room in deep conversation about Corinth and the trip before them. Left in the room were Aquila and Aristarchus. These were experienced mission team members but not part of the team that would be leaving tomorrow. They stayed behind to help rearrange the room. Sosthenes had been here but he had gone with Stephanas and Fortunatus to prepare for their journey homewards to Corinth. Earlier in the evening Stephanas had prayed for Ephesus and Asia, and this caused Aristarchus to ask Paul a question "What have you felt about staying behind in Ephesus whilst the others leave? Paul had intended leaving in a few weeks for Corinth and Macedonia, but it had been postponed because of new possibilities in the province of Asia for the gospel. His time in prison had opened further links through the military, and through them to some of Caesar's family. Paul recognised God had opened a door for the gospel and so had felt he should stay for a bit longer. He had told Aristarchus some days ago, and Aristarchus had managed to change his schedule so he anticipated being able to accompany Paul to Macedonia with Gaius. Paul said he hoped to see those leaving tomorrow later in the year and for the moment wanted to make the most of the opportunities present in Asia. Together they put the room back in order and the others left the house leaving Paul on his own in the room. He sat down and began to process in his mind some of the events of his time in Ephesus. Into his mind flooded conflicting thoughts and memories; for it had been the best of times and the worst of times.

When he had arrived he had found the local synagogue and also found some believers. The believers were small in number and because of Apollos' earlier influence had only been baptised in the baptism of John the Baptist and did not know anything of the Holy Spirit. Paul had therefore baptised them in the name of Jesus and the Holy Spirit had then come in power. This was the start of miracles, healings and wonders which had accompanied him throughout his stay. During this time there had been a demonstration of the kingdom to a greater extent than anywhere else he had ever been with remarkable miracles so far unheard of anywhere else in the world.

The first three months of his stay in Ephesus had been wonderful. He had been a blessing to the existing church and had been received into the local synagogue which was at that point closely linked to the church. But after the first few months of church growth and rapid development, the novelty factor wore off, and some in the synagogue opposed him. False ideologies in religion and in culture since then had constantly dogged his steps throughout his stay and there had been many a battle to fight in prayer.

Paul recalled in an instant some of the things that had happened to him. Two events remained deep in his thoughts whilst others passed quickly. These were the rejection and expulsion from the synagogue early in his stay and also the recent imprisonment he had shared with Aristarchus during the winter that had just passed had been so hard he had despaired of life. These two events he recalled because they affected his past and present life in Ephesus. The expulsion from the synagogue had brought him enemies, some of whom had remained constant thorns in his side – not least Alexander the coppersmith who was part of the synagogue and business community in the city. Ephesus was a proud city not afraid to use the law against so called troublemakers, but fortunately the Jews were a minority and unable to wield any influence to attack Paul, but the anger of some still simmered.

For about two years after leaving the synagogue Paul had taught each day in the school of Tyrannus without too much trouble but then a few months ago there had been an open move of repentance on the part of those involved in the occult. Expensive documents containing occult rituals, recipes and spells for healing and cursing, which in many cases were family heirlooms passed down from one generation to another, had been publicly burnt in the market place. This had created quite a stir particularly amongst some of the local families but also amongst those who profited from the various religious practices which Paul opposed. They had turned against Paul and his companions and used their influence to put Paul with some of his friends in prison. Paul had not known what his fate might be and there was the real prospect of execution in the arena.

Paul had never found life in Ephesus easy, and his time in the fortified prison near the harbour was indeed a trial. The immediate effect of his imprisonment was the ending of the meetings in the hall of Tyrannus. Others tried at first to carry it on because they wanted to be in Paul's place of honour and influence, but it soon petered out. Meanwhile prison life was difficult and Paul was openly mocked by many inside and outside the prison. News of his plight spread to Philippi and Paul had been gladdened by the arrival of Epaphroditus who had travelled from Macedonia across the sea and visited both Paul and Timothy in prison. He brought some provisions and ointments which made life a little more bearable for them. Epaphroditus however had caught a fever from the poor conditions in prison made worse during the winter and nearly died. Fortunately he got well and then Aquila had risked his life by intervening in the legal process and personally vouching for him so he could leave the prison no longer under a death sentence. Aquila had suggested he did not return to his previous house but should stay in his business house. There was ample space for Paul because he and Priscilla had moved in the autumn to a farm just outside the city.

Paul now knew it was time to leave Ephesus, but he also knew he had made good friends in Ephesus and that God wanted him there at the moment. The difficult times could not erase all the good things that God had done through Paul's stay. Every day for two years until his sudden imprisonment, Paul had debated about Jesus in the hall of Tyrannus and through this many had found faith. Some visitors to Ephesus had then returned to their towns in Asia to found churches or increase the church life where they lived. Amongst these Paul had formed some deep friendships which he would never forget. Many of whom lived in parts of the province of Asia Paul himself had never visited. He knew of the churches and places through their connection with Ephesus, and he counted many of them his close friends. Paul had built on these friendships over the months by sending teams to encourage the churches in the region.

The expansion of the church in Asia had been rapid. Converts like Epaphras from Colossae had travelled frequently to and from Ephesus to spread the teaching they heard from Paul. Some visitors who became converts Paul appointed as leaders. It seemed ages since he had ordained Archippus to head up the church in Laodicea (but was actually just a year or so). Laodicea was the biggest city in the Lycus valley, and in a key location. John the apostle had founded the church there as well as others in the cities of the region.

Paul knew his time at Ephesus was ending. He was already in his heart leaving all this behind and Paul was unclear of the future, but it seemed a new door of opportunity had opened so he had delayed his trip to Corinth and would stay instead in Ephesus until Pentecost and then make his trip towards Macedonian and Corinth. The change of plan was brought about by some of the officials in the province, some of whom were connected with Caesars household, becoming interested in Christ. There were now further opportunities for the extension of the gospel in Asia. This was indeed an open door which he felt he needed to stay in Ephesus for a bit longer, but the next few days would not be easy Paul thought to himself, little knowing how true his thoughts were.

Paul in Reflection

Paul turned to pick up the Hebrew Scriptures which he had had since a youth. He was in one of the lower living rooms near the hall at a quiet time of day when the sun was hot. He was reading a few verses, as he did each day, and today he was reading from the book Exodus about Moses in the desert approaching a burning bush from which God spoke. Paul knew this desert well. After his conversion, he had spent two years in Arabia which in Moses' day was called Midian. It was in that same desert place that Paul had found his full understanding of the gospel of Jesus Christ. How strange, he thought, that he should receive the gospel in the same place that Moses got the law. It was during that time Paul first recognised how grace affirmed and superseded the law. This is the message he had preached to the synagogues of the cities where he had travelled. At Ephesus he had also spoken about this in the hall of Tyrannus. Some of his sermon notes from his lectures he had included in the letter to the Galatians and he intended including more of these in a general letter to the church in Rome. Paul had built on the revelation he received in Arabia, but he had never departed from it. He had spoken daily in Ephesus for over a year and the revelation he received in Arabia was still relevant and bearing fruit.

When in prison, and unsure of what the future might hold, Paul had decided to include some of the revelation he had received since Arabia so it could not be forgotten. He had written a general letter and this he had sent to the churches in the region. He called it the letter to the Laodiceans because Laodicea was the largest city in the area, but he was glad it had been read out in all the churches. Tychicus and the Ephesians intended keeping the letter safe in Ephesus as a teaching resource for new

Christians in the region. Paul was grateful for this idea for he knew he was to leave Asia behind for Greece in a few weeks time.

Paul had taught for fourteen years the revelation he had received in Arabia before he met all of the twelve in Jerusalem at the church council there to lay before them his revelation, so they could decide whether they agreed with what Paul was teaching. It was during that time that what Paul taught was affirmed by the whole church. Since then he and Barnabas had started their missionary work. Paul was grateful to the council of Jerusalem because it forged the basis of teaching for the nurture of converts which Paul used in every church he visited. As instructed at that council, he would teach according to its decrees so the Christian teaching on sex and idolatry was always part of his teaching package. This he had taught in Corinth and Ephesus. The council in Jerusalem was central and foundational to everything that had happened since. Paul recalled how the council of Jerusalem would not have happened unless he had had a vision. It was now nearly 14 years since that event happened. He rarely spoke about it, but he had been caught up to one of the dimensions of heaven. During the vision he had been instructed to go to Jerusalem and lay before the apostles the revelation he had received in the deserts of Arabia. How important it was that he had obeyed God then. His missionary call and the shape of his ministry had been forged in the council of Jerusalem and Paul had played his part by helping to bring the gospel to all the earth.

Paul returned from his thoughts back to the scriptures he was reading where God reveals His name to Moses. "I am that I am". Paul reflected how God was and is and is to come. He thought when people meet God they see Him in the past carrying and guiding them; they also see Him in the future leading them forward in hope and promise and they also see Him in the present in encounter, spoken word and actions of the Kingdom. Meeting God always involves these three levels. Paul reminded himself that when God is absent from man's thinking, sight in life shrinks to the present because when there is no revelation from God or eternal perspective the future is uncertain. The past is also painful without God either because the past brought pain - (and only God can heal the wounds), or because the past was good and is now over and past. If the view of life shrinks to the present, all that is left is instant gratification, to live for a moment which passes. Meeting God changes everything. Meaning of life is difficult to find amidst instant passing experiences or empty activity. But knowing God brings so much more because it brings a relationship with God and inner strength to our present, a re-evaluation of our past and a hope for our future. Paul turned his thoughts to prayer recalling the times Jesus had met with Him and the calling he had on his life. He waited in God presence receiving strength in his life, and then he stood up, putting the scriptures securely in his small shoulder bag, and went through the hall up the stairs to the upper room where Sosthenes was waiting ready to write the final part of his letter. The topic was to do with the end times...the future destiny from our present.

1 Corinthians Chapter 15-16
Overview

Becoming clear and certain about ultimate destiny

We are made body soul and spirit. Thousands of Christians know the change in their souls. They know Jesus has forgiven them and they are different on the inside, but many can be still uncertain about the future of their body. They may have attended Sunday school or an Alpha course and heard about Jesus and the Bible but during that time heard little or nothing about the future destiny of the body. They may believe in the resurrection of Jesus from the dead but are unclear about whether their body will go through a similar transformation. This is precisely the situation of the target audience to whom Paul is writing in Chapter 15, and for those who think this is somehow unimportant – we need to remind ourselves that there is a whole chapter in scripture devoted to this and therefore it is very important indeed.

The central issue Paul refers to is referenced in verse *12."If Christ is proclaimed risen from the dead, how can they say among you that there is no resurrection of the dead?"*

He addresses this issue by first looking at the historical fact of the resurrection of Jesus from the dead, and then drawing the implications of that resurrection for their present position. If Jesus did not actually rise from the dead it means:

a. Faith is not real, (verse14)
b. Those who have spoken to them the gospel are liars, (verse 15)
c. Their sins are not forgiven (verse 17)
d. There is no eternal life after death (verse 18)

The rest of the chapter includes revelation about the body at the end time when Jesus returns. This covers the verses 21 onwards and the climax of which is verses 51-53.

His motive for so doing is not just to pass on revelation, so that we know a few facts about that time, but he does so because we need to know about it now. His reasons are without an eternal perspective.

a. We are to be pitied (v19), because without eternal perspective our life's journey does not bring the honour our obedience to God deserves. The world loves its own but we are called out of the world, so the world hates us. If our only focus is the here and now, being a Christian has few apparent benefits. Life can get tougher because we are Christians. We face ethical dilemmas about our choices we would not face if we were not Christians. In our private worlds also we cannot be at ease with our sin as we once were before being a Christian. In addition as a Christian we are misunderstood or slandered because of our faith if not actively persecuted. Some are not given favour or work or the same rights as others, undeservedly being treated as an enemy or a fool all because of faith.

b. We are in jeopardy (v30) and need the eternal perspective to stabilize us on the inside. This is a necessary focus for our position. Being a Christian in a world that hates can be dangerous and scary. Prison, torture and threatening assault is an experience for many Christians in various parts of the world. This is nothing new. Destruction of churches and the murder or rape of Christians has occurred throughout the history of the church to the present day.

c. We have no basis for sacrificial obedience. (v32). If we lose the eternal perspective, our focus is narrowed to the present tense – what feels good for the moment or what satisfies the present demands. Sacrificial obedience never feels good at the time and will require us to deny some current needs. It is done with a higher purpose than our present needs. But if we lose eternal perspectives, future consequences of our actions or past hopes are dimmed, and it is the demands of the present which rules our life's choices. In such a context selfishness thrives.

d. Morals die (v 33). Moral actions come from the question "Why we do what we do". They stem from a conscience based on values from our past and hope drawn from our future. When we shrink our world down to our present running away from our past and ignorant or not making decisions with regard to our future, we can live life and love without morals. Within our past are things we do not want to face, and some of those things we can face and rise above only with the knowledge of our forgiveness through the cross and knowing within the love God has for us individually. Within our past lies the information which unlocks our identity and inheritance. To deny our past means we are not aware of our full identity, and unable to build on the inheritance and opportunities others through their values have passed onto us. Guilt and Pride join forces to persuade us to forget the past, but we do so at our peril causing the watchmen of our souls to be muted and weak. This is true for a nation as well as for us as individuals. If we deny our past a nation's Institutions can be weaker in their assessments of what is evil and what is good.

The future equally has importance as it brings a meaning to lives which are not dependant on the passing acclaim of men and which roots us in the truths of our eternal existence. This provides us with hope which remains amidst disappointment and personal pain or loss, and can rejuvenate our present lives enabling us to live in a blessed place within and become a blessing to others.

What does the Bible say about this resurrection day elsewhere?

Job knew there was a resurrection of the body at the last day (19:26) and Daniel learnt about this from an angel who disclosed what was in the heavenly decrees called by the angel "scripture of truth" (Daniel 12:2, 10:11).

Jesus explained about this in his teaching contained in Matthew 24:29-31; 25:31-32 (see also Mark 13, Luke 21). John in Revelation (especially 20:11-13) and Paul in 1 Thessalonians 4:16, but also here in this chapter 15 especially verse 51-53

A summary of these verses is as follows:

One day Jesus will step from the unseen dimension of heaven into the visible creation. He will come in the clouds of heaven. Just as Jesus stepped out of the visible creation into heaven at the ascension so the same phenomena accompanies his return. His return is marked by a shout for this is a day of creation. The end of the old creation and the arrival of the new. There is an archangel voice summoning the angelic host and a trumpet call announcing the momentous day. As Jesus comes, heaven and earth flee from his presence and the angels are dispatched to gather those who are God's people who are alive at the time of his return. Because they are of the new creation, they do not flee from his presence unlike the rest of creation, but they are changed instantly with resurrection bodies. There is then a gulf fixed automatically between those who are driven away by the presence of God because they are of the old creation and those who are not. The holy presence of God like the glory of God is physical and not just moral. Evil cannot stand in His presence. The division into who is of God and who is not will be obvious on that day before the books are opened to show the detail of our lives. Judgement then happens for all creation. Those on the divide near Jesus are commended in detail, for their sin is already dealt with at the cross so is not mentioned. They have already passed from death to life. Judgement day for God's forgiven people is commendation, followed by decrees regarding future destiny/responsibilities in the new heaven and new earth linked to those commendations. The others on the other side of the divide discover the full horror of their foolishness and sin and are not able to enter the new heaven and new earth and are banished from God into "hell" sharing the same judgement as the devil and his angels. The unseen creation is judged as well as the seen.

Chapter 16:
Closing business and greetings

Greek text commentary Chapter 15

1. I reveal to you,

Paul is bringing revelation, a download from heaven, to do with the last days and specifically the resurrection of the body. The Creed reminds us that this doctrine is equal in importance to the forgiveness of sins and the value of the church and is closely linked to the doctrine of eternal life. This chapter is right up there in the premier league of Christian truth and Paul has revelation about this here.

The Greek verb has the meaning "make known something" so Paul is imparting fresh revelation, rather than as most translations imply, that Paul is recalling something they already know. His revelation does not lie in the content of the gospel for he has proclaimed it already and they have heard it. The revelation as we shall see lies more in the implications of that gospel.

In this chapter Paul talks about the consequences of not believing in the dead being raised or not believing in the resurrection of Jesus. He also reveals something about the nature of the resurrection of our bodies and the end times.

brethren the good news which I proclaimed to you (evangelised you) which also you received

The gospel to be effective has to preached and has to be received. Without the preaching there is no invitation to respond and without receiving the gospel the potential of the gospel and its promises remain unfulfilled. This is not a one-time event. Whenever we grow more into the kingdom, or increase our effectiveness in Christ, there is a receiving of an invitation. This invitation may be activated immediately we first hear it or activated years later as we remember it spoken or read it again. It is only activated when we receive the invitation into our hearts. Receiving a promise of the gospel into our hearts means agreeing with it, aligning our lives to it, trusting and obeying it. We are transformed through it.

Certainly since the reformation the gospel has been a message which is cross centred. It was at the cross that Jesus paid the price for our sin so we can be forgiven and our grief healed. At the cross we can be freed from the accusations and regrets about our past and we can also receive healing from the effects of the sins of others on our lives.

But the gospel in Acts and in 1 Corinthians 15 is not cross centred. It is resurrection centred

> *Acts 1:22 - Beginning from the baptism of John, unto that same day that he was taken up from us, must one be ordained to be a witness with us of his resurrection.*

> *Acts 2:31 - He seeing this before spoke of the resurrection of Christ, that his soul was not left in hell, neither his flesh did see corruption.*

> *Acts 4:2 - Being grieved that they taught the people, and preached through Jesus the resurrection from the dead.*

> *Acts 4:33 - And with great power gave the apostles witness of the resurrection of the Lord Jesus.*

> *Acts 17:18 - (Paul) preached unto them Jesus, and the resurrection.*

> *Acts 17:32 - And when they heard of the resurrection of the dead,*

This chapter 15 mentions the gospel but it is not a chapter about the cross; it a chapter about the resurrection. The cross has the importance of a sacrifice for our sin, but it is the precursor to the new creation, to the new order of the Father's purpose which turns the old order upside down. It is the resurrection of the dead which is the central point on which the Kingdom of God comes.

By emphasising the cross, the resurrection of the dead can become simply a proof that Jesus is God. Jesus was indeed God, but it is as a man that he dies and rises from the dead. Jesus ushers in a completely new order which anticipates the new heaven and new earth where God's will is done on earth as it is in heaven. He starts a dynamic reordering where everything in heaven and on earth can be brought together under His headship (see Ephesians 1:10), and where the old divisions and power bases are changed in the new order (Daniel 7:12). In fact the first shall be last and the last first. Everything is turned upside down and all is made new.

Without the resurrection life, the gospel can become a sterile message around the cross empty of the offer of life. Without the resurrection, the cross becomes just an example of Jesus' suffering providing at best inspiration or reminder of His love, but missing the wonderful new order of creation and authority or life of the Holy Spirit that the resurrection offers us. Without engaging with the Holy Spirit in our experience, we miss the point. He dies not to primarily show us the character of God but to redeem us from our sin so we can enter the new life he offers us and enjoy the Kingdom of God in its impact on the earth. It is this which makes the cross important.

So the more we have understood Jesus' teaching about the Kingdom of God, the more our understanding of the gospel has moved from the reformation emphasis of the cross to the resurrection emphasis in the New Testament. In the gospel we can enter a new heaven centred life in which the Holy Spirit who is the first fruits of that inheritance (Ephesians 1:14) brings transformation to ourselves and our communities. This is the good fruit of the Kingdom of God.

Making the cross central rather than the resurrection has allowed a "Be Good Gospel" to emerge in the church. This gospel message is: "We are all sinners; we can never please God; Jesus came to earth to die for our sins; if we ask him into our lives he will forgive us. " – so far so good- but then its message is "When we respond to this invitation we can now try to be good doing what we think Jesus wants us to do and being a faithful member of the church" This is not the gospel. Jesus does not save us to be good. He saves us to be a new creation! The "be good gospel" has no message about no supernatural connection through which Jesus transforms lives; no power; no expectation of encounters with God; no mention of the actions which flow from faith or the risk taking lifestyle of a Christian empowered by the Holy Spirit. The true gospel of the Kingdom has its basis in the resurrection of Jesus from the dead. The cross is the end of the law, but the resurrection moves us to a new place "against which there is no law" (Gal 5:23). "Be good" has no place in the new order.

> **in which also you stand** *(a permanent position rather than just a passing phase)*
>
> **2. through which also you are saved if you hold fast to the message which I proclaimed to you unless** *(The phrase εκτος ει is used in 1 Corinthians 14 verse 5 with same meaning here of unless.)* **you believed in vain.**

Paul is saying the reality of salvation requires us holding fast to the message. We will look at this in a moment. What does Paul mean by "unless you believed in vain"? Is he saying that it is possible to have a real faith which does not bear fruit? No, because he states the importance of faith for salvation

Romans 1:17 - For therein is the righteousness of God revealed from faith to faith: as it is written, The just shall live by faith.

Romans 3:22 - Even the righteousness of God which is by faith of Jesus Christ unto all and upon all them that believe: for there is no difference

Romans 5:1 - Therefore being justified by faith, we have peace with God through our Lord Jesus Christ

Galatians 3:11 - But that no man is justified by the law in the sight of God, it is evident: for, The just shall live by faith.

Paul also does not grade faith. Faith is a response to the word of God and that faith is always the real deal. *Romans 10:17 - So then faith cometh by hearing, and hearing by the word of God. Galatians 3:2, Received ye the Spirit by the works of the law, or by the hearing of faith?*

We who know the above still read this verse and miss the point about empty faith. We read it as if Paul is not being serious but rhetorical - as if Paul is saying that you are bound to receive salvation if you hold fast to your faith because we know that faith cannot be in vain. But Paul is saying more. He does not add words without a meaning and purpose - he is saying something profound to do with the theme of empty faith.

Empty Faith. It is possible to hold fast to what you hear without it doing any good. This is because we hear it with "empty faith". Empty faith can be present amongst those who hold fast the word of truth. They are there in churches. They believe and act like Christians but there is no salvation in their experience. Faith is empty when it is all talk, just principle led or where there is a non engagement with the genuine "you" on the inside. How do we recognise "empty faith"? There is a hearing and a knowing but no change in life and no activation in experience within. This is a sign faith is empty (or in vain). You can meet some who appear full of faith on the outside but believe lies on the inside. The truths they hear, quote and hold fast to never seem to do anything for anyone. The reason is that any truths they hear are swamped by the lies within. This is believing in vain. Salvation is not a head knowledge to learn at school or debate with others but a life changing experience. Those who hear the invitation of Jesus to this new life and respond to it, will hold fast to the truths they hear. This response is in action. It may be in attending church, reading the bible or starting to pray or it may be in very different ways of behaviour or attitude to life. These actions if they come from faith bring about salvation into inner life experience. We begin to experience and live the truths we have believed in.

Holding fast the Message produces salvation in all cases where faith is full.

The τινι λοψω is singular and it is all about the word of God he spoke which they believed. Paul like Jesus before him was a sower of the seed, and the Corinthians had to keep the word so they would bear fruit. Jesus in his parable of the sower recognised that not everyone would do so. Those who bear fruit are those who hold fast to the word (Mark 4:12). Jesus saw some would let go of the word sown because of suffering whilst others would be distracted by anxiety or pleasures Paul is endorsing Jesus teaching by saying they have to keep hold of the words sown so their faith bears fruit,

It is therefore possible to respond to the gospel and remain fruitless simply because we do not hold onto the truth we hear. Holding onto it means owning it as from God and operating according to it. Sometimes to hold fast to the word means holding onto the church we belonged to, or the spiritual

274

disciplines we adopted in obedience to God. Our faith needs to be partnered by us pressing into further intimacy with God, belonging to His family on the earth (church) and to personal obedience on the inside so fruitfulness and profit from that faith can be experienced and known. We seek to align ourselves to the word we trust and it is from this standpoint that we find our faith activated and not in vain. This threefold aspect of obedience, belonging and acknowledging God at work are in my opinion the bedrock of maturity in church members and by contrast some stay outside a dynamic faith within because they have not acknowledged or pressed into all three of these sectors. One or two out of the three sectors will not do.

---

3. For I handed to you first *The word "first" is unlikely to mean "of first importance" (as it is sometimes translated) for the word relates in the sentence to "you" not to the gospel that Paul handed on. The verse therefore means either "the gospel I handed you the first time I came to Corinth" or "I handed to those of you who were first to respond to the gospel")* **what also I had received, that Christ died for** *(on behalf of)* **our sins according to the scriptures** *"According to the Scriptures" means what is in line with the Old Testament. This is a reminder that (a) definition of sin and prophesies pointing to a deliverer are prophesied in the Old Testament and (b) the details of the way that Christ was betrayed and died is also in the Old Testament (Psalm 22, Isaiah 53, Zechariah 11:13 12:10).*

4. And that he was buried and that he rose on the third day according to the scriptures

---

Again his resurrection is prophesied in the Old Testament. At the first outpouring of the Spirit on the church (Acts 2) Peter immediately quotes Psalm 16:8-11 as a prophesy about Jesus' resurrection and in his next sermon in Acts 3 he is quoting from Deuteronomy 18 about "God raising up a prophet " - the verb taking on greater significance when seen as a prophecy about the resurrection of Jesus. We know from Acts 4:33 that it was the resurrection of Jesus that was the major reference point in the proclamations and in the works of the kingdom. I think Peter got this understanding from Jesus' teaching after his resurrection and before his ascension .Acts 1:3. Part of his teaching must have involved the resurrection that, with the ascension, opened the way for the kingdom to come to men and in this context there must have been some references to the Old Testament prophesies which Peter and the others referred to post Pentecost.

There is prophecy about Jesus' burial (Isaiah 53:9) but whereas the other aspects of Jesus' death and resurrection were referenced in the gospels as having prophecy with them the burial is not so. Every aspect of Jesus' life was prophesied in the Old Testament but Paul is not primarily making that point here. He is saying that in the Old Testament was written the fact that Jesus would die for our sins, and that in the Old Testament that he would rise from the dead. They are connected together, but from the resurrection as its central point not the cross. It is the real holiness of Jesus which means he does not see corruption so he can rise from the dead, Acts 2:31, Psalm 16:8-11. Jesus really died on a cross, but death can only happen where there is sin - for the wages of sin is death. The only way Jesus who was sinless could die was by bearing our sin. When Jesus rises from the dead, death could not hold him because he was holy. This means Jesus has indeed paid the price for our sin and it is no more for he has died bearing our sin but is now holy and death cannot hold him. The perfect sacrifice has indeed been perfect, or else he would not have been able to be raised from the dead.

5. And that he appeared to Cephas *Cephas is the Aramaic form of Peter. It is interesting that Greek Corinth should know Peter not by the Greek form of his name but the Aramaic one. This is because Cephas was what he was called when he visited Corinth. We might know him as Simon Peter, but Corinth and the other churches knew him as Cephas which was the actual name Jesus had called him.* **then to the twelve.** *Acts 1 explains how there were still twelve even after Judas Iscariot's suicide*

6. Then he appeared to over five hundred brethren at one time of which many remain up to the present day, but some have died. Then he appeared to James

This is James the brother of Jesus who did not believe in Jesus during his earthly ministry. This verse shows James was not one of the five hundred and

276

a reminder James became a member of the church after the initial resurrection appearances had passed. He became the leader of the Jerusalem church. It is significant Paul mentions Peter and James for these are the only apostles whom Paul met at the first (Galatians1:18-19). The subject under discussion at that point in Paul's life with Peter and James was probably the resurrection of Jesus from the dead. Paul had after all met Jesus on the Damascus road.

then to all the apostles

The apostles are a wider group than the twelve who are mentioned in verse 5. I suspect it is referring to the 120 in the upper room at Pentecost, and referenced those Jesus sent out who followed him) for example Luke 9:1; 10:1.) The followers of Jesus were both male and female. There were not just male apostles (see Romans 16:7 apostle Junia (female name). The twelve were a distinct group in a foundational sense for the church, but they were not the only ones moving in the gift of the apostolic. In the last 30 years or so we are having to relearn that this apostolic gift is more than a foundational gift for the historic founding of the church but apostolic men and women are sent to start works of the kingdom and found churches in every generation.

8. Last of all as if by a miscarriage, he appeared even to me.

9. For I who am not worthy to be called an apostle, am the least of the apostles, *Qualification to be one of the twelve was not apostleship or else Paul could not have been an apostle. There were others who were apostles who had never met Jesus in his earthly ministry. The twelve however were distinctive because they had been chosen to be "with Jesus". It is all about Jesus and their relationship to Him not their "apostleship". This is why the candidates to replace Judas Iscariot to complete the twelve are not qualified through their spiritual anointing of apostleship but according to those who have been with Jesus from the beginning. Paul would never have qualified to be one of the twelve, but it seems he sees he is equal in apostolic authority to them* **because I persecuted the church of God.** *Paul is writing about the earliest events of his life before his conversion over twenty years previous.*

10. But by the grace of God I am what I am, and his grace towards me did not happen in vain, but I laboured more abundantly than them all. But not I, but the grace of God with me.

11. Therefore whether I or those (other apostles) **so we preach and so you believe** *All have the same message and therefore whoever they have listened to whether it be Paul or Peter or one of the others, it is same faith they share because faith is a response to the word (Romans 10:19). (See v.14 below)*

He has now completed the facts of Jesus' resurrection of the dead which most Christians in Corinth would already know. He is now moving into the revelation they do not yet know and which he wants to bring to them.

12. If Christ is proclaimed risen from the dead, how can they say among you that there is no resurrection of the dead?

13. If there is no resurrection of the dead, then Christ is not raised either.

The resurrection of Jesus and past events

Now follows 5 consequences that have to be drawn if Christ is not raised

Consequence 1

14. If Christ is not raised, our proclamation surely is empty and your faith is empty also. *Note again the link between the proclamation made and the faith engendered. Note also that the faith shares the same characteristics as the proclamation (in this case emptiness). What is at the heart of a proclamation is transferred through the faith of the hearer into their lives.*

Consequence 2

15. We are also found to be lying witnesses of God *(because they have witnessed to the bodily resurrection of Jesus from the dead as real. If it is not real, they are false witnesses).*

Because we have witnessed about God that he raised the Christ who was not raised if the dead are not raised. *To Paul and the apostles the purpose of witness is not just to teach about the historic facts, but it is more to make God known through witnessing to what He has done. They are false witnesses of God if they have been saying God did something He did not do. This is more than being mistaken about an historical fact or doctrine. Paul and the other apostles would be false witnesses of God if there was no resurrection. This is serious and personal for Paul and the others. They become witnesses who cannot be trusted in their proclamation about God.*

Consequence 3

16. If the dead are not raised then Christ has not been raised.

17. If Christ has not been raised your faith is futile - you are still in your sins. *Jesus was raised from the dead because He was holy (sinless). Death had no right to hold Him as death only has power where there is sin. This is why from the Old Testament passage Peter in Acts 2:27 is as important as a prophecy of Jesus' resurrection. Jesus on the cross took upon himself our sins (he experienced the separation from God – hence his cry from the cross "My God why have you forsaken me). As he was considered a sinner, because of our sin, Jesus dies on a cross, but because he was sinless He was raised from the dead. This means our sin was fully dealt with at the cross, and Jesus was indeed sinless so he could do this. Because sin was dealt with, death could not hold him. If Jesus was not raised from the dead, it means our sin was not dealt with at the cross and so we are still in our sins despite our faith in Jesus.*

Paul has finished his 5 reasons why it is foolish to believe that there is no resurrection from the dead. He shows the resurrection of Jesus is central to their current practices and beliefs. He has other consequences he wants to make clear, but first he needs to reveal more; He is moving from their current practices and beliefs to their experience.

The resurrection of Jesus and final destiny

He must first make a connection between the resurrection of Jesus and final destiny so he can introduce consequence 6 and 7.

20. But now Christ has been risen from the dead, the first fruits of those who have died.

21. For since through man (came) death, and through man (came) the resurrection of the dead.

22. For just as in Adam all die, so also in Christ shall all be made alive.

23. But each in his own order. Christ the first fruits, then those who belong to Christ in his Parousia

There seems 3 distinct "orders" in resurrection.

    (a)   Christ on the first Easter day has his resurrection body – i.e. a body distinct from his old body. Lazarus when he was raised from the dead had his old body and at some later point died in old age, Jesus however has an eternal body in a different order,

(b)   Those who belong to Christ in his "parousia."

(c)   The resurrection at the last day

This is strange as we would think of there being two not three groups. Christ at Easter day and the resurrection at the day of judgement (when it is the end of all things) (Daniel 12). But Paul does refer to those in Christ coming with Christ on that last day. In Revelation John references Christians who are part of the first resurrection (those who are born again) do not need to fear the resurrection to judgement. (Revelation 2:11, 20:6). The full resurrection body like Jesus had is also there for those who belong to Christ at his coming and then at the end there is a resurrection for all and then judgement.

Parousia means presence. It takes the meaning of coming because its root meaning is being beside. It has more of an idea of arrival than of travelling. At Jesus' arrival, Christians move from the old creation to the new. This is referenced later in the passage when Paul refers to the trumpet sounding and we shall be changed

Parousia is a term for the second coming of Christ, being a shorthand of the same expression used in 2 Peter 3:12 which could be translated hasten the Parousia (coming) of the day of the Lord.

Matthew 24:3 records the question the disciples ask him. "What will be the sign of your parousia (coming) and when will the end be". This has the same distinction as in these verses between the parousia and the end. It could be that the Parousia references the time frame when God is coming, but as said earlier the Greek is more about the arrival and presence of Jesus than on the journey. The arrival of Jesus breaking forth into the creation is marked by angelic hosts being visible as the unseen world is manifested in the visible world as the latter is fading away to destruction

The Parousia is also marked by those who have died in the Lord coming with Jesus in the clouds. When we ask Jesus into our life we are born again and this is what the bible refers to as the first resurrection, the fulfilment of which is our bodies are resurrected to match the change in our souls. This transformation can only happen once the new creation materially is present. The bodies are of a new order which is part of the new creation. This new creation starts at our conversion (2 Corinthians 5:17) but is completed at the second coming of Jesus.

24. Next is the end when he hands over the kingdom to God and Father whenever he will abolish *the word "whenever" used here implies the abolishing of every rule and authority and power can happen at the time of but also before rather than after (see verses 25, 28) the handing over of the kingdom to God the Father. This is the way Paul describes judgement day when the books are opened. This is the resurrections of all* **every rule every authority and power** *Power does not need "every" with it as power is power wherever it is, whereas authority and rule is diverse varying in both form and scope. In the case of rule and authority every form and every type and every expression of it is abolished by Jesus so nothing can stand before the throne of God.*

25. For it is necessary for him to rule until he puts all enemies under his feet. *The age of the Kingdom on earth lasts whilst enemies are not under the authority of Jesus. "Rule in the midst of your foes" Psalm 110:2 (see also Psalm 23:5). The Kingdom is not conflict free. It is contested, disputed, and attacked. We as sons of the kingdom experience this. The martyrs, the controversies and the persecutions of the church of God are all part and parcel of the age of the kingdom on earth.*

26. The last enemy he will abolish is death,

27. For he has brought all things under his feet. The abolishing of death is made possible somehow by the bringing of all things under his feet. Death's power is broken when he cannot exercise any control; when he can no longer hold the dead in death. The resurrection of the dead at the last day *(see John 11:24, 25)* **is the sign of death being abolished.**

> **Whenever he says that all things have brought into submission, it is clear that the exception is the one who has subjected all things to him.**
>
> **28. When he has subjected all things to him the Son himself who has subjected all things also will be in submission to Him in order that God might be everything in everything** *This phrase "Everything in everything" has been used in the way God works (12:6) through spiritual gifts in His people. Here the same phrase is used again of the results of the universal, global work of Jesus*

    a. The word of the church is a foretaste of what Jesus Himself will facilitate at the last day. What we experience now in the body of Christ and Holy Spirit life is fulfilled even more so in the whole of creation seen and unseen. The character of God does not change, but Jesus makes it manifest.

    b. When He is all in all, God is at work. Our obedience of the Lord should lead us to a place where God is all in all. We recognise God in every aspect, in every deed, in every thought, and in every action. As a result our relationship deepens to further surrender

He now brings in **Consequence 6**

This relates to their practice of baptising on behalf of those who have died. Paul makes the point that this practice indicates there is a future destiny which is in turn shows there must be a resurrection of the dead.

> **29. Otherwise what are they doing who are getting baptised on behalf of the dead? If actually the dead are not raised, why indeed be baptised on their behalf?**

Now comes **Consequence 7.**

Paul says in the next verse if I adopt a "this world only" view point with regard to life, morals become corrupted. What is the point of sacrifice?

30. Why also are we endangered every hour? *This has echoes in Philippians 2:1-23; Colossians 1:29, 2:1 (See Appendix for the imprisonment of Paul in Ephesus)*

31. Every day I die as surely (νη) as is my boast of you, brethren, which I have in Christ Jesus our Lord.

32. If from a human point of view *"human point of view" is the same expression used in 1 Corinthians 9:8 κατα ανθρωπου: κατα with accusative means towards or in the direction of. The human point of view in 1 Corinthians 9 is contrasted with God's perspective. People may see Paul fighting with wild beasts but Paul sees a supernatural dimension of conflict behind the natural and if there is no resurrection, there is no purpose to the fight.*

This event with wild beasts is not mentioned in the list of what Paul had endured which he gives in 2 Corinthians 11:22-33 though he does mention imprisonments in 2 Corinthians 6 :5 which could have been a precursor to this event mentioned here. But there is no mention of this in Acts either. Because there is no explicit reference to this elsewhere in the New Testament, it does not mean this did not happen.

I fought with wild beasts in Ephesus, what profit is there for me? *We do know Paul had some serious life threatening events whilst at Ephesus. He admits in his second letter 1:8 that he despaired of life during his stay and to the Romans (16:3) how Priscilla and Aquila had risked their lives for him in Ephesus. These might have been one of those occasions.* **If the dead are not raised, let us eat and drink for tomorrow we die.**

33. Do not be deceived, Bad company *(ομιλια means company or sermons/speech)* **corrupts good ways**. *This is a quote from Menander's lost play Thais, which said "Bad Company (ομιλια) corrupts good character.". Menander was a Greek playwright who often moralized. and was a well-known proverb of the day as although the play is lost, we know of it from the quotes later writers wrote.*

However strong you may feel your morals are, without an eternal perspective, your morals will change. Without an eternal perspective, you will be influenced by the speeches you hear or the people you meet; the friends you have, or the people who hold different values or beliefs to you who seem good, nice people. There will also be the tragic stories you will hear or encounter, or the cultures you walk in which threaten to change your morals, and will succeed if no eternal perspective whatever strengths you may feel you have now. Thus Paul says "Do not be deceived".

34. Be righteously sober and do not sin. For some have ignorance of God (among you). I say this to put you to shame.

35. But someone will say, "How are the dead raised? What sort of body do they come?

36. Foolish (one) *(word for "not thinking" rather than for being ignorant)* **What you sow does not make life if it does not die;**

37. And what you sow is not the body that it becomes, (for) you sow but a naked grain, it could be of wheat or some other variety,

38. But God gives it a body as he wished, and to each of the seed its own body.

39. Not all flesh is the same flesh. But there is one sort for mankind and another flesh belonging to animals, another type of flesh belonging to birds another of fish. *He now broadens this beyond living creatures (see v 41) to the whole of creation*

40. And there are bodies in the heavens *(planets, stars and possibly angels)* **and there are bodies on the earth** *(mountains glaciers etc.),* **The glory of the heavenly bodies is different from the glory of the earthly bodies.**

41. There is one glory of the sun, another glory of the moon and another glory of the stars.

Their glory is different because their impact is different because their purpose is different. Glory is always linked to purpose. **And a star differs from a star in glory** *there is no star the same*

42. So also is the resurrection of the dead.

a. There is no person the same, so our glory will be distinct according to our character, calling and relationship with God (which will involve our obedience to Him).

b. The glory of the resurrection is different from the earthly body we once knew. This is the theme of the next verses

It is sown in corruption, it is raised in incorruption.

43. It is sown in dishonour; it is raised in glory. It is sown in weakness, it is raised in power.

44. It is sown a physical (soulish) body, it is raised a spiritual body. *Now we have a physical body whose life is defined by the soul what it feels, desires, touches or decides; but one day we will have a different resurrection body not defined by our soul but by our spirit. Then what will matter will be whether we have a spirit that is alive or dead; awake or asleep able to move freely or curled up within itself.* If there is a physical body, there is also a spiritual body.

45. As it is written the first man Adam became a living being. *(Genesis 2:7)* The last Adam a life-giving spirit.

Paul is perhaps bringing out the text of Genesis 2:6, 7. Verse 6 mentions God making Adam from the ground, and then verse 7 God formed him into a living being through breathing on him. Paul takes these verses from Genesis and says it does not just refer to the first Adam in the garden. This is more than the formation of Homo sapiens. It refers also to God's plan throughout history i.e.to take the earthly human he has made and make them a living spirit. This verse refers to Jesus. He is the really true Man who was both of the earth and a true giver of life through the Spirit. His ministry of life to the world started when he was breathed on in his baptism though he was conceived in the womb of Mary through the Holy Spirit. He was a real Man and life giving in the spirit.

> **46. But it was not the spiritual which was first but the physical then the spiritual.**
>
> **47. The first man was out of the ground so is earthy, the second man from heaven.**
>
> **48. As such is the earthly man so also are the earthly ones, and as the heavenly one, so also are the heavenly ones**
>
> **49. and likewise we bear the likeness of the earthly (man) and we bear the likeness of the heavenly (man).** *We also are designed to become those that not just bring life during this earthly journey but our bodies will be transformed into resurrection life glory!*
>
> **50. I say this, brethren, that flesh and blood is not able to inherit the kingdom of God, not does corruption inherit incorruption.**

The sources are different. The life does not come from the earth but from heaven (verse 47). Whilst it is true that the earthly body came first and then the heavenly spirit was breathed into that mortal frame, Paul makes clear that was is of the earth does not bring about what is from heaven. This heaven will one day break into our earth like a thief in the night. The old order of earth first and then heaven will be ended. The first will be last and the last first. During our earthly lifetime, God has us to make the first move before He responds. He waits for the five loaves and two fish before feeding the 5,000. He has ordered the first creation in such a way that humans can make a difference. They can bring heaven to earth by their prayers, obedience and declarations. But the final change from corruption to incorruption; from mortality to immortality does not come from any source except heaven. Now in this life, God waits for us to make the first move; at the new creation with a new heaven and a new earth, it will be heaven initiated and it will be not dependent on anything we do at all

51. Behold I show you a mystery *(remember he stated he was speaking revelation to them in verse 1).* **We shall not all die (sleep) but we shall all be changed**

52. In a moment, in the momentary glance *(Greek word ριπη means this)* **of an eye, at the last trumpet. For the trumpet shall sound,** *Paul in I Thessalonians 4:16 says this happens at the time when Jesus steps out of the unseen realm into the visible creation. Jesus also talks about a trumpet sounding at the last day to send the angels to gather the elect (Matthew 24:31), and Paul also recognises in I Thessalonians 4:16 that there is angelic activity at the time of the sounding of the trumpet. Jesus says the trumpet heralds the unseen creation and seen creation coming together (the angels are sent to gather the elect). So Paul then writes* **and the dead shall be raised incorruptible and we shall be changed.** *The unseen soul and spirit of man is clothed with the new resurrection body.*

53. For it is necessary for this corruption to be clothed with incorruption and this mortality to be clothed with immortality.

54. Whenever this corruption is clothed with incorruption and this mortality has been clothed with immortality then will be the word (fulfilled) that is written "Death has been swallowed up in victory.

55. Where, O death, is your victory, where O death is your sting.

56. Sin is the sting of death; The power of sin is the law.

57. But thanks be to God who has given us the victory through our Lord Jesus Christ.

58. So, my beloved brothers, Be firm, unmoveable, abounding in the work of the Lord at all times, knowing that your labour is not in vain in the Lord.

Chapter 16

1. Concerning the collection *(λογια is a form of λογεια meaning collection)*

This is the collection he had promised the church in Jerusalem he would make wherever he went. The original intention was to help with the famine which occurred under Claudius in Judea in 54a.d which was in line with the prophecy Paul had received from Agabas before the council of Jerusalem (Acts 15). That famine had already occurred by the time Paul is writing this letter but he is still making a collection. This shows that Paul is adhering to the collection principle regardless of world events. Famine had struck Corinth just before Paul first visited the city. He may for this reason have been reluctant to initiate a collection in the newly forming church, though he did spend over a year there. This collection may be unfinished business which Paul needed to complete with the Corinthian church.)

which is for the saints, as I have instructed the churches of Galatia *he does not mention Macedonia here as they are also being approached about the collection at this time. Only later, when successful, does he mention the collection from Macedonia to the Corinthians in his second letter (2 Corinthians 8, 9)* **so even you have done.**

2. On the first day of the week *(Greek "on the first of the Sabbath")* *This is the phrase used to mean Sunday. The same phrase is used Matthew 28:1 translated first day of the week , See Mark 16:9; Luke 18:12 where Sabbath means the week that followed it and not just the Sabbath day which was each Saturday.* **Each of you should privately put (aside) to store whatever he has prospered to ensure that when I come, there are no collections.**

3. When I arrive, whoever you will consider through letters *Paul needs to know who they recommend to receive the gifts in writing so he could have this documentation as he organises this collection. Paul wisely does not want individuals complaining that either Paul has stolen the money* *or redistributed it according to what he thought was right or changing it according to the needs when he arrives in Jerusalem.)* **I will send these to bring your gift to Jerusalem.**

4. If it is possible for them to come with me they will travel with me.

5. I will come to you when I have passed through Macedonia. For I am passing through Macedonia.

6. I will stay with you, hopefully *(τυχον literally means "may it happen". It is used in a similar way to the interjection "hopefully" or "if God will it" that we might use in English)* **or even spend the winter** *Paul has delayed his trip thinking at this point that he would pursue the opportunity he has in Ephesus for the gospel so instead of setting out for Greece in the Spring he will do so after Pentecost and then arrive in Macedonia for the winter. This time schedule is changed by events in Ephesus (see Appendix 58A.D. and 59A.D. (See Acts 19:29-20:1)* **in order that you may send me onwards to wherever I may go.**

7. For I do not want see you on a passing visit for I hope to spend some time with you if the Lord permits.

8. I am staying in Ephesus until Pentecost. *He must be still intending to visit Corinth and then go from there to Macedonia (2 Cor 1:16) as we know from Acts 20:1, 2, he goes instead to Macedonia (see 2 Cor 9:2) and then onto Greece.*

9. For there is a door opened for me which is large and active, and many stand against us.

An opportunity has opponents as well. We know from his second letter and also from Acts that Paul does not go to Corinth as he intends here. The combination of the open door and the opposition is the cause of the delay. The opposition could be false teachers, as he references in his later speech to the Ephesian elders at Miletus (Acts 20:28-30) Here Paul refers to false teaching and possible false leaders arising in the churches to lead astray or devour the sheep. There was also we know the build up against Paul in the business community which would culminate in the riot which would propel him from Ephesus towards Corinth. This was unknown to Paul at the time of writing. The open door, on the other hand, was known to Paul, and must refer to new opportunities which could have come through contacts made during his recent imprisonment. If as I believe the Philippian letter was written from Ephesus immediately before this epistle, there is a reference in the Philippian letter to Caesar's household (Phil 4:22). Members of the Praetorian Guard were supervisors over the military who guarded the prison as well as oversaw all major aspects of Ephesian life where military personnel was required. It is quite possible that a member of Caesar's household who was either part of or protected by this praetorian guard detachment in Ephesus, had become a Christian .If influential members of the Romans empire were becoming Christians, it would make sense for Paul not to pass this opportunity by, and he is therefore delaying his journey until Pentecost before going to Corinth. On the other hand the open door could be the repentance from witchcraft which probably led to a reaction of Paul's short imprisonment and finished his days of teaching in the hall of Tyrannus. We know from Acts that the widespread conversions did threaten to change the culture of Ephesus to the extent it affected the sale of idols. With the shaking of the principality's authority and advance of the Kingdom of God, it would not be unreasonable to assume there were many new opportunities for the gospel. Revival in Asia (not just in Ephesus) is causing Paul to delay his journey to Corinth. He had known a door close when he was trying to enter the proconsular Asia 8 years before. He is not going to fail to go through the door now it is open to him.

10. If Timothy should come, *This shows that the letter would arrive before Timothy gets there. This is because Erastus is the postman for the Corinthian letter. It was only Timothy who would go to Macedonia. If the Philippian letter was written just before Timothy's departure from Macedonia in Acts 19, the fact that Erastus was going direct to Corinth would account for Timothy but not Erastus not being mentioned in the Philippi letter. Both would* *however go to Corinth. Erastus first followed by Timothy* **Be careful that he be without fear among you, for he works the work of the Lord as I do.**

11. Let no-one despise him, but send him forth in peace in order that he may come to me. I am waiting for him with the brothers.

12. Concerning brother Apollos. I have invited him many times to come to you with the brothers. And every time he is not willing to come at this time, but he will come when it will be a suitable time. *(Apollos may not have wanted to come to Corinth with all the controversy of the divided groups around Paul, Apollos and Peter. Apollos may have felt it would be more suitable once this situation had been resolved).*

13. Watch, stand in the faith, be courageous, rule.

14. Everything about you should be in the love (of God).

15. I appeal to you brothers. You know the household of Stephanas because he is the firstfruits of Achaia and they have appointed themselves to the service to the saints

16. in order that you may be drawn under such as these *(place of safety and accountability)* **and to every team work** *(place of activity and fruit bearing)* **and labour** *Paul is here affirming Stephanas and his household and thus it seems this is where the leadership of the Corinthian church was rather than with Fortunatus or Achaicus who were assisting him.*

17. I am grateful for the coming of Stephanas and Fortunatus and Achaicus because they have made up for my missing you all *(The Greek is literally these have filled what is lacking of you).*

18. They refreshed my spirit (as they do) yours. Recognise these.

19. The churches of Asia *These are the churches of Ephesus plus those Paul wrote to. Paul wrote to the Christians in Colossae (Colossians 1; 2) which was upstream from Laodicea which itself was just over 90 miles from Ephesus. Hierapolis (Colossians 4:13, Philemon) was across the valley 6 miles away from Laodicea. All three cities were in a valley where the Lycus River flows into the Maeander River. Paul writing in 58A.D. is writing unaware that in 3 years these cities would be devastated by an earthquake. The Roman historian Tacitus (Annals 14.27) says the earthquake occurred in the seventh year of Nero which would be 61AD Colossae was destroyed and never rebuilt. This accounts for the letters of John in Revelation not including Colossae in its writing. Laodicea however was large enough and wealthy so it was rebuilt without Roman aid.* **greet you. Aquila and Priscilla, with the church that meets in their house, very much greets you in the Lord.**

20. All the brothers greet you. Greet each other with a holy kiss.

21. The Greeting of Paul is in my own hand. *The earlier part of the letter has been dictated but this Paul writes himself writing the words. This is a way Paul authenticates the letter as really from him. (see 2 Thessalonians 3:17, also Galatians 5:11). The ones he writes after 1 Corinthians do not have this same authentication. The reason could be that those who brought the letters to the churches were by this time well known as Paul's team and so did not need the same level of authentication within the letter themselves. Authentication was important to stop churches trusting deceptive or false teaching because they thought it was from Paul when it was not.*

22. If anyone does not love the Lord, let him be anathema. Maranatha. *Meaning our Lord come.*

23. The grace of our Lord Jesus Christ be with you.

24. My Love be with you all in Christ Jesus Amen

Departure

Time was fast approaching for the sailing. It was morning and there was a gentle breeze. Ideal conditions for the trip said someone in the group behind him as the group walked through the colonnades down to the harbour. Paul turned to agree. It was a very good day. The Church had expected the sailing to take place today and had gathered the previous night to commend Timothy and Erastus for the mission trip to Macedonia and onto Corinth in the same way as Paul had first been commended by the church in Antioch for his first mission trip with Barnabas. Timothy and Erastus were accompanied by a team who would help them on their arrival to first Macedonia and then Corinth. Sosthenes was holding the letter he and Paul had written. Paul looked around at the team which included most if not all of the influential people in the Corinthian church, and he said how he looked forward to joining them in Corinth. The Macedonians Gaius and Aristarchus stood with Paul as the rest went through the gathered throng towards the boat. They thought in a week or two they would also go when accompanying Paul to Corinth and then onto Philippi.

Timothy and Erastus said goodbye and embarked on the trading vessel. The ship was bound eventually for Spain taking its wares westwards from where it would return along the ancient trade route. The proposed journey followed the coast northwards towards the Black Sea and then across from Troas to Neapolis the largest seaport in eastern Macedonia. Timothy would leave there and go from this major trading city along the Via Egnatia to Philippi. The ship would pick up further goods at Neapolis and then sail down towards the second largest seaport in Greece Piraeus at Athens, and then it would follow the coast around Achaia towards Lenchaeum Corinth's west facing port where most of the group would disembark unless the weather allowed a stop earlier at the smaller east facing port of Corinth Cenchrae, but according to the captain, a stop there was unlikely. The ship would then go to Italy and finally Spain, taking not a few weeks to complete the journey. When the group disembarked they would gather the whole church in Corinth and Erastus would read and deliver the letter Paul had dictated. The Church would then make ready for Timothy and then Paul's direct visit to them.

That was the plan but none of them knew what lay ahead. Paul's plans, as he watched the ship get ready to depart, were to sail direct to Corinth and from there to travel to Macedonia and then return to Corinth to stay the winter and onto Jerusalem for Pentecost next year. Paul and Timothy had planned this but this was not to materialise. It would bring much disturbance amongst the Corinthians friends who he had just said goodbye to. They would feel the dismay at his broken promise. He would be propelled from Ephesus going direct to Macedonia before making his way to Achaia and Corinth. The seeds for this were already sown but Paul and his companions did not know it.

The boat was soon made ready and started to inch its way from the quayside. With a final wave, Paul and his friends turned back to walk up the slope to the city determined to take up the opportunity for the gospel expansion before him. What none knew at this time was the dangers of the murmurs of the business community since his exit from prison and the growing influence of Christianity amongst certain key leaders in the province. In just a few weeks the silversmith Demetrius would use the fear of the economic downturn caused by rise of Christianity and the related decline in idolatry to call together all those linked to the sale of idols and cause a riot. This riot was on a city wide scale and meant Paul was no longer safe in the city. He had to leave the city for Europe. He would never see Ephesus again, but the seeds Paul had sown were deep, effective and the churches in the province of Asia flourished. Paul left them in a much better place than when he arrived. He had used his talents well. Gaius and Aristarchus were caught up in the riot and they were forced to sail to their home country Macedonia. Corinth would be visited but there was going to be a much longer delay than any had anticipated.

Acts 19:21-24

After these things were ended, Paul purposed in the spirit, when he had passed through Macedonia and Achaia, to go to Jerusalem, saying, After I have been there, I must also see Rome. [22] So he sent into Macedonia two of them that ministered unto him, Timothy and Erastus; but he himself stayed in Asia for a season. [23] And the same time there arose no small stir about that way.

2 Cor. 1:8-10

For we would not, brethren, have you ignorant of our trouble which came to us in Asia, that we were pressed out of measure, above strength, insomuch that we despaired even of life: [9] But we had the sentence of death in ourselves, that we should not trust in ourselves, but in God which raises the dead: [10] Who delivered us from so great a death, and doth deliver: in whom we trust that he will yet deliver us;

Acts 19:24-41

[24] For a certain man named Demetrius, a silversmith, which made silver shrines for Diana, brought no small gain unto the craftsmen; [25] Whom he called together with the workmen of like occupation, and said, Sirs, ye know that by this craft we have our wealth. [26] Moreover ye see and hear, that not alone at Ephesus, but almost throughout all Asia, this Paul hath persuaded and turned away much people, saying that they be no gods, which are made with hands: [27] So that not only this our craft is in danger to be set at nought; but also that the temple of the great goddess Diana should be despised, and her magnificence should be destroyed, whom all Asia and the world worships. [28] And when they heard these sayings, they were full of wrath, and cried out, saying, Great is Diana of the Ephesians. [29] And the whole city was filled with confusion: and having caught Gaius and Aristarchus, men of Macedonia, Paul's companions in travel, they rushed with one accord into the theatre. [30] And when Paul would have entered in unto the people, the disciples

suffered him not. [31] And certain of the chief of Asia, which were his friends, sent unto him, desiring him that he would not adventure himself into the theatre. [32] Some therefore cried one thing, and some another: for the assembly was confused; and the more part knew not wherefore they were come together. [33] And they drew Alexander out of the multitude, the Jews putting him forward. And Alexander beckoned with the hand, and would have made his defence unto the people. [34] But when they knew that he was a Jew, all with one voice about the space of two hours cried out, Great is Diana of the Ephesians. [35] And when the town clerk had appeased the people, he said, Ye men of Ephesus, what man is there that knows not how that the city of the Ephesians is a worshipper of the great goddess Diana, and of the image which fell down from Jupiter? [36] Seeing then that these things cannot be spoken against, ye ought to be quiet, and to do nothing rashly. [37] For ye have brought hither these men, which are neither robbers of churches, nor yet blasphemers of your goddess. [38] Wherefore if Demetrius, and the craftsmen which are with him, have a matter against any man, the law is open, and there are deputies: let them implead one another. [39] But if ye enquire anything concerning other matters, it shall be determined in a lawful assembly. [40] For we are in danger to be called in question for this day's uproar, there being no cause whereby we may give an account of this concourse. [41] And when he had thus spoken, he dismissed the assembly. Acts 20:1-2 And after the uproar was ceased, Paul called unto him the disciples, and embraced them, and departed for to go into Macedonia. [2] And when he had gone over those parts, and had given them much exhortation, he came into Greece.

Appendix A
Corinth in the missionary journeys of Paul
Acts 18:1-22

After these things Paul departed from Athens, and came to Corinth; [2] And found a certain Jew named Aquila, born in Pontus, lately come from Italy, with his wife Priscilla; (because that Claudius had commanded all Jews to depart from Rome:) and came unto them. [3] And because he was of the same craft, he abode with them, and wrought: for by their occupation they were tentmakers. [4] And he reasoned in the synagogue every Sabbath, and persuaded the Jews and the Greeks. [5] And when Silas and Timotheus were come from Macedonia, Paul was pressed in the spirit, and testified to the Jews that Jesus was Christ. [6] And when they opposed themselves, and blasphemed, he shook his raiment, and said unto them, Your blood be upon your own heads; I am clean: from henceforth I will go unto the Gentiles.

[7] And he departed thence, and entered into a certain man's house, named Justus, one that worshipped God, whose house joined hard to the synagogue. [8] And Crispus, the chief ruler of the synagogue, believed on the Lord with all his house; and many of the Corinthians hearing believed, and were baptized. [9] Then spake the Lord to Paul in the night by a vision, Be not afraid, but speak, and hold not thy peace: [10] For I am with thee, and no man shall set on thee to hurt thee: for I have much people in this city. [11] And he continued there a year and six months, teaching the word of God among them.

[12] And when Gallio was the deputy of Achaia, the Jews made insurrection with one accord against Paul, and brought him to the judgment seat, [13] Saying, This fellow persuadeth men to worship God contrary to the law. [14] And when Paul was now about to open his mouth, Gallio said unto the Jews, If it were a matter of wrong or wicked lewdness, O ye Jews, reason would that I should bear with you: [15] But if it be a question of words and names, and of your law, look ye to it; for I will be no judge of such matters. [16] And he drave them from the judgment seat. [17] Then all the Greeks took Sosthenes, the chief ruler of

the synagogue, and beat him before the judgment seat. And Gallio cared for none of those things.

[18] And Paul after this tarried there yet a good while, and then took his leave of the brethren, and sailed thence into Syria, and with him Priscilla and Aquila; having shorn his head in Cenchrea: for he had a vow. [19] And he came to Ephesus, and left them there: but he himself entered into the synagogue, and reasoned with the Jews. [20] When they desired him to tarry longer time with them, he consented not; [21] But bade them farewell, saying, I must by all means keep this feast that cometh in Jerusalem: but I will return again unto you, if God will. And he sailed from Ephesus. [22] And when he had landed at Caesarea, and gone up, and saluted the church, he went down to Antioch.

Paul & Corinth

Paul remained in Corinth for 18 months. He then went via a brief visit to Ephesus on his return to Antioch. Paul returned after some time to visit the Galatian and Phrygian provinces helping the disciples to form churches and go out in mission. These were making secure the areas he had been before, rather than reaching new areas for the gospel. When he arrived in Ephesus, the province of Asia was new to him as a missionary. His arrival at Ephesus was accompanied by power encounters and miracles of the Holy Spirit. He stayed 2 years. It is towards the end of his time in Ephesus that Paul wrote this first letter to the Corinthians and within the year he visits the province of Achaia and its capital city Corinth and he stays 3 months in the province. It is during this time that he wrote the epistle to the Romans as at end of his letter he sends greeting from members of the Corinthian church. We can see from Romans 16:23 that by this time the Corinthian church has grown from the single church meeting in the house of Justus next door to the synagogue into a network of churches.

Corinth the city

Corinth was the capital of a Roman province. It was a city which prospered with a large, busy and important harbour to the west and a smaller one at Cenchrae to the east connected by a paved road. Corinth was built on the land which connected the southern Peloponnese with mainland Greece, so it was favourably placed on the east west trade across the Mediterranean and also controlled the land route between north and south Greece. From the earliest days this advantageous position had made it wealthy. Homer calls Corinth wealthy in the Iliad (ii.570), and though it had suffered destruction by the Romans so there was no longer an indigenous population from the earlier period, after it's refounding by Julius Caesar in 44b.c. there had been a new elite – primarily war veterans and others with close links with Rome. These became wealthy through trade, Corinth itself was rebuilt as a Roman city and Corinth through its close links with Rome and the Empire grew richer than any of its previous generations.

History of Corinth

Corinth was called by an even earlier ancient name Ephyrē of which little is known, but because Homer described this as in the valley of Argos, it might be there was a close link between the city Argos founded at a similar time to Mycenae. By the time of the Trojan War in the 12th century bc Corinth had become a major city state in its own right taking its place alongside Mycenae, Sparta, Pylos etc. Homer states that for the Trojan war Corinth provided with Mycenae twice the amount of ships of any other contributor under the command of Agamemnon. As mentioned above This ancient city. was destroyed by the victorious Romans, and for 100 years the city did not exist. Julius Caesar however restored it (about 44 B.C.) and colonised it with Italians, mainly discharged soldiers who were rewarded for their service with a new life at Corinth. It became and felt more of a Roman city than a Greek one. The Jews also came to Corinth, and they were in large enough numbers to start a synagogue. Archeologists have found part of the superscription above the door of this synagogue verifying what we already know from the Acts of the apostles.

107 years after Corinth's rebuild by Julius Caesar, Paul arrived from Athens. He was in Corinth when Gallio arrived as governor in July 51AD. Ephesus was the capital of the Roman province of Asia, whereas Corinth was the seat of government for the Roman province of Achaia. Junius Annaeus Gallio was the son of Seneca the rhetorician and brother of Seneca the philosopher, and was the Roman governor of Achaia. An

inscription dated 52AD. naming Gallio found at Delphi says that he was a 'friend of Caesar', and dates his governorship to AD 51 or 52. This dates the time Paul made his first visit to Corinth (Acts 18). We know also that there was a famine during the reign of Claudius which affected Judaea in 45 AD and Greece in 50AD So Paul was definitely at Corinth the following year, and could have arrived in 50AD when the famine effects were still present in the city.

As the church first emerged in a city where they were recovering from a difficult famine, Paul may have not pushed the Jerusalem collection side of his commission and so several years later when he has decided to return to Corinth he sends Timothy and Erastus to take up a collection for the poor in Judaea according to the wishes of the Jerusalem church council (Acts 15). This collection seems to have been successful for he mentions it in Romans (Romans 15:26) where he indicates that he has already received the collection to bring to Jerusalem.

This accounts for mention of the helping of the poor in Judaea coming to the Corinthians through Timothy and Erastus as they come with the first letter of the Corinthians. We know from the second epistle to the Corinthians that Timothy and Erastus' appeal to the Macedonians for help for the Judaean church was well received and they gave generously but it is written before the Corinthian response. Paul intended to visit Corinth and collect this to take it back to Jerusalem, and there is some doubt as to whether this collection will materialise (2 Corinthians 8 & 9). So we can see that when 2 Corinthians was written, Romans had not yet been written.

The general culture of the Corinthian society before its destruction by the Romans which the Greeks associated with Corinth was immorality, and so in Greek of an earlier era the verb "to act like a Corinthian" meant to be immoral. Corinth may have retained some of these ancient characteristics in Paul's day. Although Paul included teaching to prevent immorality at every place he went, there is evidence from Paul's letter that immoral lifestyles were part of life in Corinth, and therefore his teaching especially relevant there.

1 Corinthians 6:9-11 - "Know ye not that the unrighteous shall not inherit the kingdom of God? Be not deceived: neither fornicators, nor idolaters, nor adulterers, nor effeminate, nor abusers of themselves with mankind, [10] Nor thieves, nor covetous, nor drunkards, nor revilers, nor extortioners, shall inherit the kingdom of God. [11] And such were some of you: but ye are washed, but ye are sanctified, but ye are justified in the name of the Lord Jesus, and by the Spirit of our God". (Cf Chapters 5-7 and 9:27)

Acts 18 records that the reason Aquila and Priscilla were in Corinth was because Clauidus had ordered the Jews to leave Rome. This is why Paul met them when he came to Corinth. Claudius brought in this policy in 49AD and Paul arrived in Corinth for the first time before 51AD. Aquila and Priscilla had been in Corinth about a year before Paul first met them. Although displaced from Rome, they eventually returned (Romans 16:3 Also Priscilla is probably buried in the catacomb below the city which is named after her). They formed a close bond with Paul moving with him from Corinth and living in Ephesus when Paul left Corinth the first time .Paul met them again when he stayed in Ephesus. This must be in 56 or 57A.D. as Paul spends time in the Levant and Asia Minor before arriving there. When he arrived, it was probably a year after the Mother of Jesus had died and John the apostle had gone to Rome. According to eastern tradition Mary lived eventually in a house on one of the hills just outside ancient Ephesus until she died 29 years after the death of Jesus. Jesus was about 33 years old when he died and was born in 5b.c. (Herod the King died in 4b,c, and therefore Jesus died on the cross in 27b.c (Pontius Pilate being in Judea 26-36a.d). Mary died therefore in 56A.D. John the apostle according to Tertullian went to Rome where he was present when the persecution of Christians happened under Nero (for Domitian is far too late) and was exiled to Patmos. John writes the book of Revelation from there, but he does not remain there. According to legend John dies at Ephesus at the end of the first century, and there is every reason to suppose John lived many years in Ephesus as an old man before his death as some of the apocryphal writings also indicate.

Aquila and Priscilla went from Ephesus to Rome soon after Paul left Ephesus as they are in Rome when Paul writes to the Romans a few months after departing from Ephesus for Corinth, having written both 1 Corinthians and 2 Corinthians

The Corinth Erastus Inscription

When Paul wrote from *Corinth* to Rome in AD 58/9, he included greetings from *Erastus*, who is described in his epistle (16:23) as the city *treasurer*. In 1929 Archaeologists discovered a stone inscription in a block of marble as part of a paved square near the theatre "Erastus, commissioner of public works (aedile), laid this pavement at his own expense". An aedile was the contact person between the authorities and the ordinary people. They administered a district and had assistants (quaestors) who were treasurers. You served for a year and could not serve for two years after your year of service. He also met Gaius who looked after Paul and was rich enough to have a property where all the house churches could gather (Romans 16:23) He also met a woman Chloe who was either single with slaves or a single parent. She was perhaps a business woman working in Corinth. Stephanas and his family was part of the foundation of the church (Stephanas was one of the first people to be converted to Jesus (I Cor 16:15)). Other foundational members of the new church were Crispus the converted ruler of the synagogue and his family as well as Justus who was the first host of the new church. Justus was a Gentile who had in the past had leanings towards the Jewish synagogue but welcomed Paul when the synagogue threw him out (Acts 18:7) He lived next door to the synagogue so the geography was interesting to start a "rival" meeting to the old synagogue services. There was also Fortunatus who according to eastern Orthodox tradition knew Stephen who was stoned when Paul was a student in Jerusalem and not yet a believer, and Achaicus mentioned in 1 Corinthians also features as a saint in the eastern Orthodox lists. Included in this delegation may have been the successor to Crispus as ruler of the synagogue, Sosthenes, who must have been converted after Paul left Corinth the first time because he is with Paul in Ephesus when he writes 1 Corinthians (1:1)

It seems that the church which Paul founded in Corinth had a wide variety of people some wealthy but most not so; and the Jews were a minority amongst the majority of Gentiles. This would explain Paul in Romans 16:21 sending greetings from the Corinthian church, he includes as a special category Lucius, Jason and Sosipater as his fellow Jews. It may be that Paul particularly appreciated contact with Jews who were Christians like he was, but he formed deep relationships with many non-Jews as well (e.g. Trophimus from Ephesus with whom he is seen in Jerusalem and which brings about his arrest there. Acts 21:29)

Appendix B
Background to 1 Corinthians

51AD - 56A.D.

Acts 18

18 Paul stayed on in Corinth for some time. *(Late summer 50- spring 52 year and a half Acts 18:11)* Then he left the brothers and sisters and sailed for Syria, accompanied by Priscilla and Aquila. 19 They arrived at Ephesus, where Paul left Priscilla and Aquila. He himself went into the synagogue and reasoned with the Jews. 20 When they asked him to spend more time with them, he declined. 21 But as he left, he promised, "I will come back if it is God's will." Then he set sail from Ephesus. *(Early spring 52AD)* 22 When he landed at Caesarea, he went up to Jerusalem and greeted the church and then went down to Antioch *(53AD)*. 23 After spending some time in Antioch, *(54A.D.)* Paul set out from there *(54-55A.D.)* and travelled from place to place throughout the region of Galatia and Phrygia, strengthening all the disciples. (55-56A.D.) 24 Meanwhile a Jew named Apollos, a native of Alexandria, came to Ephesus. He was a learned man, with a thorough knowledge of the Scriptures. 25 He had been instructed in the way of the Lord, and he spoke with great fervour and taught about Jesus accurately, though he knew only the baptism of John. 26 He began to speak boldly in the synagogue. When Priscilla and Aquila heard him, they invited him to their home and explained to him the way of God more adequately. 27 When Apollos wanted to go to Achaia, the brothers and sisters encouraged him and wrote to the disciples there to welcome him. When he arrived, he was a great help to those who by grace had believed. 28 For he vigorously refuted his Jewish opponents in public debate, proving from the Scriptures that Jesus was the Messiah.

56A.D. - 58A.D.

Acts 19

While Apollos was at Corinth, Paul took the road through the interior and arrived at Ephesus. *(Early 56a.d)*. There he found some disciples 2 and asked them, "Did you receive the Holy Spirit when you believed?" They answered, "No, we have not even heard that there is a Holy Spirit." They were baptized in the name of the Lord Jesus. 6 When Paul placed his hands on them, the Holy Spirit came on them, and they spoke in tongues and prophesied. [7] There were about twelve men in all. [8] Paul entered the synagogue and spoke boldly there for three months, arguing persuasively about the kingdom of God. [9] But some of them became obstinate; they refused to believe and publicly maligned the Way. So Paul left them. He took the disciples with him and had discussions daily in the lecture hall of Tyrannus. [10] This went on for two years, (*56-58A.D. For three years Paul was at Ephesus (Acts 20: 31). For the first 3months he was in the synagogue then after a short delay of a few days he was 2 years teaching in the Tyrannus hall, then 8 months in Ephesus post Tyrannus. This book assumes 1 Corinthians was written in the spring of 58A.D. after a 3 month winter imprisonment prior to a rapid expulsion from Ephesus in the summer of 58A.D.when he left for Macedonia,*) so that all the Jews and Greeks who lived in the province of Asia heard the word of the Lord. [11] God did extraordinary miracles through Paul, [12] so that even handkerchiefs and aprons that had touched him were taken to the sick, and their illnesses were cured and the evil spirits left them. and the name of the Lord Jesus was held in high honour. [18] Many of those who believed now came and openly confessed what they had done. [19] A number who had practiced sorcery brought their scrolls together and burned them publicly. When they calculated the value of the scrolls, the total came to fifty thousand drachmas. [20] In this way the word of the Lord spread widely and grew in power. [21] After all this had happened (*57 winter.*), Paul decided to go to Jerusalem, passing through Macedonia and Achaia. "After I have been there," he said, "I must visit Rome also." [22] He sent two of his helpers, Timothy and Erastus, to Macedonia, while he stayed in the province of Asia a little longer.

1 Corinthians is written at this time

1 Corinthians has been written from Ephesus (1 Corinthians 16:19); he stayed whilst Timothy went ahead (1 Corinthians 4:17 16:8-10).

The Riot in Ephesus

[23] About that time there arose a great disturbance about the Way. [24] A silversmith named Demetrius, who made silver shrines of Artemis,

brought in a lot of business for the craftsmen there. 25 He called them together, along with the workers in related trades, and said: "You know, my friends, that we receive a good income from this business. 26 And you see and hear how this fellow Paul has convinced and led astray large numbers of people here in Ephesus and in practically the whole province of Asia. He says that gods made by human hands are no gods at all. 27 There is danger not only that our trade will lose its good name, but also that the temple of the great goddess Artemis will be discredited; and the goddess herself, who is worshiped throughout the province of Asia and the world, will be robbed of her divine majesty." 28 When they heard this, they were furious and began shouting: "Great is Artemis of the Ephesians!" 29 Soon the whole city was in an uproar. The people seized Gaius and Aristarchus, Paul's travelling companions from Macedonia, and all of them rushed into the theatre together. 30 Paul wanted to appear before the crowd, but the disciples would not let him. 31 Even some of the officials of the province, friends of Paul, sent him a message begging him not to venture into the theatre. 32 The assembly was in confusion: Some were shouting one thing, some another. Most of the people did not even know why they were there. 33 The Jews in the crowd pushed Alexander to the front, and they shouted instructions to him. He motioned for silence in order to make a defence before the people. 34 But when they realized he was a Jew, they all shouted in unison for about two hours: "Great is Artemis of the Ephesians!" 35 The city clerk quieted the crowd and said: "Fellow Ephesians, doesn't all the world know that the city of Ephesus is the guardian of the temple of the great Artemis and of her image, which fell from heaven? 36 Therefore, since these facts are undeniable, you ought to calm down and not do anything rash. 37 You have brought these men here, though they have neither robbed temples nor blasphemed our goddess. 38 If, then, Demetrius and his fellow craftsmen have a grievance against anybody, the courts are open and there are proconsuls. They can press charges. 39 If there is anything further you want to bring up, it must be settled in a legal assembly. 40 As it is, we are in danger of being charged with rioting because of what happened today. In that case we would not be able to account for this commotion, since there is no reason for it." 41 After he had said this, he dismissed the assembly. (Paul leaves Ephesus for Macedonia. This is different from his original plan which was to visit Corinth and then go into Macedonia (2 Corinthians 1:16). His need to leave rapidly for his own safety forced a change in the travel plans. This may have been because the Macedonian members of Paul's team were those who had experienced most trauma over the riot (see above Acts 19:29) but it is more likely to have been because Paul wanted to hear a reply from this letter sent with Timothy before arriving in Achaia, and so had arranged for Titus to travel to Corinth and then meet them in Troas where he hopes for news from Titus about the Corinthians (2 Corinthians 2:12-13). The events post this time you will find in Appendix C.

Appendix C
Background to 1 Corinthians

58A.D. - 59A.D.

Paul writes in1 Corinthians 16:8 about Pentecost in 58A.D. "But I will tarry at Ephesus until Pentecost". In Acts 20:16 Luke refers to the following year Pentecost when he writes "For Paul had determined to sail by Ephesus, because he would not spend the time in Asia: for he hasted, if it were possible for him, to be at Jerusalem the day of Pentecost. This is Pentecost in 59A.D. after he has successfully fulfilled his promise to visit Achaia and Corinth (which was the main city of Achaia). It is from here that he wrote the epistle to the Romans. It is during this second visit rather than the first time he visits Corinth when he writes this because he mentions the collection (15:26) which he has gathered from Macedonia and Corinth which reflects the background of 2 Corinthians. It also is after the time he has decided to visit Rome which Luke tells us in Acts 19:21 it was during his stay in Ephesus a few years after his first visit to Corinth.

So what happened during this year?

Summary

Paul made a decision not to go back with the Corinthian delegation. His original plan has been to travel to Macedonia via Corinth and then return to Corinth (2 Corinthians 1:15, 16) from where he would travel to Jerusalem, but instead he delayed his trip to Corinth (Acts 20:1, 2; 2 Corinthians 1:23) and decided to go to Macedonia first and then onto Achaia. (He will not actually reach Corinth until over a year after he says goodbye to the Corinthians from Ephesus (2 Corinthians 9: 2) .He wants first to know the result of his first letter to the Corinthians before arriving in Corinth and has arranged for Titus to meet him at Troas (on his way to Macedonia) with news. Titus may have been with Timothy and Erastus but this is unlikely because he is not mentioned in 1 Corinthians, so he was sent to Corinth from Ephesus when Paul had to leave suddenly with instructions to meet at Troas.

Timeline - 58A.D.

APRIL/MAY Paul is surprisingly forced to leave early from Ephesus (probably before Pentecost in May 58A.D.and he travels first to Troas

MAY/JUNE at Troas an open door for the gospel occurs. (2 Corinthians 2:12) Troas is on the North west coast near ancient Troy south of the Black sea. Paul stays in Troas delaying his arrival in Macedonia.

JULY/AUGUST Paul wants to see how his first letter to the Corinthians has been received before approaching them face to face. He is anxious about Titus not coming with the expected report from Corinth (2 Corinthian 2:13) so he travels onto Philippi (July/August)

AUGUST/SEPTEMBER He travels on the main road westwards from Philippi - the via Egnatia to the border of Illyricum (Romans 15:19 – note the close tie up with the time here in Romans 15:26) (August/ September)

OCTOBER/NOVEMBER/DECEMBER and then goes southwards through western Macedonia (Epirus) to Nicopolis (Titus 3:12) (November) where he spends the winter

JANUARY/FEBRUARY Paul travels the 128 miles to Corinth via other places in Achaia arriving in Corinth completing his 3 months in Achaia. When in Corinth he also visits more places in the Achaia province.

Romans is written during this time (when he is at Corinth) and he states in Romans 15:19 that his mission scope had been from Jerusalem to Illyricum which was a Roman province west of Macedonia The Via Egnatia was the main road built by the Romans for east west transportation to and from Rome. It went through Philippi and Thessalonica and travelled westwards into Illyricum. Paul then went southwards towards Achaia where en route was Nicopolis, an important port from which Paul could get a boat to Corinth which would be the best way to travel rather than attempting to cross the mountains of Delphi to approach the isthmus of Corinth. Travelling from Illyricum southwards he would come through the southern "Old Epirus" region which from 146bc had been part of the Roman province of Macedonia. The administration capital of this part of

Macedonia was Nicopolis from where Paul could travel by ship to Corinth. It is during this time that the letter to Titus is written. He winters in Nicopolis awaiting Titus. Paul then travels to Corinth and after a stay there completes his three months in Achaia. (Acts 20:3) He intended to catch a ship to Syria (Acts 20:3) at least a month before the Passover of 59a.d (March) at the latest but it could have been earlier).

Because of a plot to his life, he walked overland to Macedonia probably by the route through the east side of Greece joining the Via Egnatia around Thessalonica the capital of the province of Macedonia. He then joined his companions for Passover at Philippi (Acts 20:6). Paul's companions followed by Paul revisit Troas where such a good move of God had happened earlier in the year (Acts 20:6) and after a week left by ship from Troas via Miletus where he drops Timothy off to travel with the elders of the church back to Ephesus (where Timothy becomes their bishop). Paul returns to Jerusalem for Pentecost probably with Aristarchus from Macedonia (Acts 27:2), but definitely with Trophimus from Ephesus (Acts 21:29) and is arrested. (Acts 21:33)

Detail

Titus 3:12 "When I shall send Artemas unto thee, or Tychicus, be diligent to come unto me to Nicopolis: for I have determined there to winter."

Nicopolis was a city founded by Augustus after his victory at Actium. Some commentators mention that Paul could be referring to another Nicopolis in Thrace (modern Bulgaria) but this Nicopolis was founded around 40 years after Paul died by the emperor Trajan in the wake of victories he had won in that part of the empire.

So why was Paul in Nicopolis? When could he have possibly been there? There is one possibility. It could be at the time he is visiting Corinth for the second time. The period of time we are looking at is described in Acts 20:1-3 "And after the uproar was ceased, Paul called unto him the disciples, and embraced them, and departed *(from Ephesus)* to go into Macedonia. [2] And when he had gone over those parts, and had given them much exhortation, he came into Greece *(Achaia)*, [3] and there abode three months *(in Corinth we assume for most of that time)*. And when the Jews laid wait for him, as he was about to sail into Syria, he purposed to return through Macedonia."

The key phrase is in verse 2 "Achaia" This province included Euboea, Attica, the Cyclades, Thessaly, Peloponnesos, Aitolia, Akarnania, the Ionian islands, and the southern part of Epirus. (Arkarnia and the southern part of Epirus had a capital city which was Nicopolis). Nicopolis had been part of Achaia since 27BC and remained so during Paul's lifetime (but not so later in the 1st century AD). So Paul visited the city alongside other cities in the province of Achaia of which Corinth was the major one. When Luke writes Achaia he means the province and not just Corinth, and the 3 months Paul spent in Achaia was not just spent at Corinth. Paul wrote the epistle to the Romans from Corinth because he includes greetings from the Corinthian church at the end of his epistle. He mentions he has been in the province of Illyricum, and must have therefore travelled through this to reach Corinth. This would have taken him to Nicopolis. He could have then travelled probably by boat the short distance to Corinth from there. He winters in Nicopolis before sailing to Corinth. He stays about 3 weeks to a month in Corinth before sailing to Jerusalem for Pentecost. "Wintering in the 1st century meant staying in a port waiting for the weather to improve to make it safe for sailing again. It could last from November to February. He has to celebrate Passover in Philippi due to a threat on his life changes his plans (Acts 20:3-6). If Passover was in April that year (as is likely) he would have left Achaia in mid-March. But because of the plot he travels to Macedonia by road from Corinth. Because of the time loss because of his overland route he has Passover in Philippi rather than as he had originally planned in Jerusalem.

There is also a reference in 1 Timothy1:3 to Paul talking about Timothy's role in Ephesus when Paul was going to Macedonia. Timothy was not with him when he travelled to Macedonia prior to visiting Achaia, but he is with him as he goes to Macedonia because of the change of route because of the plot on his life. This would be the perfect time for this, for we know Timothy was with Paul in Achaia travelling with him back towards Syria (Acts 20:4). This is then the time that Timothy becomes bishop in Ephesus.

If this is so AD 58 and AD 59 become clearer. But we can add even more detail.

Titus during this time

2 Corinthians 2:9-13 For to this end also did I write, that I might know the proof of you, whether ye be obedient in all things. [10] To whom ye forgive anything, I forgive also: for if I forgave anything, to whom I forgave it, for your sakes forgave I it in the person of Christ; [11] Lest Satan should get an advantage of us: for we are not ignorant of his devices. [12] Furthermore, when I came to Troas to preach Christ's gospel, and a door was opened unto me of the Lord, [13] I had no rest in my spirit, because I found not Titus my brother: but taking my leave of them, I went from thence into Macedonia.

If verse 10 refers back to the discipline Paul outlined for the person in 1 Corinthians 5 as many think likely, then the mention of Troas would probably be the port Paul visited on his way from Ephesus to Philippi before visiting Corinth himself .Timothy had arrived in Corinth some weeks before with the first letter. Paul mentions his unrest which caused him to move on to Philippi despite the opportunities at Troas because of his anxiety over Titus. He says in the Corinthian letter (2 Corinthians 2:13) that his anxiety was because Titus was coming with a report to him. He was waiting for news of the reaction to his first letter. The plan was that Titus would be reporting back to Paul after Timothy's safe arrival. It is Titus who tells Paul the disappointment the Corinthians feel because he has not come at the time he promised as well as some further issues stirred up by his first letter. (See 2 Corinthians 1:17-23) Paul writes then a second letter and sends this back with Titus who will visit Corinth. Paul then travels overland from Philippi to Corinth and Romans 15:26 tells us that the collection Paul asked for from the Corinthians (2 Corinthians 8 & 9) he got. (As we have seen earlier the letter to the Romans is written from Corinth at this time)

So why is Titus in Crete? It could be he went to Crete after delivering the second epistle to the Corinthians. He had been given the task to complete which he had started when Paul had left Crete. Titus 1:5 (ASV) [5] For this cause left I thee in Crete, that thou shouldest set in order the things that were wanting, and appoint elders in every city, as I gave thee charge;" Titus then travels onto Crete to help appoint the elders. This seems to be an ongoing situation as Paul envisages sending Tychicus and Zenas and Apollos to provide further help – presumably the teaching base necessary for elders and the church to be formed.

The problem is we have no record of Paul in Crete except on his journey from Caesarea to Rome as a prisoner. He does seem to have had some freedom during his voyage, and he did have companions with him on the journey of which Titus could have been one. The problem is the invitation of Paul to Titus to join him in Nicopolis, and the visit in Crete has no mention no mention in Acts (and also no mention of Titus). Luke's interest seems to be on Achaia and especially Corinth. He does not mention Illyricum or the possibilities Paul may have had for the gospel then. There probably was some foundations for the gospel work laid by Paul for contact with Illyricum was taken up again later whilst Paul was in Rome when he sent Titus to Dalmatia (2 Timothy 4:10) which was in the Illyricum region probably beyond where Paul himself had been on his travels from Philippi to Nicopolis and then onto Achaia. His focus seems to be around the arrest of Paul and the events surrounding him as he goes to Rome.

Titus 1:5 does show Paul was in Crete but when? It is likely that Paul is reminding Titus of the time he was commissioned to do the task he is now doing in the same way Paul reminds Timothy of the call he has from him re. Ephesus (I Tim 1:3). It seems that Titus had been originally given the job some years before which he is seeking to complete with the help of others. The Cretan mission is not recorded in Acts. A reason for this may be because this happened when Luke was not around to record it. Luke stayed in Ephesus the first time Paul passed through the city and he probably started the writing of his gospel then. Paul meanwhile returned to Jerusalem and Antioch (Acts 18:21-23) and then visited Galatia and Phrygia where he spent "some time" Acts 18:23). He then travelled onto Ephesus (Acts 18:24) where he spent over two years. The time between the two visits to Ephesus is a part of his life without Luke and it may be that the Cretan mission happened during that time. It may also be because Luke is concerned to record the advances of the kingdom and in Crete there was nothing new that has not been recorded before. Ephesus for example was special for on Paul's arrival from the Galatian churches revival broke out in Ephesus and there were new examples of miracles accompanied by the whole region becoming changed. He does not give the same detail about Corinth or other places simply because what he has already shown Jesus doing through His spirit has been told elsewhere previously in his book.

So the probable time a mission to Crete could have happened is when Paul left Luke in Ephesus whilst he returned to Jerusalem and Antioch where according to Acts he "spent some time" and before he went to Galatia and Phrygia which finished with his staying in Ephesus. This would mean he was in Crete on our timescale in 54A.D.

Appendix D
Possible Timeline of Paul's Life

Year	Paul	World events
6B.C.	Jesus born	
4B.C.		March 13th King Herod dies and various rebellions which King Archelaus fails to properly deal with delays the implementation of taxation
c. 4A.D.	Born—an Israelite—in Tarsus of Cilicia (Acts: 2:3;Phil 3:5) A Roman citizen by birth right (Acts 22:28)	Augustus adopts Tiberius and recognizes him as the successor
6A.D.		Archelaus deposed by Rome and exiled. Quirinius of Syria implements the census and taxation
14A.D.		Census of Caesar and Tiberius. Lyvia poisons Augustus; Tiberius comes into power
20A.D.		Aretas King of Nabateans has a daughter Phasaelis who married Herod Antipas, Otherwise known as Herod the Tetrarch

25A.D. 25/26	Jesus baptised in river Jordan (Luke 3:20,21) John the Baptist arrested	When Herod divorced Phasaelis to take his brother's wife Herodias, mother of Salome
26A.D.	Jesus' second year of ministry	Phasaelis fled to her father King Aretas IV invaded Herod's holdings, defeated his army and captured territories
27A.D.	John the Baptist killed Last year of Jesus' ministry	Pilate begins serving as procurator of Judea
28A.D.		Crucifixion of Christ
30A.D.	Paul At the school of Gamaliel, Jerusalem (Acts 22:3	
33A.D.	Present at Stephen's stoning (Acts 7:58; 8:1) Persecutor of the church (Acts 8:1-3;Phil 3:6)	
34/5A.D.	Conversion on the Road to Damascus (Acts 9:1-9) Goes to Damascus (Acts 9:10-19) Travels to Arabia and remains there (Gal 1:17)	
36A.D.	Paul in Arabia	Imprisonment of Herod Agrippa by Tiberius Pilate is recalled to Rome

37A.D.	Paul Returns to Damascus then exits the city for safety (Gal 1:17; Acts 9:20-25; 2 Cor 11:32-33) Goes up to Jerusalem (Acts 9:26-29; Gal 1:18)	Caligula becomes emperor at the death of Tiberius King Aretas receives Damascus from Caligula When King Aretas rules Damascus Paul escapes (2 Cor 11: 32)
38A.D.	Goes back to Tarsus for safety (Acts 9:30)	
38/9A.D	Barnabas travels to Tarsus in order to seek Saul (Acts 11:25) Goes to Antioch with Barnabas teaching and many people (Acts 11:26	
39A.D.	Agabus prophesies a famine (Acts 11:27-28)	Herod Antipas deposed by Caligula and exiled to Gaul
41A.D.		Caligula murdered Claudius declared emperor
42A.D.		Famine in Rome
43A.D.	Aid sent to Jerusalem through Barnabas and Saul (Acts 11:29-30)	
43/44A.D.	Barnabas and Saul return with John Mark (Acts 12:25 Barnabas and Saul "separated" and sent out (Acts 13:2-3) They travel from Antioch to Seleucia, to Cyprus (Acts 13:4)	Death of Herod Agrippa I. Claudius appoints as procurator of Judea Crispius Fadus who brings peace 44-46A.D.

44A.D.	While on Cyprus they go to Salamis and Paphos (Acts 13:5-12) From Paphos they go to Perga of Pamphylia where John Mark departs for home (Acts 13:13) Ministry in Antioch of Pisidia (Acts 13:14-50) At Iconium (Acts 13:51 to Acts) Flees to Lystra and Derbe, preaching the gospel (Acts 14:6-7) In Lystra Paul and Barnabas are mistaken for gods (Acts 14:8-18) Stoned at Lystra, supposed to be dead, but re-enters the city (Acts 14:19-20) Departs with Barnabas to Derbe, preaching the gospel (Acts 14:20-21) They return to Lystra, Iconium, and Antioch to strengthen disciples and appoint elders (Acts 14:21-24) From Pisidia they returned to Antioch of Syria and reported their journey to the church (Acts 14:24-28) Paul has vision to lay his teaching before apostles Galatians 2:2 referenced in 2 Cor 12	Death of Aretas King of the Nabateans
45A.D.	Council of Jerusalem (Acts 15)	
46/7A.D.	Paul teaching in Antioch	
47/8A.D.	Paul mission to Derbe, Lystra, Iconium (Acts 16	

48A.D	Phrygia and Galatia (Acts 16:6 They sail from Troas to Neapolis (Acts 16:11) To Philippi where Paul meets Lydia (Acts 16:12-15) Paul and Silas imprisoned after casting out a demon from a slave girl (Acts 16:16-25) Prison doors opened miraculously and the jailer saved (Acts 16:25-34) Departs from Philippi (Acts 16:35-40)	Herod Agrippa II (son of Agrippa I) sent from Rome to the small kingdom of Chalcis in Syria and has right to appoint high priest in the temple in Jerusalem
48/49A.D.	Passed through Amphipolis and Apollonia (Acts 17:1) At Thessalonica preached Christ, but had to flee (Acts 17:1-10 At Berea he leaves Silas and Timothy (Acts 17:10-14)	Claudius expels Jews from Rome and blames it on "Chrestus" (a reference to Christ)
49/50A.D	Arrives in Corinth (Acts 18:1-17) Paul meets Aquila and Priscilla recently come from Rome	Gallio the Roman Governor in Corinth arrives
51A.D.	Stays in Corinth	Paul writes 1 Thessalonians & 2 Thessalonians
52/53A.D.	Paul returns to Antioch after stopping at Ephesus, Caesarea, and Jerusalem (Acts 18:18-22) Stays in Antioch until 54A.D.	Paul writes Galatians Herod Agrippa II trusted with the tetrarchy of Philip. Moves from small kingdom of Chalcis to Northern Israel
54/55A.D.	Crete?	Claudius poisoned by his wife Nero becomes Emperor

55/56A.D.	Travels through Galatia and Phrygia strengthening the disciples (Acts 18:23) Arrives in Ephesus late 55 or early 56A.D.	Mary mother of Jesus dies in Ephesus early in 55A.D. John goes to Rome
56/57A.D.	Arrives and stays Ephesus (Acts 19:1) Preaches daily in Tyrannus Hall	Writes Philippians. Colossians, Ephesians, Philemon
57/8A.D.	Stays in Ephesus then has to exit quickly Goes to Troas and Macedonia (Acts 20:1)	Writes 1 Corinthians Writes 2 Corinthians
58A.D.	Travels to Greece (Acts 20:2) via Illyricum and Nicopolis (part of Achaia) and then onto Corinth	Assassination of Agrippina, the mother of Nero

59A.D.	Leaves Corinth & goes back to Macedonia (Acts 20:3) At Troas (Acts 20:4-12) Assos, Mitylene, Chios, Samos, Togyllium. (Acts 20:13-15) Paul exhorts the Ephesian elders at Miletus (Acts 20:15-38) Cos, Rhodes, Patara, Phoenicia. (Acts 21:1-2) At Tyre (Acts 21:3-6) At Ptolemais (Acts 21:7) At Caesarea (Acts 21:8-14) At Jerusalem (Acts 21:15-25) Paul gets arrested in the temple and causes a mob (Acts 21:26-36) Before the Sanhedrin (Acts 22:30;Acts 23:1-10) Jesus tells Paul that he will bear witness of him in Rome (Acts 23:11) The plot against Paul's life (Acts 23:12-22) Sent safely to Felix the governor (Acts 23:23-35) Paul before Felix (Acts 24)	Seneca losing his good influence with Nero but still able to bring a sense of stability in the policy of the Roman empire despite the personal excesses of Nero
60A.D.		Earthquake destroys Colossae, Hierapolis and Laodicea. Only Laodicea is rebuilt immediately
61A.D.	Paul before Festus (Acts 25:1-12) Paul's appeal honoured - turning point towards Rome (Acts 25:12) Paul before Agrippa (Acts 25:13 to Acts)	Nero appoints Festus

61/62A.D.	Paul sent to Rome by ship. Arrives in Rome (Acts 28:14-16) preaches the gospel without hindrance for two years (Acts 28:30-31)	Seneca retires from any influence with Nero
63A.D.		Festus dies in office
64/65A.D.	Paul arrested and executed	64A.D. The Great Fire in Rome; Major persecution of Christianity starts in Rome. This is a change in policy. 65A.D. plot against Nero discovered. Many executions. Even former friends including Seneca die. 67/68A.D. Nero declared an enemy of Rome, flees and dies

Appendix E
The imprisonment of Paul at Ephesus reflected in the New Testament epistles
Introduction

Traditionally Paul wrote Colossians and Philemon from his time of imprisonment in Rome. But Colossae was destroyed in an earthquake and no longer existed by the time Paul reached Rome. This section looks at whether we can recognise Paul's imprisonment from Ephesus from the letters he wrote.

The possible imprisonment of Paul in Ephesus at first glance seems unlikely as it is not mentioned in the book of Acts, but there is a tradition that Paul was imprisoned in a prison which used to overlook the harbour. If so, it might be connected to the incident referred to in 1 Corinthians 15:31 when Paul possibly refers to facing wild beasts in the arena presumably at Ephesus from where he wrote 1 Corinthians. It is reasonable to assume that if this was so it would involve some imprisonment for Paul prior to such an event. Whilst it was not usual for Roman citizens (though it was common for others like Jews, lawbreakers, outcasts and foreigners) to be beaten or to have to face wild beasts in the arena, it did sometimes happen. (Eusebius[4] mentions how a Christian Attalus had to face the wild beast even though he was a Roman citizen because the governor wanted to please the crowd.[5] Elsewhere in Acts Paul is imprisoned and beaten despite being a Roman citizen though often because the authorities did not know he was such. It could have been the same in Ephesus.

The book of Acts only mentions one imprisonment during his missionary journeys up to Paul's time in Ephesus (Acts 16 in Philippi) yet Paul when he is writing 2 Corinthians either at the end of his stay in Ephesus or more likely after leaving Ephesus mentions several imprisonments (2 Corinthians 11:23). Clement of Rome writing at the end of the first century agrees. He states Paul "was seven times in bonds".[6]

There is indeed no mention of imprisonment in Ephesus in the book of Acts, but there is also no reference in Acts to an imprisonment in Rome either. Acts 28 says how Paul is free to move around (not in bonds). There was according to tradition a later time after the period covered by Acts when Paul was imprisoned and martyred in Rome alongside a general persecution of Christians after the fire of Rome and there is no reason to doubt this.

Luke does not include everything about Paul in Acts as 2 Corinthians 11 details many events not recorded in Acts. Perhaps he did not record the imprisonment because it was short and of little significance in the general mission of what was happening at the time both in Asia, Ephesus itself and the mission into Europe.

Pauline Epistles
Can we get any clues from the writings of Paul about whether he was imprisoned in Ephesus?

Philippians
Philippians is a letter which is definitely written when Paul is in prison (Phil 1:7, 13,). It is traditionally regarded as being written from Rome. But could it have been written when Paul was imprisoned at Ephesus?

1. The imprisonment referred to in Philippians and Philemon is different from the imprisonment mentioned in the Pastoral Epistles which were during the time when Paul was imprisoned in Rome (2 Timothy1:17). Timothy is not with Paul in the Pastoral Epistles (for he is in Ephesus. 1 Tim 1:3) whereas Timothy co-writes Philippians and Philemon. (Philippians 1:1; Philemon 1:1) as a fellow prisoner with Paul or at least a frequent visitor to his confinement.
2. Timothy is to be sent to the Philippians (Phil 2:19) after they receive the letter from Epaphroditus (Phil 1:5) who had been sent earlier as news of Paul's imprisonment had reached Philippi (Phil 4:18). Epaphroditus was the postman for the Philippi letter, followed up by a visit from Timothy who was going prior to Paul coming to Philippi (Phil 2:24). This is exactly the situation

described in Acts 19:22 and 1 Corinthians where Timothy is sent to the Macedonians and then to Corinth to prepare for Pauls coming after him (I Cor 16:10; 16:5).

The epistle to the Philippians refers to the first visit of Paul described in Acts 16 but not his second visit in Acts 20. This would indicate the letter being written before either his imprisonment in Caesarea or Rome. This makes more sense written in the time described in Acts 19:22 where Paul is planning to visit Macedonia but sending Timothy ahead.

The mention in Philippians 1:13, 14 that the whole of the Praetorian Guard have heard the gospel is often used as a proof text for the letter being written from Rome. But Ephesus was a major military base with some members of the Praetorian Guard there. Corbulo the Ephesian commander had been promoted to general over the whole of the region in readiness for probable war on its eastern flank with Parthia. Whilst Paul has been in chains all the Praetorian Guard hearing the gospel is more likely to be true in Ephesus than in Rome. In Rome the praetorian guards numbered 9000 but at Ephesus, because it was a provincial centre and a major military centre providing the supply line to the build-up because of the unrest in the East. There was a detachment of praetorian guards with other soldiers who are probably "the rest" mentioned in Phil 1:13. In Ephesus the Praetorian Guard acted as supervisors over the other soldiers. Included in this elite band could be members of Caesar's household who were converted (hence Phil 1:12) and sent greetings to the church through his letters (Phil 4:22).

Corbulo, a successful military general, was appointed military governor of Asia and arrived in Ephesus in 52A.D. On the death of Claudius, Nero promoted him in 54A.D. to be in charge of all regions of the Roman Empire linked to Asia eastwards. General Corbulo was appointed to deal with the Parthians and more specifically their ally the Armenians. He built up the legions transferring them from the Germanic front where he had been victorious in 47A.D. so he could make a successful assault on the Armenian king in 58A.D. Corbulo was closely linked to the Imperial family. He was brother in law to Caligula and father in law to the future emperor Domitian. He had been a consul as early as 39AD and he was part of

Caesar's household which meant his career was affected by the changes in emperor and the politics of Rome. This shows that it is reasonable to expect members related to Caesar to be present in Ephesus and imprisonment seems to be the most logical way contact was made between them and Paul.

Philemon, Colossians and Ephesians

Philemon was written from prison or perhaps on his release. In Philemon 1:10 Paul makes reference to his chains as a recent but perhaps past event. He is talking in Philemon 1:22 of possibly coming to Colossae to stay with him so it might be that the immediate danger is past. Certainly Onesimus who was a fellow prisoner is now free. His mention of Epaphras as his fellow prisoner (Philemon 1:23) could mean he is still in prison (see also 4:12) Colossians indicates Onesimus is free (4:8, 9) whilst Paul is not (4:18)

Could this be from Ephesus rather than Rome?

It is likely that Philemon and Colossian epistles (and Ephesian letter because of its many parallels to the Colossian epistle) were written at the same time.

The restoration of Onesimus to Philemon who lived in Colossae a town about 120 miles east from Ephesus makes more sense from Ephesus than it does from Rome.

Philemon (as did Epaphras (4:12). lived in Colossae. There was a common route between Ephesus and Colossae, and it is reasonable to assume Onesimus travelled that route and was then caught as a runaway slave and imprisoned in the port of Ephesus. The alternative is to imagine him being able to successfully catch a boat to sail as a runaway slave to Rome, to be then recognised as a runaway slave and imprisoned. This is not impossible, but the probability lies with an imprisonment in Ephesus rather than Rome.

If the traditional view is accepted that Paul wrote Colossians from Rome when imprisoned there under Nero, there is a major difficulty. Colossae no longer existed. It was destroyed in an earthquake which occurred according to Tacitus[7] in the seventh year of Nero 61AD. Laodicea was rebuilt soon afterwards by the resources of its own citizens, but Colossae was left a ruin and no longer lived in. Hierapolis mentioned in the epistle to the Colossians (4:13) also remained in ruins until rebuilt by the Romans in the early part of the second century. On this dating Colossians must have been written before Nero's persecution of Christians in which Paul was imprisoned. If so, it was not from Rome, and Ephesus is a very good candidate.

Could these have been written in Rome prior to Nero's persecution of the Christians in which Paul was executed? Could it be written when Paul was under house arrest after his arrival in Rome described in Acts 28:30 as "living in his own rented house and receiving all who came to him". It seems from this that he could not leave but there were no other restrictions placed on him "no-one forbidding him" (Acts 28:30) In Colossians , however, he at least twice mentions "his chains" which indicates a circumstance different from the freedom he knew for two years described in Acts. The letters are not therefore written in a period in Rome prior to his imprisonment by Nero.

Eusebius (who is a much later author and unlike Tacitus is not an historian writing at the time) has an alternative date for the destruction of Colossae by an earthquake which he says is during the 10th year of Nero's reign (64AD) According to the book of Acts Paul was in Rome for two years, and then the book ends. Tradition says he was then executed by Nero. Nero's attack on Christians was a change of policy we can date. It was after the fire in Rome in July 64AD If Paul was arrested in 64AD or 65 AD his arrival in Rome would be before 62AD or 63 AD This is possible. But the letters from prison must have been written post July 64AD when, even on Eusebius' dating, any letters to Colossae would be unlikely to have arrived in a city which still existed. There would have been no Philemon living there to be reconciled to Onesimus his slave. An earlier imprisonment for Paul in a city other than Rome seems more probable as the background to the writing of these epistles.

The letters could have been written from Ephesus. Timothy, who is closely associated with the city becoming eventually its first bishop, is with Paul at the writing of Philemon whereas Timothy is at Ephesus during Paul's imprisonment when he writes the Pastoral Epistles. We also know Paul had impact throughout the whole region of Asia (Acts 19:26) where we know there were at least seven major churches because of the letter to Revelation (2,3) and Colossae was at least one other. Letters to the churches in Asia whilst Paul was in Ephesus is possible.

If Paul is writing Colossians and his letter to the Laodiceans (Colossians 4:16) to be taken by a team to support the churches whilst he is in prison in Ephesus, Colossians 2:1 makes a lot of sense. He is definitely writing Colossians from prison (Colossians 4:18 - see also 4:3).This of course has implications for Colossians which is also written when Timothy is with him, and refers to Onesimus (the slave of Philemon (Philemon 1:10)) as part of the team (Colossians 4:9). Colossians then becomes a pastoral letter written during the Asian revival from Ephesus and before he wrote 1 Corinthians when Paul is looking to depart from Ephesus to visit Corinth. If this is the case there may be also reference to some of the trials and arguments he was having (1:29; 2:1) during that time in Ephesus. We know according to Acts that at first Paul was well received at Ephesus by the Jews (Acts 19:8) but then after 3 months there was a reaction and so he held alternative meetings for two years in a neighbouring hall. These meetings enabled many to hear the word of God and as a result impacted the whole of the Roman province of Asia (19:9-10). These daily debates in Ephesus suddenly ended (Acts 19:21) and Paul then purposed to go to Macedonia and Greece. The conjecture in this book is that the debates finished because of the imprisonment of Paul and his friends.

There are early writings indicating Paul was in prison in Ephesus. In the Monarchian Prologues, the prologue to Colossians reads "After he had been arrested, he wrote to them (the Colossians) from Ephesus."[8]

One of the arguments for an authorship of these letters from Rome not Ephesus is that one of the letters written at the time of the others was the epistle to the Ephesians, which if to the Ephesians could not have been written in Ephesus. But the ancient text has no mention of Ephesus (Ephesian 1:1) though it does come in later texts. There is a mention of another letter circulating with the team who Paul has sent to Colossae and then onto the Laodicea (Col 4:16). Scholars speculate whether the letter we know as the letter to the Ephesians was actually the letter to the Laodiceans. In which case the letter is not to the Ephesians but rather from Paul who is in Ephesus to the Laodiceans.

The Philippian, Colossian, Ephesian letters and Philemon letter would fit better within the Acts chronology rather than outside the time covered by Acts as some of the names in the epistles mentioned are mentioned as Paul's companions at the time of his stay in Ephesus.

A name from the Colossian epistles is Tychicus (Col. 4:7) who Acts 20:4 describes as from Asia and were present with Paul after his visit to Corinth. He seems active therefore during Paul's stay in Ephesus and there is no mention of him in Rome.

Aristarchus (4:10) Paul's fellow prisoner who is present in the riots of Ephesus (Acts 19:24ff) but also accompanies Paul (Acts 20:4) to Rome (Acts 27:2). Aristarchus in Colossians is a "fellow prisoner" and he was in Ephesus with Paul to escort him to Macedonia (Acts 190. He is mentioned with Mark in a similar list in Colossians 4:10 and Philemon 1:24. He is recorded as going with Paul from Macedonia (after his second visit to Corinth) to Asia (20:4) and he is on the boat trip to Rome (Acts 27:2) so he could be a fellow prisoner with Paul at Rome, but there is no mention of him in the pastoral epistles alongside the rest of the team who have been or were with Paul through this ordeal "2. Tim 4:10. Acts 28:30 says how Paul was not imprisoned for two years after his arrival in Rome, and whilst he may have been under some sort of supervisory order, was free to live in his own rented house; and free to meet any who came to see him. There were no restrictions. It seems therefore that Aristarchus as a fellow prisoner is more likely in Ephesus than Rome. Mark, Justus are added as Jews in his team with Aristarchus (Col 4:10, 11). This could be either Rome or at Ephesus, but Epaphras who is mentioned next is from Colossae.

Evidence from Romans

The book of Romans which is written from Corinth as Paul sends greetings to Rome from Erastus the city treasurer and mentions Phoebe and Gaius. This is written during the second visit of Paul to Corinth. He mentions in Chapter 16:7 a time when he was imprisoned in which Andronicus and Junia were also imprisoned with him. This reference comes after the reference to the first convert in Asia and would therefore put it possibly after Paul's arrival in Ephesus and certainly after the only imprisonment mentioned in Acts during his missionary journeys (the one in Philippi). This could be a reference to a possible imprisonment in Ephesus.

---

[1] C.K. Barrett (1986) *First Epistle to the Corinthians Black's New Testament Commentary* p124, A & C Black

[2] C.K. Barrett (1986) op cit

[33] David Martin, Emeritus Professor of Sociology at the London School of Economics, told The Sunday Times. Read more at http://global.christianpost.com/news/ordained-women-priests-outpace-men-in-church-of-england-77553/#9eZS85GgwuZyU5Zb.99

[4] Eusebius *Historia Ecclesiastica* Book V, Chapter 1, 44,50

[5] Ralph P. Martin (1960) *An Early Christian Confession : Philippians 2: 5-11 in Recent Interpretations*, The Tyndale Press, London

[6] Ralph P. Martin op cit p.28

[7] Tacitus *Annals* 14.27

[8] see D.J. Theron (ed) (1957) *Evidence of Tradition*, Bowes & Bowes, pp80,81 for text and translation quoted in Ralph P Martin op cit p29